FRENCH

PERSONALITIES

AND

PROBLEMS

BY

D. W. BROGAN

HAMISH HAMILTON

LONDON

First published September 1946
Reprinted December 1946

PRINTED IN GREAT BRITAIN
BY WESTERN PRINTING SERVICES LTD., BRISTOL

To
DARSIE GILLIE

CONTENTS

PREFACE

I HAVE chosen the pieces reprinted in this volume from out of a much larger body of contributions to various periodicals on French topics. I have excluded straight political reporting and, with one or two exceptions, all controversial articles. It would have been pedantic to apply this principle with excessive rigour, as the exclusion of political controversy from the discussion of modern French life and culture would involve the ignoring of many of the living forces in that culture. The article "Nationalism: Past, Present, Future," has been included here to round off the discussion of the problem of nationalist doctrine in modern French controversy.

I have, with a few minor exceptions, left the texts exactly as they were first printed. That has involved inconsistency and repetition, but the alternative is submission to the temptation to display hindsight. The minor modifications have been confined to the correction of misprints. The text of "Alexander the Great" had to be reconstructed from memory as I had no copy of the article.

I have to thank the editors of *The Times Literary Supplement*, *The Manchester Guardian*, *The Glasgow Herald*, *The Evening Standard*, *The Spectator*, *The New Republic*, *La Bataille*, *La France Libre*, *The Fortnightly*, *Politica*, *The Virginia Quarterly Review* for permission to reprint articles that appeared in their pages.

Cambridge, *15th December*, 1945.

D. W. BROGAN

FRENCH PERSONALITIES AND PROBLEMS

I

ALEXANDER THE GREAT
(1942)

IT seems a long time ago; a bored little boy of nine, on a very wet afternoon in a damp house in Ireland, lamenting the waste of a single day of a holiday. He rummaged round and in a cupboard found an old flat book bound in yellow pasteboard. The title, the author meant nothing to him, but there were pictures. There was a man in some kind of ecclesiastical costume looking at a man in some kind of fancy dress over an ornamental table. Below was the legend "The Shade of Richelieu." The little boy began to read— and rain and wasted holidays were forgotten: Paris replaced Donegal. It was *Twenty Years After*.

The experience that befell me that day must have been the experience of tens of thousands of boys and girls in the English-speaking world, in each generation since Dumas began the great chronicles of the history of France that are taken so much more seriously outside his country than inside it. In Dumas's lifetime, Thackeray called him, with only a minor dose of irony, "Alexander the Great." A generation later, Andrew Lang was to say that the death of Bussy d'Amboise was the best thing of its kind since the slaughter of the suitors in the *Odyssey*. And I am sure more people than myself, on their first night in Paris, have gone to the Pont Neuf, not merely to see Henri IV, but to see the spot where D'Artagnan found Planchet spitting into the river in so philosophical a fashion that the Gascon knew at once that this Picard was the man for him.

In France, Dumas is "an amuser," a very good thing to be; outside France he is an enchanter—which is a still better thing to be. And he is a great creator of the vision of France held by foreigners. To Frenchmen this judgment may seem absurd; it is more justifiable to think of Simenon as a serious novelist than of Dumas as a creator of a great legend. But I think the French are wrong, that in Dumas they have not only one of the great story-tellers of the world, but a story-teller who has made France, French history, French people part of the memory of their own childhood and their own dreams for thousands of American, English, Scotch, Irish boys and girls, who later come to know and admire more subtle productions of the French spirit than *The Three Musketeers*, but who, for all their devotion to *L'Éducation Sentimentale*, or *A l'Ombre des Jeunes Filles en Fleur*, never forget the moment when France and Paris suddenly came alive, came off the map into the imagination.

Of course, Emma Bovary and Adrienne Mesurat and Oriane de Guermantes live with a fuller life than do Madame de Chevreuse or the other gallant ladies lifted by Dumas in a brisk piratical fashion from the *Memoirs* of Cardinal de Retz. The view of French life got from *The Three Musketeers* is certainly tuppence coloured. Is it any the worse for that, any the worse for offsetting the admirable but depressing pictures of French life we get from the great masters, with something more optimistic, exciting, even inspiring? Of course, if you come to reflect on it, or it is pointed out to you, there is something a little odd in the fact that those heroes of all healthy boys, the Musketeers, live very cheerfully, with no bad conscience at all, on the money of infatuated females. But it seems only right that foolish middle-aged *bourgeoises*, or even duchesses, should provide the necessary pistoles which the heroes need to pay for horses and dinners at inns and gold baldrics and all the other necessities of life. Their needs are simpler, raise fewer doubts in the reader's mind than do the more sombre ambitions of a Julien Sorel or any of the climbing heroes of Balzac.

There is, no doubt, a too cheerful view taken of economic conditions under Richelieu; there is a lack of the sense of the People; these innkeepers, these valets, the *roturiers* who provide the background, the comic relief, the goods and services for the gentlemen, have not yet heard of the Rights of Man. But they are men, so are the gentlemen; and they are all Frenchmen.

Dumas is not a subtle artist, but in the long series of the Musketeers there is traced, with real if broad art, the lesson of "the contagion of the world's slow stain." Aramis dries up, becomes a kind of aristocratic Pierre Laval. Perhaps the authorities of the cathedral of Vannes are right, like the authorities of the cathedral of Autun, in not permitting a memorial in their cathedral to its most famous bishop. But the other side of the process is shown in the double progress of d'Artagnan. For the ambitious, aggressive young Gascon, a French version of the "capable Scot," grows in moral dignity to the end, resisting the seductions of Mazarin as he had resisted the threats of Richelieu till he dies, nobly and appropriately, with the marshal's baton at last in his hand. Here is ambition, energy, courage doubly rewarded.

In modern France and in modern French literature, there was, at any rate down to 1940, a natural reaction against *panache*, a natural hostility to the extravagances of French history which have cost France so dear. In no country is there so little naïve Napoleon worship as in France. In no country has there been so determined an effort to replace the hero by the mass, in no country has such great comic and ironical talent been devoted so whole-heartedly to explaining and explaining away so heroic and fantastic a history. There is a great deal to explain away; there is St. Louis and the Crusades (*Gesta Dei per Francos*); there is St. Joan; there are the long, savage and heroic Wars of Religion. There are the great soldiers and the great explorers: Turenne and Du Lhut; Vauban and La Salle. There is the grand siècle and the Revolution; there is the Empire, the épopée, the most expensive overdose of glory a nation ever fed on—till the Germans set a new standard of folly in that department. In the nineteenth century, there was the creation of the overseas Empire and the disasters of 1870, following on the profitless victories (profitless for France that is) of the Crimea and Italy.

No wonder there was a reaction; no wonder Flaubert added more and more items to his collection of exemplifications of human folly; no wonder Remy de Gourmont asserted that he would not sacrifice the little finger that he used to knock the ash off his cigarette to recover Alsace and Lorraine. Debunking became so much the mode that it took real courage to face the cultivated and sophisticated French intellectuals with the old, sentimental, un-rational passion for the heroic. 1914–18 showed how much of the old spirit remained, and how easy it was, under different verbal forms, to evoke the *furia francese*. But the aftermath showed how widespread the literary, sophisticated view had become. It was a bold man who could defy the sophistical pessimism of Alain or the

humour of Georges de la Fouchardière. No great soldier had less
general acceptance of his glory in his own country than Foch. The
real beneficiary of the campaign against glory was Pétain. There
was a *real* general, cautious, rational, sceptical, pessimistic, the
antithesis of Foch with his absurd, irrational belief in faith, in the
offensive, in the moral aspects of war and command. Alone among
the *grands chefs*, Pétain was pretty nearly exempt from the irony of
Le Canard Enchaîné. He was the hero of one of the most important
sections of *Les Hommes de Bonne Volonté*. Every war was a bloody
mess; war *à la* Pétain was less of a bloody mess than war *à la* Foch.
And the military needs of France were discussed (as far as they
were discussed at all) in a highly rational, prudent, economical
frame of mind. What was forgotten was the wisdom of the German
saying: "a wholly rational army would run away."

It was not a wholly rational act to hold the Bastion Saint-Gervais
at La Rochelle, or to indulge in absurd conspiracies in Belleisle-
en-Mer. It was not a totally rational emotion that made the French
infantry, surrounded at Blenheim, burn their standards and ask in
tears: "What will the King say?" It was not a totally rational calculation to ignore the prudential arguments of MM. Pétain and
Laval in 1940, and refuse to let France pass into the rearguard of the
triumphant and invincible march of the Third Reich. It was very
much in the spirit of Dumas, even of such unideological heroes as
Coconnas, of such unthinking heroes as Porthos, of such victims of
the point of honour as Athos, of such French combinations of calculation and recklessness as d'Artagnan.

And it is that side of France that Dumas has made comprehensible
to us, without teaching, merely by exemplifying. The France that
we learned to know as little boys was that France, the France of
long straight roads and crowded streets, of heroic follies and
ostentatious, almost vainglorious courage. From Dumas, it was easy
to move on to the *coureurs de bois* and the heroic Indian fighters,
men and women, who made Canada, and left their traces all over
the American west. Ney and Montcalm; the priggish Lafayette
and the gloriously eccentric Bailli de Suffren; the men of the
Grande Armée and the Marne; all were easily comprehensible to
the properly initiated little boys and girls of the English-speaking
world. We could understand the story of the Chevalier d'Assas
(which I have known bring tears to the eyes of a junior member of

the greatest of American families) and we could take our Céline or Zola without serious damage.

Mr. Shaw once wrote: "Dumas *père* was what Gounod called Mozart, a summit of art. Nobody ever could, or did, or will improve on Dumas's romances and plays." It is a noble tribute to Dumas as an artist, but Dumas was more than an artist, he was in his own way a kind of moralist. And he preached a morality to France, and a truth about France to foreigners that has never been less out of date than in this iron age. He is at least as modern and rather more helpful than Flaubert. Of course, as Renan regretfully admitted, "M. Homais avait raison." And the French are proud, perhaps too proud of being right in the intellectual sense, of seeing through everything and everybody, above all through themselves. It is a virtue that can become very easily a serious fault. M. Georges Duhamel noted in the last drab and depressing year before this war, that France was abandoning not merely the Maginot Line, but the Descartes line, losing her moral as well as military pre-eminence. She also appeared to be abandoning the lesser but important Dumas line, garrisoned by so many lively ghosts. But since Dumas was not so much a creator as an observer and reporter of genius, the spirit of d'Artagnan and Planchet was bound to be reincarnated, at a much darker hour than France knew when the Lieutenant of Musketeers went to take orders from Mazarin in the Palais Cardinal. And we who had been properly brought up knew it must be so. Would we have been as wise if we had thought of France as the country of the father of Eugénie Grandet or the daughters of Père Goriot?

II
THE FRENCH REVOLUTION
(1943)

"On s'occupe trop de la Révolution; on publie là-dessus un tas d'histoires, de livres! . . .

"Sans compter, dit Martinon, qu'ily a, peut-être, des sujets d'étude plus sérieux!" So they talked at M. Dambreuse's party when Frédéric Moreau was being introduced to Paris society nearly a century ago. Yet when the solid, prosperous, safe business men and officials of the last years of Louis Philippe talked this way, they had so little to worry about! There were memoirs and narratives; there was the *culte* of the Girondins and the beginnings of the rehabilitation of the Jacobins. There were signs of that republican loyalty to the great ancestors which Macaulay reprobated in the case of Hippolyte Carnot. But of Mr. Thompson's "Fifty Best Books on the Revolution" only two, Bouchez and Roux's *Histoire Parlementaire de la Révolution Française* and Carlyle, had been published. (Mercier's *Tableau de Paris* was, presumably, not in Flaubert's mind.) But by 1939 the case was altered. The role of the Revolution, its decisive character was impossible to ignore. M. Bernard Faÿ, then of the Collège de France, and not yet by the grace of Vichy, Librarian of the Bibliothèque Nationale, might rather peevishly deplore this obsession.

Tandis que le XVIe et le XVIIe siècle français sont de plus en plus abandonnés, l'intérêt se concentre sur ces années 1789–1800, et les chercheurs qui s'y appliquent y apportent un zèle dont la véhémence donne à penser que, pour eux, la grande Révolution, bien qu'elle soit produite en France, est un phénomène international. Elle semble être devenue le patrimoine ou l'obsession de l'univers. Plus qu'un événement historique, elle est désormais un cas de conscience pour l'humanité.

M. Faÿ found much to deplore in this state of affairs, but we can accept his statement of the case without following him into his lamentations or explanations of the fascination for historians of the breach of the tradition of French politics and culture, any more than we need comment here on the imbecility of the attempts of his present employers to undo 1789 or 1792.

It is the first of the many merits of Mr. Thompson's book[1] that its author defies the ban of a century ago and is equally indifferent to the imputation of motives and reproaches of the *bien-pensant* salons of to-day. He is himself a "chercheur" of the most indefatigable type, as impressed as any of M. Faÿ's American colleagues with the importance of the Revolution and a complete master (so far as one human being can be) of the immense literature of a historical theme which has been studied with more care, more heat, more lavish expenditure of learning and labour than any other historical problem if we except the origins of Christianity. This merit of being soaked in the bibliography of the subject may, at first sight, seem a merit only in the eyes of scholars and a matter of indifference to the common reader for whom this book is designed. But not only would he be a very foolish scholar who ignored this first-class piece of high popularization which is so often more than that, but the common reader who does not appreciate the novelty of Mr. Thompson's approach, the pioneer character of his equipment, will not fully enjoy or profit by this book.

The jacket tells us that "to nine Englishmen out of ten the French Revolution means Thomas Carlyle." But it means not only Carlyle, but Macaulay on Barrère and Mr. Belloc (who wrote, among so many other things on the Revolution, a characteristic introduction to Carlyle for *Everyman*). And it means, too, *A Tale of Two Cities*, *The Scarlet Pimpernel* and *Orphans of the Storm*. Every schoolboy knows about the Reign of Terror and about the scandals of the Court of Louis XV, darling subject of moralists for nearly two centuries in which the school represented to-day by Mr. Cole Porter fights an ever-victorious battle with the school represented to-day by M. Pierre Gaxotte.

Thus, the Revolution and its antecedents, crimes and scandals, the last days of Danton and the first triumphs of Bonaparte are part of the common stock of historical knowledge of the average man. 14th July, 1789, is perhaps the only date beside 1066 that he can be assumed to know. But this very popularity has prevented the acceptance by the average man of some truths established by modern

[1] J. M. Thompson. *The French Revolution*. (Oxford: Blackwell.)

historical study, and the destruction of some old errors has been as hard as the indoctrination with new truths. Yet the old legend of the Revolution is dead. The modern controversies range over fields untilled by Mignet or even by Carlyle; in some ways Michelet is as out of date as Sir Archibald Alison.

There has been, in the first place, a far more formidable attack on the Revolution than any launched by Alison or Sybel. The Revolution has been treated as a disaster and an avoidable disaster, as the result of arrogant intellectual folly rather than of centuries-old historical problems at last combining to break down a political system that could not solve them.

The conviction that the leaders of the Revolution were mostly fools as well as being, in many cases, knaves, was most effectively spread in France by Taine. For Taine, France was a horse that threw its rider; in 1830 because of the faults of the rider, but in 1789 because of its own bad habits. And those bad habits came from intellectual as well as from moral errors. The men who drafted the Declaration of the Rights of Man were naïve. They saw human society as a simple mechanism; they had none of the under-standing of its complexity that was widespread in a France that had the chance to read Le Play—and Taine.

Selon eux, rien n'était plus *simple*; avec l'idée de l'homme en général, avec la notion la plus ecourtée, la plus mutilée, c'est à dire la plus inexacte, ils construisaient leur édifice imaginaire; de là leurs mécomptes; leur procédé était bon pour abattre, non pour bâtir; effectivement, parmi leurs oeuvres une seule est restée intacte et bien viable, le système métrique, parce qu'il a pour objet, non dês ames, mais des quantités.

From Taine to Bainville and to such more discreet enemies of the Revolution as Madelin, the reactionary cry has deafened many ears until, in modern France, it was in many circles a proof of credulity to believe that on the whole the Revolution was a good thing. The results of that fashion can be seen in some of the silliest sides of French reaction to-day.

But the weight of learning is on the other side; for Aulard against Taine, less certainly for Mathiez against Aulard. As more and more documents are made available, as more and more regional and topical studies are published, as more and more legends are destroyed, the picture of the Revolution becomes not clearer (it will always have a Rembrandtesque aspect) but less varnished by more or less skilled hands. Of course, there is a danger in all this of the establishment of a revolutionary orthodoxy. More men of the Left than Clemenceau treat the Revolution as a "bloc" and try to impose on a very complicated story an edifying simplicity that it cannot have. And the motives of this simplification have sometimes nearly as much to do with the politics of the age of Jaurès and Caillaux, Clemenceau and Poincaré, as with the times of the Feuillants, Girondins, Mountain and Marsh.

It is perhaps the greatest of Mr. Thompson's many merits that he has mastered the modern learning without being mastered by it. He is against the King and for the National Assembly (his account of the role of Louis XVI is free from muddling sympathy with a fairly good man who was yet a bad king). He is for the Jacobins against the Girondins. Few historical intuitions have been more fully justified by later research than Carlyle's masterly statement of the case against Lamartine's heroes. But Mr. Thompson is not a blind admirer of Robespierre (of whom he has elsewhere written so admirably) or prepared to ignore how much trouble the Jacobins and the Convention made for themselves by economic incompetence and superfluous and often murderous rigour.

The easy contempt for the men of the Revolution against which Mr. Thompson's book is a protest (it is, of course, many other things as well) has many roots. It has some specifically English roots. From the Revolution came the war, the longest and the most exhausting war that the modern English State has had to fight until our times. The tradition of hostility to the Revolution thus bred was given literary form by Burke, by Scott, by the repentant Wordsworth and Southey. To be sound on this question was a necessary condition of political and social respectability. It was a long time, indeed, before Conservatives could dare to ponder the case for the Revolution, even for the Girondins. Nor, as the general public became more tolerant of the Revolution, more moved by its achievement, did the hostility of the bigoted or timorous Tory grow less. Paris was almost as much a centre of infection as Rome was for the zealous Protestant.

It is not only in his preface but in his narrative that Mr. Thompson protests against a type of English complacency that ignores the realities of any revolutionary situation. And it is not only critical learning that saves Mr. Thompson from underestimating the tragic difficulties of the remakers of France. Living in a revolutionary age, he is better fitted than past generations of scholars were to understand some of the psychological problems. His account of the great trials, the purges, the propaganda campaigns, the role of the parties and the pressure of civil war, obviously owes something to his contemplation of recent history, although the comparison is never stressed and is not formally stated.

Of all the quarrels bred or embittered by the Revolution, the feud with the Church was the most lasting and the most important. In France, until very modern times—and in some places and some classes to this day—the Revolution was blessed or damned for its church policy. Mr. Thompson, with his usual clarity and charity, makes plain how easy it was for the actors on each side to err and how the legislative settlement of the church question was swept through the rapids over the waterfall into schism, despite the clear-sighted fears of just that disaster which were shared by all sides. As far as there was a villain, it was the old, frivolous friend of Voltaire and Pompadour, the Cardinal de Bernis, ambassador in Rome and *saboteur* of any policy of compromise. Pius VI, of whom Mr. Thompson has a poor opinion, was a victim of Bernis as well as of his own faults.

But, in more ways than one, the average reader will find the church problem, the rights and wrongs of the Civil Constitution of the Clergy, the most difficult part of the book. Mr. Thompson, with his usual command of detail, makes plain the irrational, extravagant, unedifying state of the Gallican Church, and makes the need for reform evident. But the intelligent, if in this field not learned, reader may miss more than one point. He may not remember how like the Church of England the Church of France was. The *portion congrue* of the French perpetual curate was, after all, not much less than the stipend of the Vicar of Sweet Auburn—and it was easier for a celibate priest to pass rich on it than a married parson, even in Ireland. Indeed, the *portion congrue* was not much inferior in form and rather higher in fact than the commencing stipend of a *professeur suppléant*, or of Trollope's Mr. Crawley, two generations later. An Archbishop of Bordeaux was no richer than a Bishop of Durham or Derry, nor the life of Dillon any more scandalous than

the life of Lord Bristol. The problem of reforming the old relationship between the French State and that older organization, the
Gallican Church, was difficult, perhaps insoluble. But Mr. Thompson leans, perhaps unconsciously, to the anti-clerical side. "If his
priest disapproved of him, a man might starve in this world and
burn in the world to come." He might starve if he was dependent
on clerical patronage, as a tradesman might have starved in Bar-
chester. But why burn? Priestcraft in eighteenth-century France
was probably not unknown, a superstitious reverence for the clergy
common enough, but on what theological theory did a parish priest
excommunicate or refuse the sacraments at his good pleasure and,
even if both things happened, how was God's judgment assumed
to have been coerced? The framers of the Civil Constitution may
have been morally guiltless in not allowing for the fact that the
parish priest had a special character which made the imposition of
an oath especially dangerous, but it was a bad mistake all the same.
The Pope may have been remiss in not negotiating a settlement,
but what was in fact left to the Pope by the Civil Constitution? It is
hard to see, apart from doctrinal definitions, not yet declared
infallible, what the Head of the Church in future would have had
to do with its eldest daughter who was decidedly setting up house
on her own. (Did the Pope, under the old concordat, "consecrate"
all French bishops anyway?)

There was present in the dispute over the Civil Constitution an
element in the French national temper that we find it hard to
understand or to recognize, a totalitarian dislike of rivals to the
State, both because they were rivals to the State and because they
diminished the individual's direct relationship to the sovereign.
There were to be no mediators between the individual citizen and
the nation; it was a kind of political Protestantism. Such a claim
was manifested not only in the treatment of the Church, but in the
treatment of workers' organizations, which Mr. Thompson treats
at length, and of the universities, which he deals with very briefly.
With few exceptions, the French universities in 1789 were in a state
of decay which makes Adam Smith's and Gibbon's Oxford seem
almost like a worthy contemporary of Glasgow, Edinburgh,
Leyden or Göttingen. But even if they had been more efficient,
they would probably have been despoiled and deprived of autonomy
all the same. The reader who rejoices to learn that monks and nuns

could no longer be forced by law to stay within the convent walls may not note that the would-be monk or nun could no longer enter the suppressed convents. And, although it is well to be reminded that the schismatic character of the Constitutional Church was by no means evident to all loyal Catholics in 1791 any more than the revolutionary character of the Henrician settlement was evident to Tunstal or Gardiner in 1540, it is surely going a little far to describe the bishops who sat in the Legislative Assembly as representing "orthodoxy"!

The especially bitter character of schism in a Catholic country, where the edge of conflict is not taken off by a general acceptance of the fact of dissent, will not be borne in mind by all readers. Both sides in the bitter years between 1791 and the formal abandonment of State support for the Constitutional Church were as insistent on an "église une et indivisible" as any Jacobin was on a similarly united and, if you like, intolerant Republic. Yet Jacobin intolerance had its limits—or met its master in the attachment of the French people to the earliest hopes of the Revolution, hopes so often deceived but never abandoned.

Mr. Thompson ends his book at Thermidor and he is too good a historian to see in the overthrow of Robespierre either what Macaulay saw in it a century ago or what the neo-Jacobins have seen or professed to see in it more recently, a historical turning-point wholly good or wholly bad. And it is with a deep sense of the true meaning, for France and the world, of the great movement that Mr. Thompson chooses to end, not with the fall of Robespierre but three weeks later. Louchet had tried to justify the continuance of the Terror, and was interrupted by cries of "Justice!"

"Justice?" retorted Charlier; "yes, for patriots; but for aristo-crats the Terror!" Thereupon (says the Report) "a great number of voices replied, 'Justice for everyman (*justice pour tout le monde*)!'" It was a cry from the heart of France—France which during the last five years had hoped so much and had been so often deceived. It excused Thermidor. It explained the Revolution.

So it was in 1794; so it is in 1943. To write down the Revolution as a series of crimes fed by delusion; to write off the human hunger for justice as an idle dream; these are to-day the aims of all those who, inside and outside France, by terror or by sophistry, try to undo what was done between 1789 and 1794 when, with all its faults and follies accompanying it, the modern world was born in France. And the French people has not and never will renounce its role as mother or think the anguish of giving birth to her child too great a price to have paid—and to continue to pay.

III
PROUST AS A SOCIAL HISTORIAN
(1941)

"I T is certainly, a fact that, if you go to a bookshop in any of the provincial towns of England and Scotland, you will be able to buy some books by George Eliot in cheap editions, but you will not find Marcel Proust in any edition whatsoever." So wrote Mr. Maurice Baring, in 1936, adding with characteristic fairness that Proust "was one of George Eliot's greatest admirers." Proust would indeed have been scandalized to think that a day could come when *Middlemarch* should be forgotten in its author's own country, probably even more scandalized at such a breakdown in taste, than he would have been gratified to learn that in the midst of a renewed German war against civilization, it should have been possible to produce such an admirable edition of his great book as the first collected English edition is. There is now no excuse for the provincial town to neglect either Proust or George Eliot.[1] Here is, in cheap and convenient form, an excellent edition of one of the two or three important novels since the end of the productive period of the career of Tolstoy.

Important, that must be admitted; whether great or lasting is still a question open to dispute, but "*A la Recherche du Temps Perdu*," like *Ulysses*, will not lose its importance in the history of taste, even if it appears there as a monument to the patience, to the tenacity, and to the incapacity for boredom of the early twentieth century. This new Scudéry, this new gazeteer to the *carte de tendre*, will always excite literary curiosity. Of that, at least, we may be certain. Of course, the true Proustian will think such limited fame grossly inadequate to the merit of the book; if future generations find nothing to admire in Proust but his and his readers' monumental patience, so much the worse for posterity, so much

---

[1] Marcel Proust. *Remembrance of Things Past*. Translated by C. K. Scott-Moncrieff ("Time Regained" translated by Stephen Hudson). In twelve volumes. (Chatto and Windus.)

must the Proustian view of love have sunk into our habits of thought and reading.

For to the Proustian, the whole vast work is capable of supporting endlessly repeated study. He continually discovers new ingenuities of observation, new subtleties of architectonic, new internal patterns, new parodies, new triumphs of humour. And, it must be confessed, he continually discovers new problems, new ambiguities, new surface inconsistencies, new irritations provoked by the collapse of Proust's sense of aesthetic fitness, as well as of his sense of humour, as his mania for overcrowding the Cities of the Plain was given more and more free rein. But to the student (or, the hostile critic would say, to the victim) of Proust the ambiguities, the puzzles, the improbabilities, the arbitrary fashion in which threads are apparently knit together are part of the charm. A mind so acute, so devoted, so fitted for the colossal task it undertook cannot make merely silly, merely careless mistakes. Each mistake tells us something about Proust and that is an addition to our knowledge of important aspects of western human nature. Even those parts of Proust that seemed less good, even comparatively inferior, in the first or second or third reading, earn our admiration as we, like Proust himself, think and re-think the problems of personality-in-time that he presents to us. It is not necessary to take too seriously the theoretical statement of the case at the end of *Le Temps Retrouvé*, to appreciate how successful the last parts of Proust are. It is probable that *Le Temps Retrouvé* will never have, perhaps in the wider human sense it does not deserve to have, the more general appeal of the first parts of the novel. But whatever may be the case with Macaulay's readers of the *Faerie Queene*, they are neither few nor weary who hold out until the blood of "Gilbert le mauvais" is mingled with the blood of Odette and Swann, and Madame Verdurin is the Princesse de Guermantes, succeeding a Wittelsbach as Madame de Maintenon did a Hapsburg.

There is an egalitarian bias native to this age that must be overcome if Proust is to be approached in a proper spirit of willingness to listen, to be converted. His characters are, for the most part, rich and idle and vicious. The few we are allowed to admire without important reservations are either the narrator's own mother and grandmother, who were neither aristocratic nor idle, or female servants. The standards of French family virtues are represented by Françoise and she, in a far deeper sense than the Guermantes, represents the permanent glories of the France of Saint-André des Champs or the habits of mind and behaviour of the *chansons de geste*. The Faubourg Saint-Germain as depicted in Proust is a vast Drones' Club. Cut off from political activity, hiding the degree to which it is involved in modern business, dealing with M. Nissim Bernard only at a directors' meeting or with Marcel's father only on an official board, the Guermantes clan are as apparently divorced from the current life and achievement of France as so many court nobles of old Japan, playing their part in the ritual life of the divine Mikado, while all real power, real activity was in the hands of the clan chiefs round the Shogun.

The comparison of Proust with the *Tale of Genji* of Lady Murasaki has occurred to many readers of the two books. But not only is the court world of Genji not quite so idle, not quite so divorced from political reality as it was to become and as the Faubourg had become by 1890, the culture of the Mikado's Court was more genuine. The smattering of outdated learning, the obsolescent novelties of taste that make absurd the pride of the Guermantes circle in the *esprit* of the clan, were part of the unconscious comedy of the Faubourg. It was A. B. Walkley who noted as one of the most convincing examples of Proust's art as a chronicler of the best society, that the jokes of the Duchesse de Guermantes never quite come off. So it was with her taste in art. She bought Elstirs only because Swann told her to. She admired too soon—or too late— and although these faults in taste were not confined to the Guermantes circle, though the beauty and grace of Oriane made her lapses more tolerable than the manner of young Madame de Cambremer did hers, the world of the Guermantes had now no more than an aesthetic justification. A Legrandin, like Madame de Cambremer, had links with the still living, growing, working world of the bourgeoisie that made her musical snobbery merely ludicrous, not a failure of functions.

The cruelty with which Proust exposes the intellectual nullity of the Guermantes circle is only one of the many proofs of his severity towards the aristocratic society to whose study he seemed, to some of his friends, to have narrowed his mind and given up gifts that might have been more generously, more fruitfully, spent. But whatever judgment is passed on Proust's choice of a way of life or of a literary theme, there is no flattery here of the old French aristocracy, none of Paul Bourget's reverence for the established social church. As Mr. Raymond Mortimer has pointed out, Proust is not merely critical but unjust to his aristocratic models. There must have been to hand better Christian mothers than Madame de Marsantes, better husbands than Basin de Guermantes, better friends than Robert de Saint-Loup, less fatuous diplomats than M. de Norpois, less extravagantly contrasted combinations of virtue and vice than M. de Charlus. The most hostile outside critic of the Faubourg Saint-Germain could not have done as much to reveal the emptiness of its claims to leadership as Proust has done. If these are the "notables," then the "fin des notables," the refusal of the French people to trust power to the old aristocracy, needs little explanation or justification.

The world Proust is describing is the world that had been riven by the "ralliement," by the breach between the policy of the Pope and of the King, as well as by the sullen crisis of loyalty brought about by the replacement of the elder line of the House of France by the hated junior line of Orleans. The Pope was counselling acceptance of the exile of the King and the King was a descendant of regicides and traitors. It is a weakness of the admirable translation that some of the flavour of the political and historical tone of the novel is lost. It is rather surprising that Scott-Moncrieff should not have known what a *blanc d'Espagne* was. His "Black" friends in Rome could have told him that it meant the stern, unbending Legitimists who were horrified at the succession of the Comte de Paris to the claims of the Comte de Chambord. It was proof of the daring of Oriane that she mocked at such refined scruples. To be on very friendly terms with the Duc d'Aumale was not so bold as to be on friendly terms with the Princess Mathilde, but it was bold in a society that had not forgotten either the vote of Philippe Egalité for the murder of Louis XVI or the way in which the Condé inheritance had been acquired by the descendants of the regicide. To a true *blanc d'Espagne* the claims of the House of Orleans to the throne of France were as tainted as their right to Chantilly.

It was right in Proust to have given the Duc de Guermantes a brief parliamentary career; in 1885 there had seemed for a moment to be an opportunity for the old upper layers of French society to return to that political arena from which the *nouvelles couches* of Gambetta had excluded them. But the parliamentary career of the Prince des Laumes was as doomed to futility as was the resistance of Vercingetorix in that Alesia that rises above the little Burgundian town from which the heirs to the Guermantes duchy took their title. It was the business of the Duc de Saint-Simon, so Lytton Strachey said, to be a *duc et pair*. So it was the business of the Duc de Guermantes. And not only his business, but the business of the men and women of the Faubourg. Brief visits to Twickenham, the formal parties in the great hotels of the Faubourg, seasons in the great châteaux, these were poor substitutes for the daily ritual of Versailles. The Duc de Guermantes helping on a *roturier* with his coat with a skill intended by heredity and training to be used on a royal shirt, is an example of the bad effects of unemployment on the character. He was a skilled workman unable to practise his trade and, like many skilled workmen, unwilling to learn a trade that he could practise.

What is missing in the Guermantes circle is the King. Their frivolity, their futility, their treason to their own standards is the outward sign of their inward lack. They were, in many ways, no more futile, idle, frivolous than were the courtiers of Louis XIV. But those courtiers were forced to obey, to respect, and to accept the authority of the State embodied in a man. Louis XIV was a link with reality that no courtier could ignore, and if they needed to think of nothing but a journey to Marly or even to Fontainebleau, the King had more serious preoccupations. He could afford to be ignorant of fundamental facts about pedigrees to the horror and scandal of Saint-Simon. Worse, he could knowingly refuse to admit the importance of the genealogical facts he did know. He could impose his bastards on the Court with more success than M. de Charlus did his *protégés* on the best society of Paris. He could upset the natural order of things; for reasons of State make all marshals knights of the Holy Ghost, give Berwick a rank refused him in his native land and give the real power of the State to bourgeois and the sons of bourgeois, leaving the bluest blood of France to fight over precedence, over whose wives could sit down in whose presence, and the rest of the rigours of the game. But Saint-Simon was not as cut off from the realities of power and politics as were the nobles of the Guermantes circle. There were marshals, ambassadors, bishops of the purest blood, associating and working with great commoners like Colbert and Bossuet, or nobles of doubtful title like Vauban and Villars. These nobles could not afford the luxuries of pride of a court officer like Saint-Simon, whose career as a soldier and, in a minor way, a statesman was, in any case, more serious than the political career of the Duc de Guermantes.

The pre-occupation with the theme, if not with the method of Saint-Simon, is evident all through the novel. Openly and implicitly, Saint-Simon is a point of reference. Indeed, one of the difficulties of using Proust as a social historian is created by this devotion to his great precursor. Proust repeatedly asserts that he is not writing a *roman à clef*. Only once does he depart from this rule, or this denial, to pay tribute to the generosity of a rich *café* owner, to illustrate the true generosity of the people. But it is not merely a matter of not indulging in simple equations of Charles Haas with Swann, or of Robert de Montesquiou with Charlus. It is difficult to decide, in some cases, whether the brilliant parodist of "Pastiches et Mélanges" is not in command of the novelist and of the moralist (in the French sense of the term). It is no accident that Charlus is made proud of his Bouillon descent. What Saint-Simon writes of the astonishing letter in which Cardinal de Bouillon denounced his allegiance to Louis XIV, Proust said in much the same terms of the more extravagant pretensions of Charlus. "Cette est une si monstrueuse production d'insolence, de folie, de félonie, que sa rareté mérite d'être insérée ici. Jusqu'au style extravagant qui, à force d'entasser tout ce dont ce coeur et cette tête regorgeoit, rend cette lettre à peine intelligible." In his picture of Charlus, even in details like the claim to the Brabant title, how far was Proust the pure artist or the accurate painter of Robert de Montesquiou in his more fantastic moments—and how far the learned, almost pedantic plagiarist of genius?

The repeated theme of the novel, the dissolution of society, the discovery that its unbridgeable gaps are always being crossed, its impregnable lines forced, is intelligible enough. But in its expression there are possible traces of Saint-Simon again. Good Paris society was scandalized when it learned that precedence was given at the dinner parties of the Duchesse d'Uzès to General Boulanger, and the scandal was repeated, in less dramatic form, for various military heroes of the anti-Dreyfus party. As Rochefort was forgiven his share in the Commune for his utility in the Affair and Clemenceau his role in the Affair for his services in 1917, so, in fact, the French Right has accepted, in succession, a whole series of converts from the extreme Left, the most notable in modern times being M. Pierre Laval, whose daughter's marriage in 1935 to a scion of a great provincial house which had been honoured by an alliance with the House of Noailles would have infuriated Saint-Simon and fascinated Proust. But in Proust's treatment of this theme there are traces of the anger with which mere victorious soldiers were regarded by the Duke, who saw them forced on their betters at Court by the decree of the King.

It would be idle to worry over the historical chronology of Proust, to tie him down too closely to the central point of the second Dreyfus trial, to reconcile that date with the references to the Russo-Japanese war or the aeroplane that is seen by Marcel and Albertine. More serious is the omission of the urban working population of France, where it is not composed of servants, waiters, and the like. The Paris chauffeur whom Marcel employs at Balbec is very unlike his contemporary, Mr. Henry Straker of *Man and Superman*, and Proust is remarkably indifferent to what the American song calls "social significance." His specimens of the "people" are very French in their insistence on human dignity and rights. But Françoise is a Catholic pacifist, Morel a Bonapartist. "The people" as seen by Jaurès and by many of Proust's own schoolfellows at the Lycée Condorcet, or by Saint-Loup in his first stage, avid for justice, intent on developing the revolution, do not appear at all, unless we count the dialogue between Charlus and Morel.

"Il y eut un temps où mes ancêtres étaient fiers du titre de valet de chambre, de maîtres d'hôtel du roi.—Il y en eut un autre, répondit fièrement Morel, où mes ancêtres firent couper le cou aux vôtres."

Apart from *boutades* like this, the France of Proust is apparently stable or at least as stable as anything in life ever is. Of course there has been the Revolution; it has made the Guermantes completely *fainéants* and the evolution is now complete. A few aristocratic generals recall the days, not very remote, when there was a Maréchal de Guermantes. The natural hierarchies are, it is true, less and less recognized. In Combray, the fixed order of society is respected, but its real character ignored. At Balbec, a *premier président* knows so little of the other *noblesse* as to misunderstand, completely, the position in society of the magnates whom he sees. In the old days a *duc et pair* knew the deference due to a *premier président* as the nobleman of the long robe knew the deference due to a *duc et pair*. (This point is rather lost in Scott-Moncrieff's translation because he calls the *premier président* a "chief magistrate," a title which suggests some kind of Recorder or Stipendiary. Had Scott-Moncrieff remembered his native land he would not have given a *premier président* of Caen a title suggesting a Sheriff Principal rather than a Senator of the College of Justice.) Proust, who was so careful not merely to distinguish between the imperial and the old nobility, but to give the former such ingeniously appropriate titles, just on the edge of real imperial titles (Borodino, Iéna), would not have approved this indifference to the real rank of a high official of the legal hierarchy!

A gap in the Proustian picture of the defeated and declining world of the notables is the omission not only of religion, but of the Church. This society of nobles and their dependants is not merely not *croyant*, that might pass; but there are only one or two minor ecclesiastical figures who appear at all and that briefly. The hierarchy appears only in the form of a bishop whom Oriane alone knows how to address in writing. The Orders, whose fate was so bound up with the Affair, do not appear at all. Although Proust in an article in the *Figaro* in 1904 had protested against the preservation of churches as mere museum pieces, his own attitude in his more sincere work, the novel, suggests that he was a good deal more of a tourist than of a believer or even an ex-believer. M. de Charlus had his own fantastic faith in St. Michael, and his sister, Madame de Marsantes, had her own sincere and mercenary faith. The Pirnce and Princesse de Guermantes owe to their piety their conversion to the true faith of Dreyfusism, but that is about all. It is a great gap and far from the only one. The French social historian who took Proust too seriously, or too exclusively as a source, would err even more grievously than the historian who takes Saint-Simon too seriously. But as Sainte-Beuve said in reply to the denigration of Saint-Simon by his editor, Chéruel, "Il donnait à tout ce qu'il voyait et qu'il dépeignait ensuite cette chose unique, incomparable, la vie, la *physionomie*, la flamme. Laissons les procès-verbaux pour ce qu'ils sont, prenons la peinture pour ce qu'elle est."

IV
THE PROUST TRANSLATION
(1941)

REVIEWING Mr. Leon's book on Proust some months ago,[1] I expressed doubts as to whether he was much read by the young of to-day. I was gratified to learn from some members of that vaguely defined class, *les jeunes*, that the old spells had not altogether lost their power to enchant and that one was not immediately written-off as an old fogy for preferring Proust to Trollope or Fromentin. But a more conclusive proof that my fears were exaggerated is furnished by the decision of Chatto and Windus to issue a new complete edition of Proust,[2] agreeably printed, if a little too gaily bound. It may be surmised that one does not, in these days of paper-shortage, issue twelve volumes, some millions of words, without a certain hope of a reasonable reward in the way of readers.

Here we have Proust made as clear, as intelligible and as readable as is consistent with his being Proust. And these decently printed volumes have a special attraction for those of us who began not with the French text on "papier vergé pur fil Lafuma-Navarre au filigrane," but on what appeared to be imperfectly repulped telegraph forms. And, in some editions, even the ink seemed to have run short, so that one was forced to imitate Mr. Lobel or some other great scholar reconstructing the text of Sappho from a few odd scratches on a papyrus.

As it happens, this reviewer had only read one volume of Scott-Moncrieff's translation, and that hastily. His whole impression of Proust had been got from reading and re-reading the French text. It was natural, then, to turn first of all to the translation. Translation from the French is usually bad. "We all know French," and that means that the critical reader does not, as a rule, read the English version at all, and that persons in imperfect command of English are thought to be good enough to translate from French—

[1] Derek Leon. *Introduction to Proust.* (Routledge.)
[2] Marcel Proust. *Remembrance of Things Past.* Translated by C. K. Scott-Moncrieff (the eighth part by Stephen Hudson). (Chatto and Windus.)

which they have usually mastered even less successfully. And Proust is a very difficult French author, difficult for French people as well as for us. His grammar and syntax are his own—so I have been assured by an expert—and what he had to say, in some cases, could hardly be said in words. The Scott-Moncrieff translation has been extremely highly praised; almost the only dissident voice has been that of Professor Denis Saurat, but that is a voice worth attending to, for Professor Saurat knows English and French with a perfection that few of us can claim to rival.

Which is right, Professor Saurat or the mass of enthusiastic English reviewers? Both is the statesmanlike answer imposed by the facts. The translation is good, considering the difficulties of the task more than good, but it is not quite as good as one had been led to believe. One of its faults is made evident in the literary fantastication of the titles of the different parts. *A la Recherche du Temps Perdu* becomes *Remembrance of Things Past*, *Albertine Disparue* becomes *The Sweet Cheat Gone*, *Sodome et Gomorrhe* becomes *The Cities of the Plain*. Any reader with a taste for *New Statesman* competitions enjoys these little tricks, but we have to notice that Proust (who could play them admirably himself as is shown in *Pastiches et Mélanges* and all through his novel) did not think fit to play them. He could have lifted phrases from Racine or Saint-Simon had he wanted to. He did not want to; should his translator indulge in fun-and-games not called for by his author? It is not only the titles that show the Scott-Moncrieff weakness for over-translation. Proust was technically brought up as a Catholic, yet it is most noticeable how thin, casual and bald are his allusions to the rites of the Church. The circumstances of his ancestry, of his education, of his affiliations all explain this. But Scott-Moncrieff by over-translation gives a definitely *bien pensant* flavour to very neutral phrases. Thus the "week before Easter" becomes "Holy Week"; "la Vierge" becomes "Our Lady"; "les rites de Combray" becomes "the Use of Combray." The last ingenious little joke would have been quite in place in an Anglo-Catholic novel by Mr. Compton Mackenzie, but it distorts the attitude of Françoise—and the text of Proust. Then Scott-Moncrieff is sometimes indifferent to niceties that Proust took seriously. Starting from the erroneous belief that "Droit des gens" means the "Rights of Man," Scott-Moncrieff distorted a long Proustian analogy (which Proust had used before). Marcel was not discussing his relations with his father in terms of constitutional law; he was not reproaching a domestic Charles X with the breach of his promises under the *charte octroyée*. His analogy is from international law and, of course, is carefully and ingeniously carried out.

Then Scott-Moncrieff was too afraid of the *faux amis*. It is not enough to avoid using the linguistically identical word in English to escape mistranslating the French. It is bad translation to put "chastised" for "puni"; in the context, the English for "puni" is "punished" and "chastised" is simply a mistranslation. So I suggest that the English for "prie-Dieu" is "prie-dieu" not "prayer-desk." In short, Scott-Moncrieff was too good a French scholar to have quite the necessary humility in face of his text.

But at a higher level he was admirable. He always meant something, and if he sometimes wrested concrete meanings out of Proust which were not there, who are we to complain, especially in the later volumes when the French text was highly corrupt? How good, for example, is "the vast structure of recollection" for "l'édifice immense du souvenir."

There is no space left for Proust who, after all, took millions of words to say what he had to say and died with it incompletely and imperfectly said. But for escaping from the present world there are few authors like him. That his world is strange and for ever dead as a social phenomenon does not matter. "Il en est ainsi de notre passé. C'est peine perdue que nous cherchions à l'évoquer, tous les efforts de notre intelligence sont inutiles." "A labour in vain," Scott-Moncrieff puts it. Not in vain, especially in this dark hour when the past has a charm which we find it hard to attribute to the immediate future!

V

THE RUINED TEMPLE

(1943)

I T is one of the oldest and most successful methods of revolutionary propaganda to destroy or, better still, to make ridiculous the sacred mysteries of the old order. So Henry VIII treated the great shrine of Walsingham; so the Bolsheviks treated the monasteries and shrines of Kiev. So did the feeble parodists of revolution in Paris in the autumn of 1940 treat the *arcana* of the fallen Republic. They seized the Masonic temples in Paris, in Rouen, in other cities; they profaned the shrines; they exposed to inspection and ridicule the rituals, the emblems, the archives of the Grand Orient, just as the spiritual ancestors of the French Freemasons had profaned Notre Dame and destroyed the sacred *ampoule* of Rheims, which was the visible sign of the divine favour shown the Kings of France since the conversion of Clovis. Tourists were conducted round the premises once occupied by the Lodges; the articles of the cult were exposed to irreverent eyes, and many a French Catholic must have enjoyed the ambiguous pleasures of *Schadenfreude* as he saw the tables thus turned. What was done in France had already been done in Germany, in Italy, in Russia. At the present moment Masonry is banned and persecuted in every country of Continental Europe except Sweden and Switzerland. In enmity to the Craft Moscow and Berlin are united and the brethren, so powerful, so prosperous, so confident in 1914, are now the most friendless victims of the revolutionary storm.

Whatever survives the flood, the old political organization of Freemasonry hardly can. Its day is over, whether that day goes back to the age of Solomon or to the Middle Ages or to the first stirrings of the fairy-tale romanticism of the eighteenth century or to the age of Cagliostro and Casanova. But whatever the historical validity of the Masons' own view of their history—a nice question— the Masons have played a very important role in European history. We all know that English Masons are not in communion with the most important European Masonic organization, the Grand Orient. But English Masonry is not very secretive, not very important, not very interesting. Across the Channel we are in a different world. And we always have been. One of the few hard facts about Masonic history is that the Craft was an export from Britain in the eighteenth century, that it survived among the competing organizations of the same type, the *Illuminati* and the rest, and that in the nineteenth century it became, above all in Catholic countries, the Jesuit Order of the Counter-Counter-Reformation. *Ecrasez l'infâme* was its motto, and its methods were often not much more straightforward than those employed by M. de Voltaire to forward his cause and his interests.

No doubt, in its early days, Continental Masonry was more positive than that. It seemed to offer to generous, if not to critical souls, a religious sanction for well-doing that orthodox Christianity had ceased to provide. We should not forget that Tolstoy thought the role of the Craft worthy of a central theme in *War and Peace*, and that Mozart composed *The Magic Flute* to a Masonic text as he composed Masses to the texts of the Liturgy. *The Magic Flute* as music is not notably or at all inferior to the religious music of Mozart, but the absurdity of the plot and the banality of Shickaneder's libretto should not keep us from appreciating that, in 1791, there was something moving, faith-creating even in the libretto.

> In diesen heilgen Mauern
>   Wo Mensch den Menschen liebt,
> Kann kein Verräter lauern,
>   Weil man dem Feind vergibt.

These were warming sentiments in the caste-ridden Europe that was being shaken by the French Revolution. In a few years' time the dream of a band of brothers, united by philanthropy or by Theophilanthropy, died. "Since I have seen the results of calling everybody 'Brother,' I should call my brother 'Cousin,'" said Metternich. More amiable and more credulous characters felt the same.

It is from the time of the Revolution that Continental Masonry took its fixed character. The great schism found the Masons definitely on one side of the gulf. Despite condemnations by Popes, Catholics had not uniformly felt themselves debarred from being

Masons. Freethinkers and moderately zealous Catholics could meet in the Lodges as they met in the Académie Française. But that mutual tolerance ceased. Long before the French Grand Orient had expunged all references to "the Grand Architect of the Universe" and given English Masonry an occasion, or an excuse, for breaking off fraternal relations, French Masonry and Italian Masonry were vigorous and unscrupulous enemies of "spiritualism." They might have in their ranks orthodox Protestants and orthdox Jews, but that did not matter. For these Latin versions of Mr. Thwackum by religion meant the Catholic religion, and by the Catholic religion the religion of the Church of Rome. To destroy its power and discredit its doctrines was the main business of the Masons.

There is something particularly unjust in Vichy's condemnation of Masonry, for the Craft was decidedly *attentiste* in its policy. The most romantic conspiratorial hero of the century, Garibaldi, was a Mason, but few Masons were Garibaldis. In France it was not even dogmatically Republican. It made terms with the Second Empire (the Empire of Prince Napoleon and Sainte-Beuve, not the Empire of the Empress and Monseigneur Dupanloup). But the Third Republic (and the Parliamentary Monarchy in Italy) were deeply marked by Masonry. Of course, the role of the Masons was exaggerated by their enemies. The *gens bien* in France have always been puzzled and angered by the fact that the mass of the French people do not trust them as leaders. Faced with the problem of their unpopularity, the French Right look for causes or excuses. Masonry was one of them, and Masonry was, they insisted, *an English invention*. It was in vain that the British Craft washed its hands of the Grand Orient or pointed with pride to the more respectable Scottish Rite. Masonry embodied the Revolution and was the characteristically British contribution to the ruin of France that began in 1789. This superstition was—and is—a fact of importance in Anglo-French relations.

In France the widespread national view that all politics was a racket was fostered by the activities of the Masons. It was notoriously profitable to be a member of the Craft if you were an official. After the Dreyfus case it was for a while profitable to be a Mason if you were an officer. No doubt the influence of the Masons was exaggerated. When accident revealed the workings of the system to the public eye, they were not much liked. The system of espionage organized by the Grand Orient against army officers who were practising Catholics was one of the ugliest scandals of the Republican era. And the role of Grand Master Laferre in the Chamber was another. For it was believed that Laferre owed his political importance solely to the fact that he *was* Grand Master, and that some important votes in the Chamber had already been decided on in the *couvent* of the Grand Orient.

But even before 1914 political Masonry was declining in France and Italy. In Italy, Nathan was defeated in his Roman bailiwick, and General Cadorna, although the son of the ex-priest who had taken Rome from the Pope, was regarded as an anti-Masonic general. In France, it was harder and harder to represent *le cléricalisme, voilà l'ennemi* as an adequate political programme. New social problems, new philosophical ideas were dissolving the old cadres. I can give an instance from my own knowledge. The son of one of Laferre's most important predecessors is a friend of mine. He is *croyant et pratiquant* and, in politics, mildly *centre gauche*. His son is also *croyant et pratiquant*, and was not only a member of the Action Française, but was sufficiently trusted by his leaders to be made one of the bodyguards of M. Maurras after the murderous assault on M. Blum. The same drift of the *haute bourgeoisie* from Masonry could be illustrated by other instances.

The typical Masonic politician in France was the embodiment of that *république des camarades* which nobody but its beneficiaries liked. Much of the harm done by the Stavisky affair was due to the belief that M. Camille Chautemps, the most exalted Mason in the Chamber, was protecting the interests of his Masonic brethren as well as of his brother-in-law. This view may have been groundless, but there was nothing in M. Chautemps's career before or since to make it implausible. To many sincere patriots of the Right the affair Malvy in 1917 seemed to show that Republicanism of the pure Masonic variety was near-treason. And M. Malvy, as everybody in France knows, is the father-in-law and patron of M. Peyrouton. The Masons did not invent the French taste for imputing motives or seeing treason everywhere, but their conduct did nothing to weaken that taste.

In the French provinces Masonry kept some of its old power. In the academic world it was wiser for a leading "Republican" professor or administrator to belong to the less belligerent Scottish

Rite. But the Republican *instituteur* (unless he was a Communist) was often a Mason and a zealous guardian of the spirit of the Craft. So I have known a group of schoolmasters organize a Masonic censure of a mayor who had permitted, after twenty-five years, the revival of a famous religious procession. The mayor died shortly afterwards, unabsolved by his brethren, but not, I am sure, poisoned by them. Such activities made many enemies for the Craft and did not win much respect from open fighters for *la République*. That Mussolini, and then Hitler, had banned Masonry was one of their claims to the respect of some French Catholics. That Communism also banned Masonry was one of its claims on the respect of another group of French Catholics. So Vichy banned the Masons (though it had its pet Masons as Goering had his pet Jews). Every week or so Vichy announces that "M. Untel" has been dismissed for concealing the fact that he once belonged to the Craft. And the writing of a history of France for schools, free from Jewish and Masonic influence, has been entrusted to that hammer of the Masons, M. Bernard Faÿ, keeper, since July, 1940, of the Bibliothèque Nationale and sometime Professor of American History and Institutions at the Collège de France by the grace of M. Tardieu. *Plus ça change*; there are more ways of being a Mason than by being initiated. Only Vichy could make the fall of the Grand Orient dignified. There is possibly even some danger that the Masons may appear as the "Men of Good Will" that M. Romains's hero took them to be. They were neither black nor white angels, but an interesting political machine now as out of date as the Newcomen engine.

VI
NATIONALISM, PAST, PRESENT, FUTURE
(1944)

WHATEVER views we may have of the age, the respectability and the future of the political phenomenon called "nationalism," there can be few to-day who doubt that a just estimate of its weight in the immediate future would be of the utmost importance for the safe ordering of our world. For if nationalism is declining, if its present emotional hold is due for a speedy loosening, if the nationalist doctrinaires are belated prophets of a dying system, their passion as irrelevant to the new world situation as the bulls of Boniface VIII were to the world of Edward I and Philippe le Bel, we can with prudence disregard national feeling, or make to it only the minimum concessions that tact and kindness call for. But if that often-predicted death is not imminent, we may make equally great mistakes the other way. "Stoning the prophets is ancient news," but if that is too easy a sport, it is yet a duty to recall the deception of nineteenth-century optimism, of the general belief in a political rule of reason whose palpable confutation by the facts may give us too easy a sense of intellectual superiority.

We may be making the same mistake that was made by rationalists who noted the decline of religious faith and fervour and believed that a tepid rationalism could become the ethical and political religion of all sensible men; we may be witnessing the transfer of the irrational, passionate, pathological elements that are so marked in nationalism into other not less formidable, not less disturbing, not more rational forms.

But we are less likely than our forbears to exaggerate the chances of mere rationality in politics. Freud and Jung, the modern sociologists and anthropolgists, have soaked into our minds. We are, in that sense, more humble than the men of the great age of reason, more prone to think there is something in the doctrine of original sin, more prone to think of man as a fallen than as a rising angel.

That the Sydenham Clark Parsons Professor of History in Smith College and the Woodrow Wilson Professor of International Politics in the University College of Wales should both think the subject worthy of their study is not surprising. Professor Kohn has published the first volume of what promises to be a most acute and learned as well as lengthy historical study of nationalism,[1] and Professor Carr has, in a brief and challenging tract for the time,[2] stated his position on what is one of the great questions of the day, whether or not it will be one of the great questions of to-morrow.

There is not much good writing on the subject in English and for a very obvious reason. As a man with a good digestion has no story of ills and remedies to tell, so the happy nation has no nationalist theory to explain its national well-being. Professor Kohn, with his experience of Vienna, Prague, Asiatic Russia and the United States, has been in an excellent position to observe the workings of nationalism and the realities of national problems. And that he was, for a time, a Zionist is all to the good. Nationalism is more a state of the emotions than a philosophical theory of the state, and just as no really first-class book on love is likely to be written by a eunuch, no really first-class book on nationalism is likely to be written by one to whom nationalism is as much foolishness as the Gospel was to the Greeks.

Of course, the limitation of experience imposed on an Englishman by the happy national experience of his country is not necessarily crippling. Because there is little nationalist doctrine in England it is far from following that there is little nationalist feeling. But English nationalism is so unselfconscious, so unshakable, that the shallow observer may ignore its existence. But it is there, all the same; it is to be found in obvious and even fantastic forms in noisy and convinced internationalists as well as, we may be sure, in some dupes of the Third Reich whose folly justified their incarceration in Brixton, but, none the less, did not keep them from being very English specimens of the *genus quisling*.

[1] Hans Kohn. *The Idea of Nationalism.* A Study in Its Origins and Background. (New York. To be published shortly in Great Britain by Macmillan.)
[2] Edward Hallett Carr. *Nationalism and After.* (Macmillan.)

We are, indeed, far removed from the old optimism about the necessary beneficence of nationalism. Professor Carr gives the note of his book by choosing for it a text from Acton. "Nationality does not aim at either liberty or prosperity, both of which it sacrifices to the imperative necessity of making the nation the mould and measure of the State. Its course will be marked with material as well as moral ruin." As a protest against the credulous optimism of his age, Acton's dictum is worth recalling. But it must be remembered that Acton was protesting against much more than nationalism; he regretted the victory of Lincoln's Union as well as Bismarck's Reich and for much the same reasons. He would have regarded many modern national States with horror, and such super-national States as the U.S.S.R. with more horror still. And as a politician, by supporting Gladstone's Home Rule Bills, Acton showed that he understood that the claims of nationality were not to be dismissed on grounds of mere moral and intellectual taste.

It is to be feared that Professor Carr's impatience with the phenomenon he sets out to describe has blinded him to criticisms of this kind. Modern nationalism is new; its demonstrable history hardly goes back behind the French Revolution. But that it is new tells us nothing of its present and future; it is older than international socialism, once widely marketed as its destined rival and conqueror; it is old compared with Russian Communism, which, in its institutional embodiments, may be the tamer of nationalism— or its new allotropic form.

It is a little difficult to see what weight need necessarily be given to the undoubted fact that in Eastern and Central Europe nationalism is new. So are railways, literacy, emigration to America. It is true that nationalism is still a new and struggling form of belief in Asia. But the question is: Is it growing, is it rising or falling? Professor Carr asserts, dogmatically, that it is falling, but there is not much in the way of evidence brought forward in support of this view. Professor Carr is convinced that there is much less national feeling evident in this war than there was in the last. Yet in this war, all great international movements directed against national passions have failed ignominiously. Communism has succeeded where it has run along with national feeling. But in Germany how meagre are the visible works of the millions who paid electoral service—and more than that—to the Third International. How, indeed, are we to interpret the dissolution of the Third International?

Faiths may be new, culturally distressing and yet spread and strike roots against the probabilities as seen by enlightened and disenchanted rulers and spokesmen of a more enlightened order. We have Islam to show that. Nationalism was a political necessity in the nineteenth century. The new states that grew out of the French and industrial revolutions made demands on their members that the old states could not and did not make. Not only (as Professor Carr rightly stresses) did they wage far more totalitarian war. Anatole France was profoundly right in saying that the Third Republic, between 1914 and 1918, made demands on the French people far beyond anything dreamed of by an "absolute" monarch like Louis XIV. But they made new demands in peace, too. They undertook new functions like popular education; they replaced local immunities, feudal and other systems of devolved authority, by their own officials, drawing heavily on their own claims to loyalty, trust, obedience. To make this system work at all, a myth was required. A formally rational solution was no solution. The combination of the new industrial civilization with the problem created by the decline of traditional authority created a spiritual strain that only the national state could bear. The myth was a very expensive aid to social unity; it may long have lost what utilitarian value it ever had. But to imagine that the world is ruled by rational preference is not to be a realist but to be a romantic.

The older conservatives saw in nationalism, democracy, new industry, the critical spirit applied to religion, a common enemy, "the Revolution." But that was too simple a diagnosis, for it linked two separable elements in the new political forces, democracy and nationalism. It was long enough before the Right saw with hope, and the Left with sudden anguished fear, that nationalism and liberty were not necessarily friends and allies; that one might devour the other, that the winner would be nationalism. So long as the conservative parties in Europe clung to the idea of mere restoration or a mere *quieta non movere* evasion of all problems, so long as the revolutionary parties could only conceive of the nation in arms being in arms for the principles of 1789, the confusion persisted.

Clear-sighted conservatives like Goethe might note that the old princely power, accepted in its sacred character, was dying and the causal chain that leads from the decay of the idea of the hereditary leader-king to the Führer is not hard to trace—now. It is very easy now to see that the French soldiers at Valmy, crying "Vive la Nation" in place of "Vive le roi," were not necessarily crying "Vive la République." But for the most of the nineteenth century this truth was hidden from the generations that admired Mazzini and Kossuth, lamented the wrongs of Poland (in London and Paris) or the wrongs of Ireland (in Vienna and Paris). That nationalism may be an enemy of freedom, in the old liberal sense, is now so evident that the Left-wing intellectual has made a complete turn and either hates the most potent ally of "reaction," or, a slowly obsolescent attitude, still clings, in face of all the evidence, to the belief that each new wave of nationalist passion is a mere accident, each feeble effort of anti-national, liberal, rationalistic forces is the true wave of the future.

Something of the same transformation has marked the relationship of nationalism and religion. Because of his role as an Italian prince, the Pope, in the nineteenth century, was publicly opposed to the most fashionable nationalist movement of the age. To be opposed to Italian nationalism was to be reactionary by definition or, in the case of Proudhon, to have given another proof of intolerable eccentricity. But national movements, in most countries, were associated with the national religion, above all if it was the object of suspicion or oppression by the national enemy. Whatever the Vatican might wish to do, it could not make Catholicism in Poland or Ireland anything but an obstacle to the quiet acceptance of Russian or English rule. The intensity of religious faith in these countries was, in many cases, a function of the patriotic passion which was at least as strong as the religious devotion from which it was emotionally inseparable. In other countries the substitution of nationalism for both the old reverential faith in the divinely sanctioned political order and for the acceptance of the religious standards of what had been a basically united Christendom, was more complete. The French bishops found that their authority even among the faithful had limits when they attacked the *Action française*, as they later found—some of them—that it had limits when they preached the doctrine of submission and gratitude to the Marshal. The German bishops found Hitlerism a far more formidable foe than the *Kulturkampf*. And nationalism, as Mr. Carlton Hayes has pointed out, adopted many of the ritual devices of religion. Even short of the extravagances of Nuremberg, the flag worship of the Americans is worth attention, as is the anger raised on one or two occasions by innocent English profanation of that religious symbol.

It is not only true that nationalism is a form of religious faith, it is very often a direct and obvious substitute for the older and declining Christian faith of Europe. If the alliance between Christians and Nationalists often involved odd compromises, especially by the Christians, both doctrines were protesting against the simple view of man in the world taken by the Enlightenment in Europe and by the Utilitarians in England. Both were opposed, too, to the cultivation of the critical spirit as an indisputable good in itself. Both placed an emphasis on tradition and intuition that made them natural, if not wholly consistent allies. Bonald's attack on unlimited freedom of criticism, made in defence of a society based on religious tradition, could with very little alteration be made the basis of a nationalist doctrine, asserting nothing about the supernatural world but, with Bonald, stressing the danger of such an attitude to "la société qui enchaîne nos pensées par ses croyances, et notre action par ses lois, et à l'empire de laquelle nous faisons, tous que nous sommes, un effort continuel pour nous soustraire, la société sera donc livrée au hasard de nos examens et à la merci de nos discussions."

This fear lies at the root of much of the cultural intolerance of national movements, at the insistence on the acceptance of unquestioned national values. The critical spirit becomes the "Jewish spirit," a danger to national unity in France, hypostatized into a personal devil in Germany, rightly extruded from the national spiritual life by fire and seen everywhere in disguised forms, in the assertion of any general principles of politics, in the comic spirit of a Heine, even in the comic spirit in Sinclair Lewis, for, as a cultivated German woman told a startled American, Mr. Lewis must be a Jew because his satire revealed the Jewish spirit of mockery.

If it is not an unfair criticism of Professor Carr's tract to say that it is too short, that he cannot do himself justice and is forced to an aphoristic and dogmatic style that may provoke as much resistance as agreement, Professor Kohn's book may seem, to some readers, too long. Over seven hundred pages, and this is only Volume I and we are left at the threshold of the nationalist age! But the length of the book is wholly justified. Only on such a scale could Professor Kohn illustrate the complexity of his theme; only by careful analysis of the content of the nationalist idea over a long period and many countries can the reader be shaken out of his dangerous idea that he knows it all already. Professor Kohn is especially good in discriminating between early and late forms of nationalism, for example, between the modern identification of a nation with a linguistic culture and the old, matter-of-fact cultural protectionism that made the medieval Czechs such sticklers for their linguistic rights.

Professor Kohn's learning is not without its dangers. There is involved in the history of nationalism the problem involved in the history of any dogmatic system, the problem of development. The naïve nationalist apologist, like the naïve fundamentalist theologian, may look back into the past to find there both an exemplification of his general view of national superiority and a consciousness of that view in the ancestral stock. It is very easy to show that such an approach is dangerous and breeds a totally unhistorical attitude in the would-be historian. The modern German race-and-soil theorist is hard put to it, indeed, to assimilate to his doctrine such ambiguous Germanic heroes as Frederick the Great. He is forced to import into the past a body of ideas for whose existence there is, in the usual sense of the term, no historical evidence. He is forced to evade, or to solve by drastic methods, such problems as the nature of the loyalty due in the past to an ideal of which, soberly speaking, the past knew next to nothing. He has to be a casuist of non-existent cases of conscience. Who broke up the Holy Roman Empire of the German Nation, the Protestants or Catholics? A whole national mythology may be built around an irrelevant conception of treason to a non-existent national conscience. The treason of the Constable de Bourbon is reprobated in national not feudal terms. The ambiguous role of Paris in the Hundred Years War may be glossed over; there may be a comforting assumption that all citizens of the United Netherlands rejoiced in their liberation from the Spanish yoke and that, alike in Friesland and Brabant, all right-thinking men were of the national religion of all right-thinking men, a religion which did not, in fact, as yet exist.

Nationally unfortunate peoples are especially prone to this reading of history backwards. What had become a great test of public virtue, courage and disinterestedness centuries later is, with a serious lack of historical clarity and charity, applied to an earlier period in the national history without any justice. In his resolution to redeem his own past, "Lord Jim" is perhaps unduly hard to his own past—and there are some who think that, in this condemnation of past weakness, Conrad's hero was speaking as a Polish noble on the past weaknesses of the Polish nobility and exalting a type of unbending heroism that politically minded members of more fortunate nations may find hard to understand. Survival, success, these are not for the nationalist patriot any more adequate tests of duty done than they are for the passionate Christian. There is, at this stage of exaltation, no point in the utilitarian wisdom of not losing for the national or Christian life the reasons for living. In a country like Scotland this will lead romantic Scots (of whom there are many) to be unjust to the great and politic house of Campbell and to an excessive contempt for the Balliol name; and will lead to a glossing over, in a country like Ireland, of the question of the political wisdom and, if you like, rational patriotism of unfortunate national leaders like Hugh O'Neil and Hugh O'Donnell who can thus be made martyrs to a cause which, it is probable, they could only have faintly understood. There is so much of this *ex-post facto* historiography, especially in countries with bitterly disputed national traditions and still more in countries with frequently disastrous national experiences, to make any scholar rightly sceptical of the existence of nationalist feeling before very modern times.

But the scholar can be too sceptical. It does not follow that a dogma was not held incoherently, semi-consciously if you like, until it was defined in a decree of a council or in a treatise by a recognized Father of the Church. The historian of nationalist dogma should be careful to remember that the claims of an equivalent of Newman's doctrine of development are to be taken into account, that it is not intellectually contemptible to hold the

doctrine of historical occultation, by which ingenious astrono-
mical parallel Stubbs justified his use of hypothesis in English
constitutional history. Until there is controversy, until there is a
problem of allegiance and duty, until there is a *cause célèbre*, there
may be no occasion for any formal expression of a faith already
held. It is not safe to see in the first spokesman of the creed its
inventor as well as formulator, or to be quite certain that because
all that we now mean by national feeling cannot have been present
in fourteenth-century Scotland or fifteenth-century France, that
neither Wallace nor St. Joan were real nationalist as well as
national heroes.

Some of the difficulty is illustrated by Professor Kohn's treatment of early Jewish history. He does not make it plain whether he
holds that the post-Exilic recension of biblical history represents,
pretty closely, what we mean to-day by "history," that we know,
for instance, what were the political and social ideas of the Jews
of the early kingdom as we know what were the political and social
ideas of fifth- and fourth-century Athens; that the Bible is here a
document or collection of documents that is more comparable to
Thucydides and Plato than to Plutarch. We learn in a note that:
"Even to-day orthodox Jews celebrate the Passover as if they in
their generation had been delivered from Egypt, as if national
history were alive across thousands of years in the present." No
doubt the most important fact to-day is that orthodox Jews do so
act and have so acted for two thousand years. The existence of
historically unprovable or highly improbable equivalents in national
traditions is the important fact, not their total or partial lack of
historicity. But it is of some interest and importance to know, or
speculate about the degree of historicity, and it is probable that
both with Jew and Gentile there is an older tradition behind that
given literary and self-conscious form after the Exile or the French
Revolution.

There is another danger, usually but not always avoided here.
Objective books on nationalism, books really above the battle, are
rare. It is extremely difficult to be constantly vigilant, to weigh the
testimonies as well as enumerate them. Some books tell their own
tale; few readers of a once well-known French tract *A Quoi tient la
superiorité des Français sur les Anglo-Saxons* needed to be warned

that it was not a work of objective learning before they read the chapter on "Le Péril Anglais." But there are more subtle traps. René Johannet's equivocal use of nationalist terminology is noted, but not the danger signal of his publishers, the "Nouvelle Librarie Nationale," the publishing house of the *Action française*. And the accumulation of instances in the notes sometimes weakens the argument by raising doubts as to what is meant, or as to the relevance of the judgment. Thus the English reader with a little literary knowledge will be more baffled than instructed by the dictum, "Generally the patriotic poetry of eighteenth-century England is of little merit and shows no special emphasis upon English nationalism. See, for instance, Thomas Gray, *The Bard* . . . ; Richard Glover, *Admiral Hosier's Ghost* . . . ; Mark Akenside, *A British Philippic Occasioned by the Insults of the Spaniards and the Present Preparation for War.*" And when Lord Halifax, on the strength of a phrase or two lifted from *The Character of a Trimmer*, is erected into a precocious preacher of "Blut und Boden," one is tempted to retort on Professor Kohn one of Halifax's *Miscellaneous Thoughts*, "Men who borrow their opinions can never repay their debts." There is a little too much of Germanic passion for authority in the book and, as is not always the case, Professor Kohn gives the impression of being much more sagacious than are many of his authorities. But learning has its price, which is occasional pedantry, and it is to his learning that Professor Kohn owes some of his happiest finds, like that German musicologist who explained why German prisoners of war degenerated under the influence of English march music:

The English music intended only to be an accompaniment of marchers; it did not suggest a superior authority—it addressed the individual and thus undermined discipline. Who marches behind Scotch bagpipes could not answer the question of why he wore the King's uniform as a German would do: to sacrifice my life to the fatherland if it is necessary.

The German victim of this propaganda had "brought him a kind of undesired maturity." Since the re-education of Germany is on the agenda of the United Nations, compulsory marching to "A Hundred Pipers" or "Roll Out the Barrel" or even "Non più andrai," in place of the "Badenweiler" or other more orthodoxly

Germanic march tunes might be imposed on a people who will want to march to *something*.

Words play such an evocative part in the creation and nourishment of nationalist sentiment that the newness of much of the nationalist vocabulary comes as something of a shock to the true believer. "Patrie," which has had such a brilliant career in French song and slogan, dates only from 1539 (Boulainvilliers, that prophet of *Herrenvolk* theory, still uses it, in the eighteenth century, as the equivalent of "petit pays"; the Gallic bourgeois in their climb upwards to a status equal to that of the free Franks "sont dits et censez Pairs, avec l'attribution de pouvoir être elevez a l'honneur de gouverner leur Patrie"). The patriotism which Johnson thought the last refuge of a scoundrel was not our modern patriotism, and the word nationalism came into English after most of the marks of the thing signified were visible. And Friedrich Meinecke has listed the slow growth in meaning of the very word "nation" to its modern German meaning and potency, through such intermediary stages as being a unifying conception suitable for the Prussian officers, who, whatever their provincial origin, should be inspired by an "esprit de corps et de nation." The same verbal ideal was not improbably that of the officer corps as late as July 1944, but what different emotional power had the word "nation" acquired in the minds of the vast majority of Germans, Prussians or non-Prussians!

Our present preoccupations make it natural and defensible to look with special attention at the account of the growth of German national feeling given by Professor Kohn. The price to the world of German nationalism has been so high, the more pathological forms of national feeling have been erected into great systems by the national talent for uncritical construction, that it is reasonable to think that in the German situation, if anywhere, is to be found the clue. There are some decisive dates and events in the growth of this great historical phenomenon. There was the discovery by Poggio Bracciolini of the manuscript of Tacitus's *Germania* at Hersfeld in 1445. Few tracts, so short and so tendentious, have had such astonishing fortunes as this. From those ambiguous pages the English constitution, whole systems of agricultural history, the foundations of anthropological schools have been extracted. But it was above all for the Germans that *Germania* was important. Careful selection—and the abstention from criticism called for by national pride—made possible the most gratifying discoveries. It made it possible to rejoice whole-heartedly in the victory of Hermann over Varus in the Teutoberger Wald; thus was the future seed of all that was great in European history saved from Roman corruption. *Fons et origo mali*, indeed!

In contemplating the murderous absurdities of German national-ist doctrine it is important to remember that the failure to achieve political unity in a sense *forced* the creation of substitutes for it. Because German history was unsatisfactory to Germans, because it was hard to define "Germany" and "German," there was a natural stress on race, culture, myth. Not many Frenchmen needed to worry about the lukewarm patriotism of Voltaire; the French state was there, France was there, whether the author of *La Henriade* and *La Pucelle* was a loyal Frenchman or not. But the question "War Lessing ein eifriger Patriot?" was more urgent in a country still to be made or only imperfectly made. Germans could not, they felt, adopt "pas trop de zèle" as a guiding principle of poli-tical and historical criticism.

It is true that we are inclined, too easily, to identify the political unity achieved by France and England with national unity in the modern sense. Professor Kohn rightly warns us against that. He even warns us too much. There was a great difference between Germany after the Peace of Westphalia and France after the Peace of Westphalia. That the imperialist leaders in the Thirty Years War often bore highly un-Germanic names, "Piccolomini, Gordon, Butler," that "German nobles, like Duke Bernhard of Weimar or Maurice de Saxe, served the French king" makes a point about Germany, but not a universally valid point. It was not merely the new strength of the French monarchy that made it impossible for a Luxembourg or a Vauban to think of imitating the treasons of Condé and Turenne; there was a new standard of loyalty and duty in France. It was not our standard, but it was not the standard of eighteenth-century Germany.

In the period covered by Professor Kohn, for reasons he gives in abundance, nationalism was inevitably literary, linguistic, cultural, and there is a natural tendency to hope that it can be reduced to such comparatively innocuous forms to-day. But we have to notice that such cultural nationalism has seldom been enough to satisfy nationalist passions or the needs which those passions serve. It is probably true that in a great part of the Soviet Union nationalism has been so tamed (along with other forms of individualistic choice). But that success has to be tested in the case of a western nation, with its own Catholic culture. The remedy may work, but it is going a little ahead of available evidence to be as sure as Professor Carr is that it has worked in Lithuania. And it is particularly surprising that the author of *The Romantic Exiles* has not pondered more seriously the criticism that Herzen made on such a policy a century ago:

It need hardly be said that only among apathetic and feeble peoples was nationalism allowed to develop, and only so long as it confined itself to archæological and linguistic disputes. In Milan and in Poland, where nationalism was not confined to grammar, a tight rein was kept upon it.

The truth of this judgment can easily be illustrated from these islands. In its origin, the Gaelic League was officially and really non-political. It united Unionists and Nationalists, Protestants and Catholics; all that was necessary for a common platform was a share in Douglas Hyde's resolution that "our ancient Irish nation [should not] sink into a West Britain." It was an organization that had its parallel in the Honourable Society of the Cymmrodorion. It was an organization that could be joined—and was joined—by one of the most formidable clerical beaters of the Orange drum, Dr. Kane, who was "proud to be an Orangeman but did not forget that he was an O'Cahan." It was a cause that could excite the dilettante enthusiasm of George Moore and had enough general cultural pretensions to excite the scornful resistance of James Joyce. It could insist on the redemption of Ireland by the self-improvement of the Irish people "and as we are shall Banba be." But the emotional logic of nationalism was too much for its political neutrality and cultural autonomy. The Ard Feis became something very different from the Scottish Mod or the Welsh Eisteddfod. There was a necessary union of the old nationalist, Republican, political tradition with the new linguistic and cultural tradition, a union reflected in the never-failing respect of Sinn Fein for the memory of that remarkably un-Gaelic leader, Parnell, and in the famous eulogy of the heretical and church-condemned national martyr, Wolfe Tone, by the Anglo-Irish, Catholic, Gaelic enthusiast, Patrick Pearse, who was to be Tone's successor in the national martyrology. The living national tradition against something, e.g. English rule, made the cultural movement, in spite of itself, necessarily revolutionary and militantly nationalist.

Of course in Ireland religion did play a great part. Most "Gaels" were Catholic whatever their racial origin (in the old loose sense of racial); most Unionists were Protestants whatever their family history. A ballad once deservedly popular in Ulster recounted the treason of Bob Williamson who from being "a stout Orange blade"

> married a Papish called Bridget Maginn,
> Turned Papish himself and forsook the ould cause
> That gave us our freedom, religion and laws.

And over a great part of eastern Europe the indignant protest of the Orangemen of Dungannon would be fully understood by Catholics, by Jews, by Uniats, Orthodox. This identification of religion and nationality has much less plausibility and justification in more advanced, united nations. The Presbyterian and Gaelic population of North Uist is not separated by any national barrier from the Catholic and Gaelic population of South Uist, Catholic and Protestant alike in Alès or Montbéliard are French; their quarrels, bitter enough, are still family quarrels. And in Germany the old religious differences on which French policy attempted to play long after they had enough political force to be worth counting on, have been merged in a common national, nationalist and now, it is to be feared, Nazi passion that may have replaced the Catholic and Protestant faith in the hearts of millions of the younger Germans.

In the long run this great destructive, constructive force may be doomed to disappear, to go the way of other solutions for the perennial problem of the emotional basis of the state. But, as Lord Keynes said in another connection, in the long run we shall all be dead. It is the short run that concerns us, the next generation. And it is too early to be positive that national passion is dead, dying or even seriously wounded. The miserable stage armies that the

Germans have recruited from conquered territories, General Vlasov's liberating Russians and the rest, may be the swallows of a future non-national world conflict; so may be the devotees of the Communist parties, whose violent and uncritical patriotism has its centre in Moscow, not in the countries of which they are citizens. But for the average man it is still true that the nation is his religion, the god (or Moloch) to which he makes the most extravagant sacrifices. "Nationality," said the late T. M. Healy to the then Lord Hugh Cecil, "is what men will die for. Even the noble lord would not die for the meridian of Greenwich." And in this iron age, the creeds men die for have an immense advantage over the most rational, symmetrical and persuasive doctrines that have not that claim on our attention. Professor Kohn looks forward to the assimilation of what is best in nationalism in a more integrated culture. Professor Carr hopes for a speedy decline in what he thinks a great aberration. Each has done a service in calling the attention of the free world to a problem that, for the next few years at least, must be of absorbing importance.

VII
NATIONALIST DOCTRINE
OF M. CHARLES MAURRAS
(1935)

THE Dreyfus case acted as a catalyst on French society and politics. It forced a decision which would have had to be taken, sooner or later, a decision which was taken suddenly, passionately and, for most of that generation, permanently. Was France to be forced to subordinate her life to the necessities of her external position—as those necessities had been interpreted by the spokesmen of the "revenge"? Was France to continue to keep her eye fixed on "the blue line of the Vosges"? Was she to fit all internal questions into the narrow frame of the necessities of her foreign policy?

Long before the Affair, the whole-hearted devotion of all French parties to the task of redeeming the shame of 1870 had weakened. When Gambetta announced that clericalism was the enemy, he implicitly denied that Germany was the enemy in all conditions and at all times. The simple and flamboyant patriotism of a Déroulède, the more subtle and ingenious nationalism of Barrès failed, in the adventure of Boulangism, to overthrow the parliamentary republic in favour of a military dictatorship promising an aggressive foreign policy. More serious still, neither Déroulède nor Barrès won or kept the individual allegiance of the younger generation of Frenchmen. True, the generation which came to manhood after 1870 was, in large part, moved "by those violent nationalist passions which are necessary to conquered peoples,"[1] but if many listened to Barrès, many listened to Jaurès, to Guesde, to the new scientific socialism which was spreading the name, if not the doctrines, of Marx among the intellectuals as well as among the workmen of Paris and of the industrial towns.

Socialism was positive; it even attracted nationalists like Barrès himself, who hoped to harness popular discontent to the nationalist

---

[1] Barrès. *Scènes et Doctrines du Nationalisme*, vol. i, p. 113.

cause by preaching hostility to foreign high-finance and to foreign labour. The tradition of the workman of Paris was nationalist; it might yet be kept so. But side by side with the positive doctrines of socialism, there was growing fast the negative doctrine of anti-militarism. The increasing burden of conscription; the armaments race, with its increasing strain on the stationary population of France, made Frenchmen more willing to consider the cost and value of a great army than had been the case in the years just after 1870. Barrès, himself, had some sympathy for the point of view which asked what was the use of a great army since the collapse of Boulanger had shown that the governing class was resolved to keep peace with Germany. Then the practical experience of army life which the extension of conscription had made available to the educated classes, created a market for (and possibly the supply of) anti-militarist writing. Abel Hermant and Georges Courteline depicted the army in less rosy colours than had been popular when the bourgeoisie could buy exemption from service. Scepticism of the military hierarchy had become general in radical circles, when it was realized, under the Second Empire, that military prestige was now an asset of the Right, not of the Left. On the eve of the Franco-Prussian war, Left-wing opinion was already beginning to move in the direction of a peaceful foreign policy and of a reduction of armaments.

Eighteen-seventy, for a moment, held up this development, for most of the glory of the resistance to the Germans fell to an extreme radical, Gambetta[1]; and the Commune was as much an expression of the outraged patriotism of the working men of Paris as of any socialist theory. It was the Left that refused to make peace in 1871; and it was peace, not the monarchy, that the peasants voted for when they elected the Right majority of the National Assembly. But the development of the Left into a peace party, the abandonment of the old dream of revolutionizing Europe in arms, of identifying the republic with military glory, was only delayed for a short time. The victory of the Left was a guarantee for peace, while a success for the Right would be a menace to peace, since the evaporation of the influence of the "notables" and the weakening of the political force of the Church

---

[1] The disciples of Maurras have naturally worked hard to destroy the Gambetta "legend." Cf. "Henri Dutrait-Crozon", *Gambetta et la défense nationale*.

left the conservative parties devoid of all emotional stock-in-trade,
except the last refuge, patriotism.[1] As the Church question became
the easiest way of stirring up political feeling in France, the old
alliance of "throne and altar" became, whether willingly or unwillingly, the alliance of "sabre and holy-water sprinkler." In the
Boulangist crisis of 1889 was seen the last formidable attempt at a
radical nationalism, at rousing the old patriotic fervour of the
revolutionary Paris mob; it came near to success, but it failed, and
for "the nationalists beaten in 1889, the job was to hold out until
France *produced in abundance the feelings they had sown, doubtless
prematurely.*"[2] They had to wait, as Barrès put it, for their teachers
"to reconstruct for us our certainties."[3]

It can hardly have been expected by Barrès, or by anybody else,
that this task would fall to a Provençal journalist, a friend of Barrès
and an ardent nationalist, indeed, but better known as a literary
critic of a rigorous type than as a politician. Yet it was this poet and
critic who was ready for the emergency, because he had a doctrine
where his allies had only passions. Barrès, for all his theorising,
was no thinker, but to M. Charles Maurras to be right was "still
one of the ways in which man may immortalize himself . . . to be
right and change the 'numerous and ricidulous fancies' of one's
fellow citizens."[4] M. Maurras is a Provençal of Catholic family,
but not strictly speaking a "Blanc du Midi," since his parents had
been seduced by the Second Empire into a temporary abandonment of their devotion to the House of France. Born in 1868, he
grew up in a world in which Bonapartism and royalism were fading
out of French minds, and royalist beliefs, in any active form, faded
out of his as his religious faith had done. There remained to the
young sceptic only a conviction that in politics there were certain
laws which could be discovered and applied, and a passionate
conviction that in this world, where absolutes were not to be found,
there was one relative good so superior to all others that it could
serve as a touchstone for most departments of human life. For the
religion of his ancestors, M. Maurras substituted the Goddess

[1] During the crisis following the dissolution of 16th May, 1876, Hohenlohe wrote
to Bismarck: "The monarchist parties, however, cannot get on without a military
success to strengthen their policy in the country." (Quoted in Walter Frank,
Nationalismus und Demokratie im Frankreich, p. 62.)
[2] Barrès, *L'Appel au soldat*. (Nelson edition, p. 10.)
[3] Henri-L. Miéville, *La Pensée de Maurice Barrès*, p. 33.
[4] Maurras, *Au Signe de Flore*, p. 21.

France. He suffered, like so many of his generation, from the humiliation of 1870, and what captivity in Germany was for Déroulède and the visit to captive Metz was for Barrès, the voyage to Athens, to see the Olympic Games of 1896, was for M. Maurras. At sea, on that Mediterranean of which he felt himself to be one of the real heirs, M. Maurras realized that France had fallen lower in the world than he had dreamed. "How frightened I was to see her so small. How isolated and drifting she seemed in the world at large, how different from the conception of her which I had constructed for myself."[1] The truth was painful but salutary. France must seek to discover why she was weak and others were strong. "It is possible that this investigation will cost us a quarter of an hour of anguish. We should be the last of peoples if we were afraid of being afraid."[2] The opportunity to take stock, and to share the results of that stock-taking with his countrymen, came with the first great crisis of the Dreyfus case. The attempts of the Dreyfus family to have the case reopened had made very little progress. The condemnation of an officer for high treason had been a sensation, but as far as there had been any discontent, it came from men of the Left who asked why this rich Jewish traitor had escaped with his life, and hinted that his wealth and his origin had had something to do with it. The agitation for revision (i.e. re-trial) was very unpopular at first, and it was shunned by many prudent politicians who were afterwards to rush to the aid of the victors. In any event, the revisionists were stronger among the politicians than in the country, where the sudden moral scruples of eminent "Panamists" were not taken very seriously. But a number of faults—whether moral or intellectual[3] is a matter of controversy—involved the rulers of the army in a series of manœuvres which gave the revisionists a chance to insert doubt in the public mind and to keep the agitation alive.[4] Then, at the beginning of September 1898, the news spread that Colonel Henry, who had been deeply involved in the resistance to the reopening of the question, had admitted strengthening his case by forging a document and had then cut his throat in his cell! There was stupefaction in the camp of the army

---

[1] Maurras, op. cit., p. 44.   [2] *Anthinéa* (1919 edition), p. 265.
[3] See Georges Sorel, *La Révolution Dreyfusienne* (2nd edition), p. 69.
[4] Neither then, nor since, do M. Maurras and his friends seem to have been fully alive to the difficulty of defending *both* the honesty *and* the ability of the generals.

and its allies. Rochefort and Drumont tried in vain to stem the panic; but that honour fell to the comparatively obscure literary critic of the decidedly obscure royalist journal, the *Gazette de France*. M. Maurras not only justified the forgery, he represented the suicide as a martyrdom for France. "The article in which M. Maurras eulogized Henry is the first stage of his career. Thanks to the resounding publicity which his allies and, still more, his enemies gave him, the theorist almost unknown the day before became in one bound the councillor, the strong head of his party."[1] "Without him the Dreyfus case might only have been a three-act play . . . he kept it going for five acts and, indeed, never let it die."[2] It is an achievement of which even nationalist Frenchmen may doubt the permanent value, but M. Maurras himself has no doubts that it was "the best action and in any case the most useful action of all those for which I have had reason to rejoice."[3]

The strength of M. Maurras lay in his fundamental position, that the guilt or innocence of Dreyfus was *not* the main question. He was then and has remained convinced of the justice of the condemnation, but even if Dreyfus had been proven innocent, that

[1] Cécile Delhorbe, *L'Affaire Dreyfus et les écrivains français*, pp. 204–5.

[2] Albert Thibaudet, *Les Idées de Charles Maurras*, p. 86. The semi-official statement of the Maurrasian version of the Affair praises the famous article very highly indeed: "On the 6th and 7th of September, in the *Gazette de France*, Charles Maurras showed the patriotism, the sense of his responsibilities, the idea of national safety which moved the colonel; he saluted his 'noble memory,' and foretold that the awakened national feeling would avenge him." "Henri Dutrait-Crozon," *Précis de l'Affaire Dreyfus*, pp. 169–70.

[3] *Au Signe de Flore*, p. 82.

The defence of Colonel Henry scandalized many people at the time, and since, and it was pointed out that the *Syllabus* of Pope Pius IX, which M. Maurras was accustomed to eulogize with what might seem extravagant enthusiasm, specifically condemned, among many "Liberal errors," the doctrine that "La violation d'un serment quelque saint qu'il soit, et toute action criminelle opposée à la loi éternelle, non seulement ne doit pas être blâmée, mais elle est tout à fait licite et digne des plus grands éloges quand elle est inspirée par l'amour de la patrie." M. Maurras replied to M. Marc Sangnier, leader of a group of Christian Democrats, that the reference to a "patriotic forgery" was invented by enemies of M. Maurras, but that "Ceux d'entre nous qui ont composé leur synthèse subjective par rapport à l'idée de Patrie en ont tiré des lois un peu supérieures à l'utilité immédiate et grossière de la patrie. Cette idée de Patrie, *pulcherrima rerum*, ne leur commande rien de 'criminel' ni de 'honteux.' Elle ne sert donc point à fausser la nature humaine ni a favouriser les instincts d'artifice ou de férocité. . . . Mais en cas de nécessité? Mais lorsque le salut public est menacé? Le cas de nécessité n'est pas le cas de moralité. En cas de nécessité, s'approprier un pain n'est pas le voler, faire la guerre n'est pas organiser l'homicide; une autre loi, une loi *supreme* ou *extreme* intervient alors, et c'est d'elle que dépend en grande partie la casuistique du stratagème. Pour juger équitablement du colonel Henry, c'est surtout au point de vue de ses devoirs d'état que nous nous sommes placés." (Maurras, *La Démocratie religieuse*, p. 278.)

would not have excused the agitation which divided France, weakened the army, and imperilled the national existence. Justice was a good thing, but it was not the only or the chief thing. To the poet who asked what was the state without justice, M. Maurras replied that there had been states without justice, but never justice without the state. Professing himself a Comtist, a positivist, M. Maurras objected to the introduction of abstract ideas like "justice" into what was fundamentally a political question. Justice and many other things only existed because the nation existed, and to declare *Fiat justitia, ruat coelum* in the manner of the Dreyfusards, was to beg the question. For what if the existence of the sky were the condition of justice and its collapse the end of any possibility of justice? First of all, seek what makes and maintains states before you undertake a course of action which pursues one of the ends of the state at the cost of destroying the only means to that and to many other ends![1]

This was to raise the argument to a higher level than had been customary on the nationalist side. It was a far more defensible ground than that taken by politicians like Godefroy Cavaignac, who declared that he had no doubt that Dreyfus was guilty, but that if he *had* any doubt, nothing could induce him to keep a possibly innocent man in prison. For talk of this kind, M. Maurras had nothing but scorn and, although he appreciated the great dramatic talent which Barrès displayed in his polemics, it may be doubted if the naïve theory attributing everything to Dreyfus's Jewish origin and asserting that "Aryans" had no reason to care what happened to this foreigner, really appealed very much to the more rigorous thinker and controversialist. If Dreyfus had been of pure Lorraine or Auvergnat origin, the reasons against endangering France to free one, possibly, innocent man would have been just as strong!

[1] This argument was based, in practice, on the assertion that only by betraying fundamental secrets of the national defence could the general staff justify its action in the Dreyfus case. Such a betrayal might mean an immediate war with Germany, or when war did come, the crushing inferiority of the French army. The mutilation of the "Second Bureau," which Henry had adorned, led, according to this point of view, to Plan XVII, Morhange and the occupation of the north of France! That was the price paid by France for gratifying the hates and illusions of the Dreyfusards, and thus was justified the gloss. "*Fiat justitia*," disent les Justiciers, "*ruat coelum*." "Que la justice soit et que la mitraille nous crève," *L'Enquête sur la Monarchie*, p. 510. Henry, on the other hand, acted on Danton's principle, "let my name be infamous if only France be free." This example is mine, not M. Maurras's—although M. Maurras has more toleration for the Jacobins of the Convention than for less authoritarian republicans!

The Jewishness of Dreyfus might make it more probable that he was a traitor, and it explained the real origins of this dangerous agitation, but it, like his guilt or innocence, was irrelevant to the main issue. It was good (or necessary) that one man should suffer for the people, for innumerable innocents had suffered to create France and innumerable innocents would have to suffer in the future to save her from the sentimental revolt against the grim necessities of life which was the most respectable side of the Dreyfusard movement. These misguided men who said "*Ruat Gallia, fiat justitia*"[1] were doubly deluded, for they did not realize how fragile was the thread of life of any nation, how real was the danger to the existence of France, and, in addition to this delusion, thanks to their deplorable education, until it was too late, they could not realize what France meant to them.

The necessity of constant vigilance, of the state of siege in which artistic and philosophic doctrines had to be scrutinized to see that they helped or, at least, did not hinder the national defence was, no doubt, regrettable. M. Maurras does not profess the delight of Barrès in the separation of mind from mind by national or local tradition. He is too good a classicist for that. He does not think that because he is a Provençal and indeed a partisan of the Felibrège, he is thereby excluded from real understanding of other peoples, at any rate of other peoples in the great classical tradition. The contrast between the attitude of *Anthinéa* and the *Voyage de Sparte* is striking indeed! But the world is what it is, and the nation-state as the vehicle of the good life is *given*. No rhetoric or longing for a better past or future can alter that. There had been a time, he adds, carrying the war into the enemy's camp, when this was not so. "There was a time when the international was not the creature of the nations but led and ruled them. Before being French, Italian, English or German, the man of the Middle Ages was a citizen of a general civilization."[2] But those days are past,

---

[1] *L'Enquete*, p. 522. This argument caused great scandal at the time. G. W. Steevens, Northcliffe's star reporter, was very shocked when he heard a version of it from a judge. Yet comparable considerations were in the mind of Harcourt in inducing him to avoid awkward questions during the Jameson Raid inquiry! To-day, the argument is so widely accepted that its novelty, in the simple-minded days of the end of the last century, is easily forgotten. We are all aware how few people there are who could sincerely say, "Let both the British Empire *and* the U.S.S.R. perish as long as justice is done."

[2] *Le Pape, la Guerre et la Paix*, p. vii.

through the fault of that Reformation for which "Anti-France" has such open or faintly disguised a weakness! *Vous l'avez voulu!*[1] But it is too late to lament that paradise lost and in this age of iron, men must live in the only way they can live. It is not the noisy, verbally violent anti-militarists like Gustave Hervé,[2] it is the more moderate, more plausible, sappers of the national will to live who are dangerous; and they are numerous and must be unmasked. France must be made safe for real Frenchmen. And making a nation safe is not easy, not a task to be undertaken half-heartedly, or with a too optimistic view of the world in which the nation must live!

Tantae molis erat Romanam condere gentem, the Virigilian theme (and the Virgilian tag) recur again and again in the work of M. Maurras. His opponents who live in the clouds can indulge in fine "ideals," in the luxuries of delicate consciences, either because they do not realize the role of the national state as the condition of their intellectual or moral luxuries, or because, misled by the childish doctrines of the Revolution, they attribute to a mere concurrence of wills what is, in fact, the result of the labours and the luck of generations of men.[3] "Positively minded men do not ask of the state that it should realize any ideal, except its own duration."[4] M. Maurras would heartily agree with this view; one prizes, indeed, the richness of life made possible by the survival, in strength, of the nation; one is impoverished as that life is impoverished, but the means of richer life are to be preserved at all costs, since they are the one thing necessary. As much as Andrew Marvell, M. Maurras knows what it means to "ruin the great work of time," but he is far, indeed, from admiring Cromwell, or Bonaparte, for this type of

[1] The same argument is used to put the responsibility for modern militarism on the Revolution. The "nation in arms" is a conception of these bad new days.

[2] M. Hervé, when he was editing his anti-militarist *Le Piou-piou de l' Yonne*, wanted the colonel to plant the regimental flag ceremonially on the dung-heap. With the outbreak of war, he became violently patriotic. He was "guéri par la force mediatrice de la réalité." (*Conditions de la Victoire*, vol. i, p. 17.)

[3] On the monarchical side of M. Maurras's doctrine, the labours which have counted are those of "the forty kings who in a thousand years made France," but all states are made by men and maintained by men; by the House of France, by the English aristocracy, by the "four confederated States," which combine to misrule modern France. Right ideas are important, as far as they are guides for living men, but all ideas to be potent must be made flesh in concrete human wills, wills of a family or of families or of sects largely recruited, like the sects of "Anti-France," from groups held together by family tradition.

[4] Lucien Moreau in *L'Enquête sur la Monarchie*, p. 180.

achievement! If you believe that men are French because they want to be, you may believe that they will remain French no matter what happens to the French state, but it is not willing to be French, but being incapable of willing to be anything else that is the real mark of nationality. There is a sense in which M. Maurras's own theory of nationality is subjective, but it is a subjectivism highly conditioned by history, by geography, by family tradition. Renan was wrong in inverting the factors which go to make up a nationality, by making them fundamentally psychological and subjective, and that error is a dangerous one, since it leads to indifference to the real forces which make and maintain nations. Take example from the fate of peoples which have not been unified in the body, however united in the spirit! Should France fail to learn the lesson "we will have to begin over again the hard experience of conquered Germany and enslaved Italy. . . . France, once lost, this capital once evaporated, it will then be seen that we lived by it and that each one of us shared in its benefits."[1] It follows, then, that all who appreciate these truths must put first things first, "politics first of all—nationalist politics—politics of complete nationalism."[2]

For despite his denial of all absolutes (or rather his admission of his failure to find any), M. Maurras believes, without any doubts or hesitations, in one relative truth of so high a degree of certainty that it may, for all practical purposes, be regarded as an absolute on which his whole system rests. He believes that in the greatness of France, in her power and splendour, is, for every Frenchman, whether he realizes it or not, the possibility of the highest good he can attain to in this unsatisfactory world. If this be untrue, M. Maurras might well wish "all that the brigand apple brought and this foul world were dead at last."[3]

Who, then, are Frenchmen for whom this view of life is the one

[1] *La Démocratie religieuse*, p. 350, cf. p. 29.

[2] Ibid., p. 388. *Politique d'abord* is the most famous and debated of the Maurrasian maxims, and it lies at the basis of all his teaching on the form of the state, of the place of law, economics, the arts, etc., in national life. "Seek ye first the Kingdom of France, and its strength and all these things shall be added unto you," M. Maurras might have said, if he were in the habit of quoting—or misquoting—scripture!

[3] A clerical commentator notes that "en dépit de ses affirmations relativistes et de ses appels passagers au sentiment, le postulat de la patrie est pour lui en premier lieu une donnée de l'intelligence qui s'impose à son esprit avec tous les caractères d'un impératif catégorique." (P. Descoqs, *A Travers l'Œuvre de M. Ch. Maurras*, p. 323, third edition.)

necessary political truth which, once firmly grasped, will serve as a clue to life and duty? They are the men and women who have been made French by history; the men and women who have been moulded in their own lives and in the lives of their ancestors by the combination of the wills of men, the facts of geography, the actions of destiny (or of luck) which have caused the historical evolution of the French state. Men and women are French whether they know it, or whether they will it. Their Frenchness is *given*. It is thus a non-mystical, non-racial, "positive" doctrine of nationality. To realize that you are French, and so have certain possibilities open to you and others denied you, is to look at the world as it is, is therefore the part of wisdom.[1]

"Every kind of alteration and doctoring of texts may be attempted: no one can make of us racists or gobinists."[2] This declaration was made by M. Maurras at the height of the contoversy with the Church, but whatever its value as a reply to Catholic criticisms of his doctrine, it is a just statement of his position. It might be possible to find occasional lapses from the strict observance of the salutary rule not to mix up race and nation, but the central doctrine set out, again and again, in the writings of M. Maurras, avoids the trap into which simpler minds or thicker heads lead people so easily to fall. Being a Frenchman is, indeed, a matter of heredity, not merely of will, but it is not a matter of *blood*, of *race*. To be French is to put France before all else, to feel in the French fashion, to be at home in the physical and mental atmosphere of France and to feel uprooted elsewhere. But no degree of French ancestry can make up for divergence from the French tradition and no ancestry bars a man from being French—as long as the break with the ancestral country or tribe is complete. To be French is to have a French mind and a French heart. It is not a mere matter of choosing to be French; the choice must have been involuntary; a man who can really conceive himself as being something other than French, even if he chooses to remain or to becone a French citizen, is not a real Frenchman but a "métèque." Yet when this choice has been really

[1] Although it is not a positivist point of view, M. Maurras seems to hold also that being French is not only the fate of Frenchmen, but the most desirable fate that can, in this sphere, befall *any* man. The relativism of M. Maurras's theory of knowledge does not prevent his feeling and expressing a conviction that "they order all matters better in France"—and, if they don't to-day, it is because of the denationalizing labours of the various enemies of the real France.

[2] *L'Action française et le Vatican*, p. 286.

made, there can be no falling back on childish criteria such as appeal to modern Germany, no appeal to phrenology to assert the superiority of one type of skull over another. Was not all western Europe civilized, raised to true humanity without any necessity either of miscegenation or extermination? "A kind of ethnic grafting applied to the barbarians made of them Greeks and Romans. . . . Adoption by contact is as good as a blood tie."[1] From time to time M. Maurras has made appeals or uttered objurgations which have had a superficial appearance of "racism," but his heart and his head alike have kept him from dwelling too long in the dangerous twilight zone where grow monsters of the Rosenberg school. To say, in a moment of heat, that England is twice barbarous, once as Protestant and once as "Anglo-Saxon," is an expression of annoyance with British naval superiority; but if the Protestantism is a reality, the "Anglo-Saxonism" is merely a term of abuse. At the Olympic Games of 1896, the spectacle of "Barbarians," Germans, English, Americans, competing in that Athens where, like the Scythians of old, their only role should be that of policemen, was irritating, but what marked off these peoples from the true heirs of Hellas was not blood, but creed and language. The complete man is the heir of Greece and Rome, of Greece as the maker and of Rome as the sustainer of the civilization which we may develop but on which, fundamentally, we cannot improve. "The privileges of the strong are the natural result of a subtlety and of a clarity of mind which has no fatherland but the air of Greece,"[2] for, when she was herself and only herself "Attica was the human race."[3]

In this repeated insistence on the classical inheritance of the civilized man, M. Maurras was doubtless influenced by the problem of culture as he saw it in his youth and young manhood. After 1870, the application of the *fas est et ab hoste doceri* principle led many Frenchmen to an imitation of German methods and German ideas which was often highly uncritical. The modernization of secondary education, for instance, meant giving more space to modern languages and less to the classics—and, as M. Maurras

---

[1] *Anthinéa*, p. 296. During the war M. Maurras was provoked to repent this doctrine as far as the Germans were concerned. The hopes once held that they might some day be civilized had to be abandoned. "It is well established that the German race, taken as a whole, was incapable of promotion." (*Les Conditions de la Victoire*, vol. i, p. 24.) At heart M. Maurras probably regards all people as candidates for promotion to the rank of Frenchmen!

[2] Ibid., p. 236.   [3] Ibid., p. 56.

complained, the modern languages taught were not the kindred
Latin tongues, but German and English. Through these doors
poured a flood of new ideas, the waters of the Thames and the
Rhine poured into the Seine and the Rhône—to their pollution.
All foreign geese were swans. Kant replaced Descartes as the philosophical master of the young Frenchman. In the arts, there was a
blind admiration for Shakespeare and Goethe. The dangers which
the romantic movement made the French mind run earlier in the
century, were now doubled by the political dangers to any stable
society of the subversive doctrines of the nations which had never
known or had abandoned the healthy discipline of the Roman
Church. A good patriot like M. Jules Lemaître praised, without any
sense of his civic responsibilities, the dangerous works of Tolstoy,
and "thousands of young defenceless Frenchwomen were literally
stupefied by Wagnerian aesthetics, Ibsenian morality, Tolstoyan
political doctrine."[1] Some of M. Maurras's hostility to the novelties
which were corrupting the taste of Frenchmen was purely aesthetic.
He was himself a poet and a critic of literature before he turned to
politics and, as a leader of the "École Romane," preacher of a
doctrine hostile to the more fluid literary views of the Romantics, in
or out of France. But more serious than the decay of French versi-
fication was the decay of French self-esteem. That decay, and the
reaction against it, is the theme of *Quand les Français ne s'aimaient
pas*. It was not merely a redressing of the artistic balance, it was an
item in the refurbishing of the national armoury to restore French
appreciation of Poussin. It was a reply to the defeatist view of
French life to assert the superiority of France in the arts, while
awaiting the day when it would be possible to reassert her old
superiority in arms.[2]

As the true heir of the ancient world, France has no reason to
look outside her own borders for a lead; it is rather for her to give
a lead to her "Latin sisters" and to such parts of the world as are
capable of being raised to civilization. *Homo sum nil alienum a me
humanum puto*, so M. Maurras might turn the tag! In this identification of civilization with the classical tradition and the classical
tradition with the Latin tongues, there is a simplification of the

[1] *Pour la Défense nationale*, vol. i, p. 77.
[2] The sciences were not forgotten in this campaign, and M. René Quinton testified to the existence of enough French master biologists to make superfluous any
genuflections to German science.

question which gives more controversial than intellectual force to the argument. As an old ally and now hostile critic of M. Maurras, M. Louis Dimier, has pointed out, the whole of western Europe is the heir of Rome and the degree of inheritance is not to be computed by the inspection of the vocabularies of the national languages.[1] But the assertion of the intrinsic value of French culture, the reaction against the naïve worship of German and English methods and achievements which was marked in Quinet, in Renouvier, in Renan, in Taine, was valuable at the time, not only in restoring the national morale, but in forcing the complacent propagandists of foreign ideas to defend them as good and not merely as novelties. If there was ever any real danger of the French not thinking well enough of themselves, M. Maurras helped to prevent it from going very far!

But why was it necessary at all to be vigilant to save French culture, and the will of Frenchmen to remain French, from the snares of cosmopolitan art and ideas? The seductions of Wagner[2] were felt by such a patriot as Barrès; indeed, the literary taste of M. Maurras's chief ally, M. Léon Daudet, is very free from national exclusiveness, but if such concessions are to be deplored, or accepted as personal idiosyncrasies, very different is the case of French writers and teachers who spread foreign doctrine and admire, not only foreign art, but foreign ideas. Ibsenism and Tolstoyism and Kantism were far more to be feared than mere literary or musical fancies which, at worst, merely involve taking too seriously the claims of lesser peoples to a share in civilization. The *morality* of these northern barbarians is a dissolving force in France, and this was made manifest at the time of the Dreyfus crisis when the fighting force of the "revisionists" was found among the "intellectuals" corrupted by the official teaching of the republic.[3]

[1] M. Dimier tells us that when Mistral organized a Petrarch festival at Vaucluse he invited Rumanian, but excluded English delegates!

[2] The propaganda for Wagner in France conducted by musicians like Chabrier was not safe from suspicious criticism and, during the war, M. Barrès repented his weakness for *Tristan*.

[3] M. Maurras, perhaps because he was educated at a Catholic collège and not at a state lycée, devotes comparatively little time or space to the attacks on "Kantisme," which the brilliant polemic of Barrès made fashionable in nationalist circles. M. Thibaudet sums up, justly enough, the caricature of Kantian teaching put into the mouth of "Bouteiller," (Burdeau) by Barrès. "Belles qualités extérieures de professeur, mais parle de ce qu'il connait mal. Parait en être resté sur Kant à

But why should the official teaching of the republic be foreign, be hostile to the best interests of France? Because "the university," like all official institutions under the Republic, is in the hands of the "four confederated states" who together make up "Anti-France." The Freemasons, the Protestants, the Jews, the "métèques"—these allies are the rulers of France and they have all their own interest in indoctrinating the schools with their own anti-national view of French history. They are all loyal to France in the spirit of Arthur Ranc; "*la France, mais*"; France—but France on conditions. Each of the dominant groups has in common hostility to the central core of French tradition, Catholicism; consequently, they cannot accept France as history has made it; they must remake its past as they remake its present and its future, in the light of some general principle which will justify their conditional patriotism. In various ways, the allies are especially open to foreign ideas. "The métèques are our foreign guests, domiciled or recently naturalized, or their children. The Jews are foreigners settled in France for a longer or a shorter period of time. The Protestants are Frenchmen who, for the past three centuries, under the effects more of political than religious causes, tend to 'un-French' themselves in order to adopt the ideas of Switzerland, of Germany or of England."[1] The Freemasons and other anti-clericals, in their zeal against the Church, adopt the philosophic and religious ideas of their allies and, knowingly or unknowingly, serve to revenge on the body-politic of France old hates and old grievances. The spirit of "Anti-France" is sufficiently displayed in the teaching of French history in the schools and universities; in the shabby treatment of Joan of Arc, for instance,[2] and in the refusal to celebrate the second centenary of the victory of Villars at Denain, because, M. Maurras suggests, his memory, which ought to be dear to all good Frenchmen, is odious to the Protestants on account of his campaign against the Camisards. While honour is refused to Villars, Guiton, the Mayor of La Rochelle, "ally of England against the national unity

---

l'Allemagne de Henri Heine." (*La Vie de Maurice Barrès*, p. 176.) There is an amusing account of a difference of opinion on the merits of Kant between M. Daudet and the late Cardinal Amette in *Deputé de Paris*. The cardinal's tenderness for Kant shocked the deputy, who knew better what a danger to morals the philosopher was!

[1] *La Démocratie religieuse*, p. 90.

[2] M. Louis Dimier expands this theme in his *Les Préjugés ennemis de l'histoire de France*, originally lectures delivered at the "Institut d'Action française."

incarnate in Louis XIII and Richelieu, received, in 1911, the honours refused in 1912 to Villars. The same handsome treatment for Coligny, who betrayed Le Havre to the English. The same ill-luck for Guise, who recovered Calais from the English."[1] There is more substance in M. Maurras's complaint than is easily realized in a country which has a statue of Cromwell at one end of a short street and of Charles I at the other! "The dead speak," said a spectator when he saw a Jansenist and a Huguenot combine to pass the Civil Constitution of the Clergy; and it is never hard to remember that M. Maurras himself is a member of a Catholic family, born and bred in a part of France where the Reformation is as burning a question of the day as it is in Belfast. The successful seizure of most of the assets of patriotism in France by the Right has been met by the denigration of those assets by the Left, and the chief military memorial erected by the government of "Anti-France" was the Hoche monument at Quibéron to commemorate the defeat, in arms, of those Frenchmen whose spiritual (and in some cases carnal) descendants had just been vanquished in the Dreyfus campaign![2]

In one of the most famous and amusing of his tracts, "The Monods, painted by themselves," M. Maurras discusses the history of this eminent family of "pasteurs" and historians, and attempts to demonstrate that their constant marriages with foreigners, since the first Monods settled in France after the Revolution, have made them partisans of foreign, especially Protestant countries, filled with admiration in 1870 for the moral virtues of the German invaders, and putting their hopes for France in an imitation of those virtues by a country delivered from the servitude of Rome! The sincerity of the patriotism of the Monods, if M. Maurras were disposed to admit it, would not excuse to a Provençal of "White" origin, the impudence of the assumption that the introduction of "that awakening of the Jewish spirit and the impure delirium which we call ironically the Reformation"[3] was what France needed for her

[1] La Démocratie religieuse, p. 338.

[2] A comic example of the same spirit is afforded by the republican prudery of Lyons, which forbids the mention on the great statue in the very centre of the city that the figure is that of Louis XIV. It is officially only a monument of the skill of a Lyonese sculptor.

[3] Anthinéa, p. 242. But this was also the opinion of a Frenchman free from any family connections with Protestantism. Renan was convinced that no pupil of the Jesuits would ever be a match for the generals produced by the education of a Prussian officer. Foch had just finished his Jesuit education at the time.

salvation! That the editorship of the *Revue Historique* should be in the hands of a Monod was one of the most ominous signs of the betrayal of France to the enemies within the gates![1]

If the admission of Protestants to authority was dangerous, if it meant allowing them to display their hereditary rancour against those elements which had made France great in spite of the spirit of the Reformation, the question of the Jews was more urgent still. For most of the Protestants, whatever their injustice to the memory of Louis XIV, were Frenchmen, with only sentimental attachments to outside influences. But the Jews were not Frenchmen, since their tradition was autonomous and tribal; the Huguenots had revolted from the true national tradition; the Jews had never entered it. Moreover, their connections with other countries were not occasional or haphazard. The Protestant Monods, with their Danish and Swiss origin, were exceptional, but the international character of the Jews was permanent. Cornélius Herz, the master of corruption in the Panama case, was typical; he was at home in every country, and only returned to France, where he had been accidentally born, to plunder her. Herz, the Reinach family, the Jews who had rallied to Dreyfus, were all capable of moving elsewhere; their whole life was not bound up with France; *they* might well say that it was better that France should be ruined than that Dreyfus should be unjustly condemned, for the very emotions which made them prefer Dreyfus to France were those which made real Frenchmen prefer France to Dreyfus.

M. Maurras has a more fundamental objection to Jewish influence than its role in high finance or its international connections. The simple-minded assaults of Drumont, the more sophisticated racial theories of Barrès, do not dwell enough on the real Jewish menace, the Bible. The great merit of the Roman Church is that it has disciplined the Bible; that it has drawn as much of the poison from that book as it could. There still remains a good deal of it to mislead simple-minded people like Marc Sangnier but, since, alas, the *Magnificat* is there, we can at least be grateful that the Church does not encourage private exegesis of

---

[1] M. Maurras's anger against the Monods did not keep its original intensity. Some younger members of the family gave proof of their patriotism and, M. Maurras was informed, the happy fortune of residence on the favoured soil of France had made the young women of the family pretty, although the family tradition was quite the other way!

such revolutionary texts! Against the constructive spirit of the
Greeks (although even Greece had its subversive forces) the Jewish
spirit sets up the ideal of the individual, pursuing the orders of his
private conscience, disregarding the claims of the community,
fundamentally anarchical. That Jewish spirit was the poison that
killed the ancient world. The Romans committed the crime of permitting the semitic poison to spread—and died of it, as the modern
world will die of it too, if an antidote is not provided.[1] Luther,
Rousseau, Kant, the individualists whose doctrines are eating at the
foundations of the French state and corrupting the mind of the
French nation, are all spiritual descendants of the Jewish prophets,
and the modern Jew, consciously or unconsciously, is himself a
dissolving force since his tradition forces him to be an enemy of
our tradition. Then there are the "métèques." M. Maurras bor-
rowed this term from Athens, where the resident foreigners were
given a status which enabled the Athenian state to enjoy whatever
strength their wealth or talents brought, but which denied them
full political rights. A strong government can make good use of
such "metics," as the monarchy did of the Broglies and countless
others. But a weak government, led astray by the false doctrines of
1789, puts the "métèques" on a level with the full citizen and
commits part of the political power to men who are French by law,
but not by nature.[2]

The Protestants, the Jews, the Metics, all, it is asserted, modify
their patriotism by considerations foreign to real French interests.
They have *their* abiding city elsewhere, but why should the remaining "State" of "Anti-France," the Freemasons, that is the Radicals
and the Socialists, be also conditional in their devotion to the

[1] The necessities of an alliance with Catholics induced M. Maurras to suppress
parts of his earlier works, which were especially offensive to them, but even in their
modern versions, *Le Chemin de Paradis* and *Anthinéa* show, plainly enough, that
all that he prizes in Catholicism is what it has preserved from the ancient world.
Given the existence and the power of propagation of Jewish ideas, the Church has
been useful in so far as she has canalized them, and rendered them almost innocuous.

[2] M. Maurras used the term "métèque" in Barrès's paper, *La Cocarde*, before
he was famous and, thanks to him, it is now common in French writing. It has lost,
however, the exact meaning he wished to give it, and has become a pseudo-scientific
term for Jews (like non-Aryan in Germany) or for persons who are not Jews by
religion, though of Jewish origin. Thus it was pointed out that Stavisky was a
"métèque." It is also used, loosely and inaccurately, to describe any foreigners
whom one dislikes. So a Socialist writer, wishing to stigmatize capitalist society,
laments that "le nombre des dancings se multiplie à l'infini; les métèques au teint
olivâtre, aux cheveux luisants" perform there. (A. Zévaes, *Le Socialisme en France
depuis* 1904, p. 120.)

country to which their blood should bind them? Because they are committed by their political beliefs to a view of France as an idea, not as a thing. Their France is a vehicle for certain values, freedom, liberty, equality; it is France as the propagandist of the ideas of 1789; France as the martyr of these ideas; it is "Quinet and Michelet hailing their country with the enviable title of 'Christ of Nations.'"[1] These general principles lead them to ally themselves with the other confederated States, since these principles deny the importance of just those truths which would, if generally accepted, put Protestants, Jews and Metics in their proper place. Such principles play into the hands of the exterior as well as of the interior enemies of France, for France is not admired and loved as the country of the revolution, but in proportion to her own strength or weakness.

The revolutionary legend is not a reality but a fiction, with less and less plausibility. A preacher of that doctrine like Jaurès builds in the clouds for, whatever he may desire, the fact is that nationalism in other countries is growing, not weakening in force. In defence of their ideology, the Left-wing parties are betraying their country by giving a false picture of the outside world; by weakening the internal unity of France for doctrinal reasons, by asserting that the fight against reaction can be pursued in peace because there is no menace from without.[2] But there is a menace from without, a permanent menace, and to indulge in illusions on this score for any reasons is to be foolish, and to spread them for party reasons is to be a traitor.

Of the causes of this menace, M. Maurras gives an explanation whose very simplicity added to its propagandist force when it was first offered, but whose continued employment, after the late war, reminds the reader that a certain disdain for economics has weakened the *Action française* in its general political propaganda. The memory of 1870, of a brief war whose direct cost to the victors was more than repaid by the indemnity, and whose indirect costs

---

[1] *L'Enquête sur la Monarchie*, p. 522.

[2] In the years immediately before the last war, this controversy was fought out within the Socialist party in the attacks of Charles Andler on Jaurès's policy of trusting the pacific professions of the German Socialists, and in the *succès de scandale* of Marcel Sembat's book, *Faites un roi sinon faites la paix*. Sembat resumed the argument of Maurras's *Kiel et Tanger*. The same dilemma has arisen again since the Hitlerian revolution, with M. Léon Blum in the position of Jaurès and the *Néos* in the place of Andler.

C*

might very easily be thought to have been more than covered by the acquisition of Alsace-Lorraine, was fresh in the minds of Frenchmen of M. Maurras's generation. The growth in wealth and population of Germany might be represented to be (and in some degree was) the fruit of victory. The spoils of the new German empire as well as the petty plunder of the rank and file, might be believed to be a standing temptation to the Germans to raid, once again, the fertile lands to the west. That the French indemnity, like the French clock in Alphonse Daudet's story, might have had other effects than the despoilers of France expected, could be ignored. France was a more desirable and a richer country than Germany; Germany was overpopulated and so there *must* be repeated waves of German assault on France, raids for plunder, more ambitious invasions for dismemberment. So it was of old in the Roman Empire, so it is to-day; the barbarian still covets the lands of the civilized man. It is treason to teach that things have changed, that war no longer pays and that, with the spread of this lesson, the German menace need no longer be feared. Germany has conquest and pillage in the blood. "With time conditions have changed. The ways of life are altered. But as the nations which are Germany's neighbours have equally evolved, the relation between them has not varied and it is in vain that, between the Rhine and the Vistula, factory chimneys cover ground once thick with gloomy pines; men remain too many for the resources; their European overflow, which remains inevitable, will come about, as it has always come about, arms in hand. The arms are not those of the time of Varus and of Augustus, that is the only difference which prevents the writing of a history of Germany in the language and spirit of Veilleius Paterculus."[1]

In this passage there speaks not only the Frenchman seeing in Germany the country which has invaded France five times since 1792, but the Provençal for whom the conflict has not changed since the days when Marius defeated the *Cimbri* and *Teutones*.[2]

If this be true, then a condition of all healthy French life must be security against the outer barbarians, and all questions of

---

[1] *Le Mauvais Traité*, vol. ii, p. 369.
[2] With, possibly, a memory of "Kennst du das Land, wo die Zitronen blüh'n," M. Maurras warns Frenchmen against the horde anxious to "take again the road to the countries where our orange trees flourish." (*Les Conditions de la Victoire*, vol. i, p. 370.)

political doctrine must, before their other merits or defects are considered, pass muster from the point of view of national strength. That the national strength is very narrowly evaluated is a criticism which may well be brought against this doctrine. M. Maurras is not and does not pretend to be interested in economics. For him, that science is the weapon of sophists like Mr. Keynes, who wish to defraud France of her due.[1] The scepticism of Sir Norman Angell about the profitableness of modern war is, naturally, regarded as another liberal illusion—and a dangerous one. The lesson, if it is one, has not been learned by the Germans, who have found not that war is unprofitable, but that defeat is. Even in defeat, there are memories that stimulate this predatory people to new invasions. "In the ruin and disorder of these last years, the Germans can recall with pleasure all the profits that they kept on collecting in the countries which they occupied, from the humble little parcel that the lowest in rank of their soldiers sent off by post every week to their wives, up to the powerful machinery which they systematically tore up from the floors of Belgian and French factories to transplant to the centre of their foul country, mixed up with the masterpieces of painting, the statues, the rare furniture and all the other treasures they could find and carry off."[2]

As is almost inevitable for a nationalist writer, the pressure of his own national interests leads to deformations of doctrine. It is rare,

[1] I do not think, however, that it is quite just to say that "It is scarcely possible to find in the writings of Maurras, Montesquiou, or the others, a reference to the economic advantages of national strength. They wish France to be powerful not in order that Frenchmen may be more prosperous, but in order that they may remain French." (Charlotte T. Muret, *French Royalist Doctrines since the Revolution*, p. 220.) Remaining French involves having a share in the total patrimony of France, in which its natural richness is included. It is that which the Germans covet, not the spiritual goods which, even if they prized them, would be volatilized in their hands.

[2] *Le Mauvais Traité*, vol. ii, p. 318. The spectacle of the survivors of Verdun and Ypres, longing for the days when they were more than compensated for their risks and sufferings by the chance to indulge their national kleptomania, suggests rather a civilian point of view and gives ground for M. Dimier's complaint that the directors of the *Action française* lost touch with the mind of the soldier during the war. M. Maurras, himself, would be quick to see the limitations of a theory that reduced the resentments of the "demi-soldes" of the Restoration to a desire to have another chance to plunder Venice or Cordova! But M. Maurras attaches excessive importance to booty as a temptation to war, even when French soldiers are concerned, for he notes that the French soldier, in the late war, "had only rare chances of occupying and had no chances of taxing, exploiting or squeezing the inhabitants." (Ibid., vol i, p. 305.) The projected allotment of part of reparations to individual soldiers by a lottery system would, it was thought, have served to revive the martial spirit among French ex-soldiers!

indeed, to find a nationalist who can recognize a nationalist of another and hostile nation. M. Maurras was conscious of the great role Fichte had played in forming a nationalist opinion in Germany after the humiliation of Jena; the weakness of disruptive forces in Germany was a cause of envy to a nationalist observing their strength in France, but the step from observation to understanding was never taken. The claims of French and of German nationalism were too directly opposed, in the practical sphere of politics, for the similarities of doctrine to be allowed for. This intrusion of the pragmatic into the ideal world is best exemplified by the insistence on the break-up of Germany. The crime against France, which the republic and the empire committed in helping to bring about the union of Germany (and of Italy), is a theme on which M. Maurras and his disciples never tired of dilating. Largely because he opposed the policy of nationalities favoured by Napoleon III, Proudhon was promoted by M. Louis Dimier to the rank of "master of the counter-revolution."

The war and the victory seemed to the *Action française* to give an opportunity to undo the evil, as far as Germany was concerned. *Dividenda est Germania* was the repeated message of the new Cato to his countrymen from the beginning of the war till the collapse of the Rhineland separatist movement after the victory of the Left in the French elections of 1924. The policy was well argued on practical grounds; a united Germany, always covetous of the pleasant land of France, was a constant menace, a menace which could only be met (if at all) by a never-ending vigilance. The one hope of a permanent peace was in the undoing of the evil work of the Hohenzollerns. The spirit of Richelieu must be recalled to conquer the spirit of Bismarck. As long as the argument is kept to these narrow grounds, it is a powerful one, given the general premises, but even M. Maurras is not immune from the spirit of the age and he attempts to justify his solution of the German problem on more general grounds than those of French interests.

This involves him in a dilemma from which even his dialectical ability cannot save him. M. Maurras has, in fact, to try to persuade the world, and the Germans, that what he regards as an intolerable evil for France, is a good for Germany. On the one hand, the annexation of German territory to France, or its admission to a client relationship with France, would give Germans a chance of being raised in civilization, of being a new Alsace, and he asked why Germany should be allowed to deny to these potential Alsaces "their right to life."[1] So Germans talked in 1870 of restoring Alsatians to Germanity, of giving to the children, if not to the adult generation, the opportunity to recover the cultural patrimony stolen from them by Louis XIV! But the chances of a successful absorption of Germans into French society are not estimated highly. They might, given the weak government of the republic, merely add to the mass of "métèques," and the risk is too great to take. But more hopeful is the creation of a number of small states, owing their liberation from the Prussian yoke to France, which would thus step into the place once occupied by her under Richelieu and Louis XIV as the "protector of German liberties." There would, of course, be drawbacks from the point of view of a German, still misled by the false doctrine of Berlin, but the advantages would more than compensate for any military or political disabilities. In reparations questions, it was argued while there was still a reparations question, preference ought to be accorded to those parts of Germany which broke off from the Prussian mass. It would thus be possible to bribe millions of Germans, in the Rhineland and in South Germany, to break off their burdensome connection with Berlin. These material gains would more than compensate for spiritual losses—and these would not be very serious in any case. "The state of division would have for them (the Germans) its attractions. . . . It would be possible to make this deprivation of military *éclat* and political prestige tolerable and agreeable."[2] After all, "the task and destiny of being a member of a great state and a great nation isn't all beer and skittles."[3]

But these theories are not novel. They were preached by the French anti-militarists, in such exaggerated forms as in the dictum of Remy de Gourmont that the recovery of Alsace was not worth the sacrifice of the little finger which flicked off the ash of his cigarette! M. Maurras, so keen on the scent of anti-nationalist doctrine in France, so severe in his condemnation of the domestic enemies of French greatness, never permits himself to wonder what

[1] *Les Conditions de la Victoire*, vol. i, p. 246.   [2] *Ibid.*, vol. ii, p. 200.
[3] *Le Mauvais Traité*, vol. ii, p. 208. "Tout n'est pas rose dans le métier et dans le destin de membre de grand État et de grande nation."

a patriotic German would say and think of such arguments in the mouth of *his* countrymen! He even goes so far as to argue that the treachery of the German government frees the people of the Ruhr from any obligation of fidelity to it. "The crime and the perjury of the German state looses the Germans from the oath of fidelity."[1] That is to say, the German who says "Germany but," is free from all moral blame although corresponding conduct is infamous in a Frenchman!

The reasons for this astonishing blindness are double. One is a reluctance to admit the permanence of any change in the situation of Europe or the world which limits French power. That France and England were united nations long before Germany or Italy is an historical fact of great importance, but it is not a law of nature incapable of alteration or modification. M. Maurras sees that clearly enough when his judgment is not clouded by his passionate patriotism. He does not think it likely that Huguenots to-day would call in English troops to fight their battles—even though they have not repented of such conduct in the past! He would, undoubtedly, refuse to fight the battles of the Church or the King with the aid of Spanish or English arms, despite precedents of the sixteenth and eighteenth centuries. But although there is no place for a Buckingham or a Parma in France to-day, M. Maurras is unable to reconcile himself to the fact that there is no place for their French opposite numbers in contemporary Germany.[2]

The other cause is to be found in the concentration of M. Maurras's gaze on France and on French interests. This is his

[1] *Le Mauvais Traité*, vol. ii, p. 310. M. Thibaudet has put into the mouth of his M. Mathis a brief but sufficient refutation of this *sua si bona norint* argument. The delights of a political life on the model of Switzerland, held out to unaccountably reluctant Germans, omitted those aspects of Swiss life which a nationalist ought to sympathize with. "Il vous faut observer cependant que cette future Suisse, où la représentation de Guillaume Tell est interdite, n'a encore pour armoiries que le chapeau de Gessler." (*Les Princes Lorrains*, p. 147.) The Germanic liberties, for which M. Maurras is so anxious, would be the work of local Malvys and their emblem some equivalent of the *Bonnet Rouge* of the late Citizen Almeyreda!

[2] I have avoided discussing the royalist doctrine of M. Maurras, but one aspect of it illustrates this point very well. The relative decline of France is treated, almost always, as the fault of the various weak or rash governments which have followed the Revolution, but no place is allowed for such important factors in the world situation as the industrial revolution in England, for the rise of Russia, of Japan, of the United States, all of which were bound to have immense effects in world politics. The follies of democracy may have been responsible for the weakening of the Greek cities in the face of Macedon, but they were not directly responsible for the rise of Rome and Carthage, which made a fifth-century policy impossible in the second century.

strength, but it is also his weakness, for it leads him to naïve identifications of French interests with those of larger unities which have a decided appearance of having been created *ad hoc*. M. Maurras, who would shrink with horror from any suggestion that serious French interests should be sacrificed to any vague Latin sympathies, talks at times as if Spanish or Italians should allow real weight to such far from positive considerations as the assumed unity of interests of the three Latin powers in *"mare nostrum."*[1]

Indeed, all these general appeals are in fact invitations to other peoples to *"travailler pour le roi de France"*—and not likely to be more attractive than naked appeals to do the same for the King of Prussia! When M. Maurras extended his approval to the "pan-Celticism" of M. Charles Le Goffic, "a pan-Celticism entirely French or *entirely for the benefit of France,"*[2] he revealed the limitations of his power of appeal to peoples and ideas outside the scheme of things in which France always comes first. M. Maurras, as a teacher, might rejoice in the sacred selfishness of the Italian, even if the selfishness was exercised at the expense of France, but as a rule the Frenchman in him overcomes the doctrinaire and nullifies all his efforts to extend his principles beyond France.[3] Whenever this new Antaeus attempts to exercise his strength as a dialectician and as a political thinker, while out of contact with the sacred soil of France, he becomes weak and has to fall back on vague terms of rhetoric, of appeals to unsubstantial generalities of a kind which, had they come from a Jaurès, would have called for and received all the devastating irony of "Criton." The appeals to general European interests are almost always appeals to French

[1] "Pas un peuple méditerranéen n'est capable de rétablir à lui seul l'indépendance des mers latines. Mais le rêve ne serait pas irréalisable si l'on y travaillait à plusieurs. L'intérêt bien compris de l'Italie et aussi de l'Espagne serait de s'entendre et de s'accorder avec nous plutôt que d'aller demander la protection d'un podestat étranger qui garderait toujours allure de maître." (*Le Mauvais Traité*, vol. ii, p. 44.) The Italians, no matter what their form of government, have always been too practical, too positive in their politics, to listen to such siren songs. Such follies have been left to Germans who were surprised when England made war on her "kinsmen"!

[2] *L'Enquête sur la Monarchie*, p. 191. Italics mine.

[3] This limitation was illustrated in another department of M. Maurras's thought by his failure, during the last war, to make any attempt to understand the point of view of King Constantine of Greece who, rightly or wrongly, was displaying some of the qualities M. Maurras likes to see in a monarch. That these advantages of the royal office were exercised against the interest of France kept M. Maurras from considering seriously the question whether they were exercised in the interests of Greece.

interests very thinly disguised, hastily produced to meet some special emergency and, perhaps, not intended to do more than stuff a hole in the armour of France.

M. Maurras thinks differently, but that is because he identifies so completely the safety of civilization with the safety of France. With these premises it is easy to assert that "The case is common in which solicitude for the most general interests of man agrees in detail with the preoccupations of concrete patriotism"[1]—but when those interests do not coincide with the fears or hopes of the nation, it is treason to let the general take precedence over the particular. To do that is to fall into the trap set by Kant, to "put in the place of the precarious but real and calculable guarantees of statecraft, the absolute but unreal guarantees of justice."[2] From temptation to make such a sacrifice, M. Maurras need hardly pray to be delivered.

This strength has, of course, been also a weakness. The passionate nationalist is seldom a good judge of either the interest or the sentiments of other peoples. M. Maurras's attitude to Britain, from the days when, he was convinced, she was stimulating the Dreyfusard movement to weaken France at Fashoda, through the period when Clemenceau was the "bloody" minister of Edward VII to the later time when Clemenceau was a hero and Britain an ally to be courted, had this unity, that he never for a moment looked at the enemy, or ally, from a neutral ground. He saw her always through French spectacles. Even when he assured his readers that M. Briand's expression of contempt for golf had insulted the British nation, he displayed more clearly his dislike of Briand than his liking or understanding of Britain! These limitations of sympathy have extended to Frenchmen of the opposite political camp who were not always bad patriots for thinking that war and peace were too serious issues to be left to soldiers or that national and military strength were not necessarily convertible terms. Righteousness, or the reputation for it, *may* exalt a nation and, still more, the absence of righteousness, or of the reputation for it, may weaken a nation, even from the point of view of a positivist, as Louis XIV, Napoleon I and William II learned. That the victorious Dreyfusards strengthened France in one direction, if they weakened her in another, is a truth that M. Maurras has been unable to see, if only because he dreams of a

[1] *Les Trois Aspects du Président Wilson*, p. 85.   [2] Ibid., p. 22.

France to whom the opinion of lesser peoples matters nothing. But there has not been, for a long time, such a France or such a Europe, and if France was victorious in the late war, was it not, in part, because the world could believe that France was fighting for something more than herself and was, therefore, more willing to appreciate how great a thing France herself was—and how well worth saving?

But the controversialist who makes such admissions is not the controversialist who rallies parties and carries the day, not in the victories of the study, but of the forum. M. Maurras has been not the cloistered thinker seeking the truth, but the missionary who has, he is convinced, found it. His books are not academic treatises, but the fruits of his daily work as a journalist, bound, by the nature of his trade, to say the same thing over and over again, to simplify, to assert, to denounce. And that has been done with astonishing force, despite the necessary limitation of the craft.

M. Maurras has fought many battles, some successfully, many without apparent success. He has been, even by French standards, a ruthless controversialist, giving and taking no quarter, very ready to believe evil of his adversary and never reluctant to run the risk of calling himself, or, at any rate, his party, the just. Yet he has escaped ostracism. Men of many parties have been moved by the power of his pen to re-examine the premises of their political faiths; perhaps to hold them all the more strongly because they have survived examination in the bright light cast on them by the mind which has exposed the intellectual nakedness of many "leaders" of public opinion and of the *respublica*. Such men may not be ungrateful for the real service M. Maurras has done them. To others, he has been more than a light, he has been an inspiration to action and to belief, and to yet others he has been one of the masters in the long line of great French controversialists, with his due place in the succession of Pascal, of Voltaire, of Paul-Louis Courier. M. Maurras himself, who forgave so much to Anatole France because he "maintained the French tongue," may forgive the neighbours I have given him! French controversy is not gentle, and to a reader coming to M. Maurras's writings from a country where truth is so often sacrificed to good manners, or, worse still, to good form, the savagery of some pages may be shocking. The unwillingness of the controversialist to pay enough attention to that "tact des choses possibles" which Cavour called the mark of the statesman, may also startle the British reader. But the consistency with which a point of view has been put for nearly forty years, with an indifference to the lower rewards of political or literary activity, has its own attraction, and that consistency has been far more than verbal. From the beginning of his career down to this day, M. Maurras has applied to his own acts and his own writing the fundamental doctrine of his life, the primacy of the national interest over all other interests. It is a dangerous doctrine, but it has been for M. Maurras his guiding light and it he has followed, resolved:

> Ne placet Damnedeu ne ses angles
> Que ja pur mei perdet sa valur France.

VIII
JACQUES BAINVILLE
(1936)

THE death of Jacques Bainville and its immediate consequences
have a high symbolic value, a value that may possibly hide the
actual achievement of the man who died on his fifty-eighth
birthday. His funeral was the cause or the occasion of the assault
on M. Léon Blum and so of the dissolution of the *Action française*
and the charging of M. Charles Maurras with incitement to murder.
Over the body of the dead man of letters, a struggle has begun
which, if not a turning-point in French history, cannot but be a
turning-point in the history of a movement whose significance
has always been underestimated out of France. In the annals of the
Action française the name of Jacques Bainville must always have a
high place; in the annals of French literature his place, if less high,
will not, in this generation at least, be low.

M. Bainville was best known outside France as the author of a
phenomenally popular *History of France* and, more recently, of
a *Life of Napoleon* which was translated into English and which
revealed to many innocent readers the simple truth that the reputation of the Emperor is less contested outside France than it is
inside. But the *History* and the *Napoleon* were merely the natural
culmination of a life of letters which began when M. Bainville was
barely out of his teens.

It was by his book on Ludwig II of Bavaria that the brilliant
young Parisian made his début. He was born too late to know the
full shock of the disasters of 1870, and he turned to a German
subject—for slightly more objective reasons than were common in
the generation which was conducting a post-mortem on Sedan.
But in the subject of Ludwig there was to be seen not merely the
patron of Wagner, the emulator of Louis XIV, but the political
problem of Germany—or as the school with which M. Bainville
threw in his lot puts it, the problem of "the Germanies." M.
Bainville wrote on many subjects, some of them superficially far

83

enough removed from this problem, but never for a moment did he forget that for a Frenchman the question of his relations with the formidable neighbour across the Rhine was the primary question. It was of no avail to pretend to retire to an ivory tower like Remy de Gourmont if the covetous neighbour would not permit you to stay there. And that neighbour would not.

This is the main thesis of the *History of France*, and that book owes its power, if not its popularity, to the ingenuity with which it is asserted or insinuated in age after age that the German covets Gaul. The greatest service of Rome to Gaul was the preservation of Gaul from the German. Ariovistus was the ancestor of Blücher, of Bismarck, of William II. Probus or Julian driving out the invading barbarian or punishing him by expeditions across the Rhine are the ancestors of Philippe Augustus at Bouvines, of Turenne, of Foch, and the early raids into Germany are merely the early acts of a play of which the invasion of the Ruhr is one of the most recent but not the last episodes.

The view of French history as fundamentally a permanent watch on the eastern frontier was severely attacked, both when it appeared in the *History of Two Peoples* and in the more subtle form it takes in the *History of France*. It is open to the objections made to the work of Haller, Bainville's opposite number in Germany; it interprets the past too exclusively in terms of the present, and (graver fault still) puts the emotions of our day into the minds of men who knew nothing of them.

Why, it may be asked, should M. Bainville have felt bound to defend or palliate the errors of kings and of their ministers? Because he had been won over to the panacea for the ills of France preached by M. Charles Maurras. M. Bainville was, he told the world at least once, of lower middle-class origin. He was anxious to make plain that his royalism had nothing in common with the sentimental royalism of the old aristocratic families or, still worse, with the snobbish royalism of the upper ten. Royalism for him and for his master was the policy of common sense.

To M. Maurras the chief need of every Frenchman was security from foreign invasion. The Frenchman was so fortunate that all the world must envy him and seek to replace him. Since the Revolution,

France had been ruled by men paying at least lip-service to vague "ideals," to the "Rights of Man" under the Republic, to the "principle of nationalities" under the Second Empire. Both of these principles were dangerous to France; in their name France had been involved in fruitless wars and had even committed the supreme folly of helping to unite Germany and Italy. The beneficent policy of the old régime, seen at its highest in the policy of Richelieu, had kept away from the frontiers of France all great unified Powers. Germany had been broken up at the Peace of Westphalia; the dangerous Habsburg power had been weakened in Italy; and in the next generation Louis XIV had put his grandson on the throne of Spain. This great work the Revolution had undone. But, it will be asked, what of Napoleon who put his brother on the throne of Spain, who, not content with having weak States on the left bank of the Rhine, annexed that debatable land to France, who replaced both the House of Savoy in Piedmont and the House of Habsburg in Milan?

It was to the undoing of the maleficent influence of such Bonapartist doctrines that M. Bainville devoted his last full-length work. His *Napoleon* is an extremely skilful variation on a simple theme, a theme owing much to Albert Sorel. Napoleon fell because he could not make peace with Britain; he could not make real peace with Britain because the permanent basis of British policy was the refusal to leave the Low Countries in the hands of a great military power. But Napoleon, as the heir of the Revolution, could not give up the first and dearest conquest of the Revolution, Belgium. To hold it he had to conquer Britain. The French Navy, ruined by the Revolution, was unfit for that task, so we have the makeshifts of the Continental System leading to Spain, to Moscow, to Leipzig, to the invasion of France. The whole train of events is worked out with the clarity of a mathematical demonstration, and after the Q.E.D. comes the rider that only the King, tied to no fanciful theory but bound to consider the real interests of France (since his interests are inseparably bound up with hers), could save France. This lesson taught in books was also taught in small doses in brief articles in the *Action Française*, and in less dogmatic form in other Conservative papers. It shook faith in the Republic, but it won few, if any, fit to see the remedy in a return to the House of France.

Of this M. Bainville seems to have been conscious. He was less touched by the passion for levitical purity than is M. Maurras. He did not despise all compromises with the evil thing, and he avoided the virulence of abuse which make the writings of MM. Maurras and Daudet so amusing and infuriating. This willingness to see rudiments of goodness in bad institutions was shown in his *History of the Third Republic*, where he had to explain the paradox of the survival for sixty years of a régime condemned on doctrinal grounds to a speedy and ignominious end. He attributed this to the rudimentary powers given by the monarchical authors of the present French Constitution to the President. That pale simulacrum of a monarch was near enough the real thing to save the ship from foundering, if not from dreadful batterings at the hands of those elemental forces of politics whose existence democratic optimism denies or minimizes. There was thus a certain fitness as well as an obvious irony in the action of the *Académie française* in electing Bainville to the chair of Raymond Poincaré.

It is only three months since Bainville accomplished the difficult task of praising a great Republican without denying his complete scepticism as to the past and future of the Republic. This task was accomplished with great skill. It was insinuated that Poincaré was the product of a social system that republican institutions were rapidly destroying, that the *petite bourgeoisie* from which both Academicians sprang was being destroyed by inflation, by social legislation—and by the past and future wars to which republican follies doom France. In Poincaré there was one type of the French bourgeois, upright, incredibly industrious, animated with a conviction of French rightness that nothing could shake. It is not a type that excites much love, and, *mutatis mutandis*, the cold clarity of Bainville's mind and style had its points of resemblances with the advocate's mind of Poincaré. And they had one faith in common, for, if one despaired of the Republic, neither despaired of France, and the professional anti-clerical and the ostentatiously agnostic royalist would both have agreed that as a verdict on human history you could not improve on *Gesta Dei per Francos*. In these dark days of barbaric hysteria it is not quite certain that they were wrong.

IX

DAUDET'S CLEMENCEAU [1]

(1940)

M. LÉON DAUDET tells us at the end of this book of a conversation with Clemenceau in which, oddly enough, the friend and disciple of M. Maurras expressed his surprise that the old man did not accept the divinity of Christ. It was one of the barriers between Clemenceau and the Right majority of 1919, the "Bloc national," that the Blue of La Vendée never recanted his anti-clericalism, his faith in the Revolution. But, as he told Daudet, "We have one faith in common, you and I, and that is France."

This book is published at a moment when that faith is at its lowest in France, where a policy that would have horrified Clemenceau, a revival in more disastrous form of the illusions of M. Caillaux and the policy of M. Malvy, is being defended by the *Action Française*—to the surprise of simple-minded English admirers but not altogether to the surprise of the ghost of Clemenceau! For that tough old Vendean, proud of the Chouans who fought on the wrong side as of the Blues who fought on the right, would not have been surprised at the treason of the "Blancs du Midi," who made no real fight for their King—until an invasion and conquest made the White Terror possible. France is, alas, a country of secular feuds, and it is impossible to-day to read this violent, self-satisfied, scurrilous account of the organizer of victory without remembering all the verbal courage and violence of the men whose courage has now failed them. The testimonials from this source to that valiant *métèque*, M. Georges Mandel, read oddly at this moment, and the contempt poured on all who thought that a deal could be done with Germany, before, after and during the last war, read more oddly still.

Clemenceau was all his life attacked as the friend of England, he was slandered by those sections of French opinion which provided money and recruits for the *Action française*, and then for

[1] Léon Daudet, *Clemenceau, A Stormy Life*. (Hodge.)

the literary mud-throwers of *Gringoire*. Here we have the standard abuse of Cardinal Gasparri, of Woodrow Wilson, of Poincaré, of Briand, of all those who did not rise to the exalted standard of patriotism of the *Action française*. In quiet times Léon Daudet was the most amusing, the most vivacious and the least merely malignant of those bitter French polemists of all parties who made French journalism such good reading for foreigners. Growing up in the inner circle of the Republican ruling class, Léon Daudet had opportunities for observing human nature and acquiring a repertoire of more or less authentic anecdote that, added to very real literary gifts, put him far above men like Henri Béraud. But all the faults of the school are here, too—the contempt for the truth (the Norton forgeries were no sillier than some of those that formed the staple of anti-Dreyfusard controversy); the profound ignorance of the modern world which no amount of *salon* smartness can compensate for the preoccupation with private feuds and private follies.

How shallow all this is compared with the *Cahiers* of Barrès! Nor is the narrative very easy going for the common reader. Léon Daudet is a devotee of the romantic method in history to a degree that ought to have earned for him the most severe condemnation of M. Maurras. Hardly any part of Clemenceau's story is told in a straightforward fashion, and the reader who knows nothing of the general history of the period, or of Clemenceau's role, will find the thread of the narrative very hard to follow. And M. Daudet, who has a good conceit of himself, takes time off to relate events of his own career in a fashion that is unconsciously funny. Thus Clemenceau's famous appeal to the glories of La Vendée reminds M. Daudet of a speech he made in that department twenty years later, a speech showing up the old-fashioned Republican dogmas to which Clemenceau was inexplicably addicted. M. Daudet forgets to add that La Vendée (under clerical pressure) refused to send the representative of its true traditions to the Senate.

Of course the book, since it is M. Daudet's, has many entertaining and even some valuable passages. The highly spiced style of the original is difficult to translate, and the translator has sacrificed a great deal to an effort at idiomatic translation. It does not matter that we should have Camille Pelletan as "First Lord of the Admiralty," but to describe the École Normale Supérieure as the "Training College for Secondary School Teachers" is only accurate in the sense that describing Eton as a "non-grant-aided Church of England secondary school" would be. An excessively high proportion of the proper names are wrongly spelled, and "the illuminating affair of the fraudulent Reforms" was less like an unreported case from the note-books of John Watson, M.D., than the mistranslation suggests. M. Daudet makes great fun of the cowardly politicians who infested Bordeaux in 1914; against the *franc fileurs* of to-day many great French ghosts protest—and none with more authority than Clemenceau.

X
LÉON DAUDET
(1942)

LÉON DAUDET has died, and appropriately, at Saint-Rémy-en-Provence. He was a Parisian, and some of his most successful literary efforts were the evocations of the Paris of around 1900. *Paris Vécu* was more than a title of one of his books; it was a description of much of his life. But there remained the permanent ancestral connection with Provence; like most Frenchmen, Daudet had his own *province*. His pride in Provence had, of course, more roots than the mere ancestral fact. He was immensely proud of being the son of Alphonse Daudet and he may have suspected that the most permanent values of his father's work were associated with Provence. *Tartarin*, for all its lightness, was a more serious work than *Le Nabab*. There was another connection, too. Daudet was proud to be a disciple of Maurras, and in Maurras, a born Provençal, exaltation of the glories of all the territories of the *langue d'oc* was and is an obsession. It may be guessed that Léon Daudet did not wholly share the religious passion of Maurras for Mistral and other glories of the *félibrige*; but he was a good partisan, and if overpraising the Greco-Roman culture of the Midi was a way of showing up the treason of such Germanophiles as that renegade meridional Jaurès, then a certain suspension of critical judgment was part of the rigour of the game.

In yet another way the ancestry of Daudet, his affectation of Provençal piety, had its justification. In that barren, sun-drenched, wind-scoured landscape, with the ruins of Saint-Rémy there to commemorate the transitoriness of human power and glory, the fragility of civilization, political passions are bitter even by French standards. Not far away are the foothills of the Cevennes with their lively tradition of religious war, not far away the hills and the farms where the austere Huguenot farmers remember the fame of André Gide's grandfather, the *pasteur*. And the descendant of the *Blancs du Midi* did not forget or forgive the *Bleus*. So Saint-Rémy was not an unsuitable place for the violent polemical writer, the intolerant and unscrupulous controversialist, to die. It is not very far from there to Martigues, where Maurras retired every year to renew his hatreds and restate his unvarying dogmas. It is far, far from that northern misty city, Paris—and since 1940 Paris, under the German heel, has been cut off from the south by spiritual as well as physical barriers.

Alphonse Daudet was not a first-class novelist, and his son was not a first-class political writer or even a first-class polemical writer. Both father and son were a little too facile, a little too much of their age. Alphonse Daudet has not the weight of Flaubert, much less of Balzac; he has not the impressive tenacity of Zola. But he had great talents and once or twice he achieved something like perfection. More often he managed to record an aspect of life which the curious will always turn to with interest. His son had his father's faults, though not his father's literary amiability. He wrote too much, too easily; he was too readily content with dramatic effects. He affected roughness as his father affected sweetness. And as Alphonse Daudet was less amiable than a good deal of his writing suggested, his son was less of a blindly partisan bigot than he affected to be.

It is a speculation not wholly profitless to wonder what would have happened if Daudet had not fallen under the spell of Maurras. Of course, he gained something. His disordered mass of hates, hopes, hobbies needed an organizing principle. Maurras supplied it. It might be juster to say that the reaction against the Republican ruling class, with which he had been associated from childhood and into which he had married, was bound to come, but that reaction got form and direction from the more systematic, more controlled, more emotional mind of Maurras. More emotional, for there is in Maurras none of that humorous appreciation of the comic side of life, even of the life of one's own party or of one's deepest enemies, that is so often present in the bitterest writings of Daudet. But the Maurrasian emotion was hate, a hate which excluded all self-criticism and all charity.

Daudet was certainly a good hater, but his hatred lacked the steel frame of Maurras's temperament and self-made dogmatic foundation. So Daudet's doctrinal writings lacked the power of those of Maurras, the grace and subtlety of those of Barrès. The masters of the counter-revolution in modern France had prophets and poets enough; Daudet was the buffoon, the political warrior who found his highest delight not in acute argument or in subtle portrait-painting, but in noise, abuse, Rabelaisian jokes and schoolboy smut. He could not have written anything at the level of *La Révolution religieuse* or *L'Appel au Soldat*. He wrote political polemics at a lower level than Maurras and novels at a much lower level than Barrès. But if he was not a first-rater, he was none the less interesting and of value, if only as a symptom of a disease from whose ravages France is suffering terribly to-day.

Daudet, as is well known, was converted to more than the ancestral legitimist faith of his family. He was one of the most conspicuous converts to Catholicism of his generation. Most conspicuous, not most impressive. The religious and secular worlds alike took his frequent professions of religious faith with less seriousness than they took the faith of Péguy or Psichari or Maritain. It was not only, as an Archbishop of Paris made plain, that the spectacle of the author of *L'Entremetteuse* charging all the paynim horde as a champion of the faith had its scandalous side. Daudet's Catholicism, however deep it may have been in his private conscience, was in its public manifestations noisily political.

It was not, perhaps, as distressing to the deeply religious Catholic as was the utilitarian assessment of religion in terms of its political value which was the contribution of Maurras to the problem. But Maurras did not profess to be a Christian, to be a disciplined son of the Church, to have means of grace denied to the Jews, Huguenots, Masons and *métèques* of the neo-Royalist demonology. Daudet did. It is not beyond belief that (as was rumoured) it was Daudet who refused to compromise with the Church when the condemnation was imminent. And when the condemnation came, not many people felt for Daudet the sympathy that saints have sometimes earned in their conflicts with ecclesiastical authority. He did not even earn the sympathy felt for many of his pious followers, pushed by his intransigence into a conflict with the Church that recalled, on a smaller scale, the fight over the bull *Unigenitus*. Daudet, the Catholic, quarrelling with the Pope evoked less sympathy than Daudet, the Royalist, being disowned by the King. The world felt, rightly or wrongly, that the one was more of a blow than the other.

But it is not as a novelist or as a politician that Daudet will be remembered, but primarily as a memoir-writer, and to a lesser degree, as a critic. His family, his talents, his impudence (or his lack of diffidence) gained him admission to very varied circles in Paris, and he enjoyed all the rich possibilities that were thus opened to his talents as a chronicler of scandal. His medical training affected his mind and style, and it was Parisian intellectual and political society seen with a clinician's eye and from a dogmatic political standpoint that provides the main staple of the *Souvenirs*.

Again, as a memorialist, Daudet suffered in comparison with Gide and Jules Renard, and still more in comparison with his literary protégé, Proust. There is no great subtlety in the dramatic contrasts of the patriots and traitors. There is no great respect paid to the reader's critical judgment in the telling of the scabrous anecdotes which were piled up to show that the rulers of the Republic were knaves in private as in public matters. No historian would use the many volumes of reminiscence with anything but the greatest prudence. But he would be wise to use them all the same. They may lack truth of formal statement, but they have flavour, they have gusto. Of course, the taste is bad; Daudet smelled sexual or pathological weakness everywhere, and even his strong party spirit could not suppress his taste for scandal. No doubt Syveton was a martyr; his enemies blackguards as well as traitors; André and Combes *canaille*; yet, Daudet conveys, maybe there was something in what they said. Syveton was a good Nationalist, but the charges of "Anti-France" were not implausible.

But it is not as the compiler of a new secret history, as a Parisian Procopius, that Daudet is valuable and entertaining. He was a good witness to the internal politics of the Right; his caustic comments on the old Orleanist leaders provide materials for a new *Fin des Notables*. The incoherence of the Right, its total political incompetence, is made plain. It is also made funny. For Daudet's sense of humour, though cruel and crude, was real. It was his humour, that won him many secret readers on the Left. And it was his humour that ensured that many loyal readers of the *Action Française* began their daily political toilet by reading the Daudet leader on anything from cookery to the crimes of Pius XI before they braced themselves for the more austere article in which Maurras reasserted the immutable truths of Royalist doctrine.

Arthur Meyer, the Jewish-Catholic climber, who edited *Le Gaulois* and married Mademoiselle de Turenne, was an intrinsically comic figure, but Daudet, who knew him well, did him something like justice; his portrait is cruel but not unfriendly. It is not Proust and it is not Balzac, but it is funny. There were, no doubt, many reasons why Daudet liked being "député de Paris." He rejoiced, for instance, at being pointed out to an American lady in the Chamber as "the most reactionary man in the world." (The competition was not as severe in 1922 as it later became.) But he enjoyed his Parliamentary career not merely because he could speak and interrupt, but because his colleagues sat as models for him. The result was not as aesthetically satisfactory as *Leurs Figures*, but it was good if not clean fun all the same.

His loss of his seat, the mysterious death of his son, which became an obsession with him, the survival of the old political clans in France, the revival of Germany, the quarrel with the Church, all embittered Daudet and made his polemics more and more mere scolding, more and more mere incitements to hate and civil war. But as a critic Daudet continued to deserve respect. Here the contrast with Maurras was striking. Maurras never escaped from the narrow clique outlook of his own *cénacle*, the *école romane*. And his culture was too purely French, too purely classical, to make him a sympathetic critic. Daudet the critic was free from most of the faults of Daudet the pamphleteer. He found many of the writers, with whose political bias he sympathized, boring, and he had a weakness for some writers whose influence was, from the nationalist viewpoint, unhealthy.

As a member of the *Académie Goncourt* he helped to make some reputations, to launch *A l'Ombre des Jeunes Filles en Fleur* and, much later, *Voyage au Bout de la Nuit*. Proust was half a Jew and all a Dreyfusard, but Daudet's taste was good. Céline was, for the moment, the darling of the Left, but this brutal talent appealed to Daudet, who may (of course) have smelled the future anti-Semite and pro-Nazi in the doctor-turned-novelist. Daudet knew German and English well and he was free from the narrow "Latinism" which Louis Dimier has so scathingly exposed in *Maurras and his docile disciples*. His literary articles in *Candide*, rather than his polemics in the *Action Française*, were the best things he did in his last years.

It would be idle to conceal the fact that Daudet shares with Maurras a great responsibility for French disunion, for the Anglophobia of the *bien pensant* classes and for their equally suicidal faith in Mussolini. With the armistice the *Action Française* found itself in an impasse from which courage and magnanimity opened the only way out. Could they accept a policy that was far more abject than anything with which Caillaux and the defeatists of 1917 had been charged? What was Malvy compared with M. de Brinon, ambassador of France to Paris? Maurras, always more ready to hate than to love, chose the baser part. Daudet did not openly break with his chief. He continued to write in the *Action Française*, but while Maurras poured out his bile on the "Gaullists" who practised what he had preached, Daudet wrote reminiscences of his father, popular medical articles on how to cure whooping cough, on anything but an open defence of the policy of making France a German satellite.

To see Laval back in power and a chief of a French Government openly wishing for a German victory must have been gall for Daudet, forced to silence for the first time in his life. His death may have been a deliverance. It leaves the very French Marx deprived of his very French Engels. And it leaves a mixed inheritance of fame, a varied second-rate talent that found its best expression in chronicling the follies and faults of a society of which the chronicler was himself a representative sample. And that political talent, on its political side, helped to breed quarrels with Pope and King and to create a situation in which the son of the author of *La dernière classe* was unable to comment on the silent surrender of Alsace to the barbarians.

XI
THE GHOST OF JAURÈS
(1943)

ALBERT THIBAUDET was one of the most acute and objective critics of French life, and he seldom was more acute and objective than when he wrote: "The first year of peace needed a Jaurès, as the last year of the war needed a Clemenceau." But it was not only the first year of the peace that showed what a loss France and the world had suffered when the cretinous assassin murdered the Socialist leader in 1914. France and Europe continued to suffer from the absence of Jaurès, from the absence from the French scene of a political leader whose generosity and personal integrity were equalled by his oratorical ability and political sagacity.

As Mr. Hampden Jackson makes plain in his very timely study,[1] French Socialism got from Jaurès a moral bias, a generosity of temper, a comparative freedom from sectarian bias which it very soon lost when his moderating influence was gone. And the disunion of the French Socialist party was one of the sources of French disunity, the revival of sectarian bitterness one of the renewed plagues of France, the abandonment of the humane and humanitarian tradition one of the causes of that decline in political morality which has led to betrayals of the workers by their leaders on a scale and of a baseness that make previous treasons seem mere tolerable examples of human weakness.

But it was not only the loss to the French Socialist party that made the murder of Jaurès such a disaster. It was the loss to the French State. In his person Jaurès represented the old Republican "mystique." Even his most bitter critics admitted that he *had* represented the mystique even if, like Péguy, they asserted that he had ceased to represent it. There was in the dumpy, ungraceful, untidy person of Jaurès, a more effective incarnation of the Republican spirit than in any new streamlined Marianne designed for the

---

[1] J. Hampden Jackson, *Jean Jaurès, His Life and Work.* (Allen and Unwin.)

96

mairies of France. There was the spirit of 1789 and there doubtless would have been in the crisis the spirit of 1793.

It was natural that in his lifetime, when he was one of the two or three most famous Socialists in the world, the Socialist element in Jaurès should have been stressed and that, like Matteotti's in the post-war period, his murder should have been made more a new item in the Socialist martyrology than a great event in the general history of France and Europe. But it is plain to any non-partisan student of his career and is made plain by his latest biographer that for Jaurès, Socialism was not summed up in any economic programme, in any mere material claims. Socialism was good, was right, was inevitable because it was just, humane, progressive. For Jaurès had a faith (that may seem naïve now) in the inevitable progress of the human race, in the optimism of Condorcet and of the scientist-politicians of the Revolution. Although it was not and is not the wont of French Left-wing politicians to quote Holy Writ, Jaurès would have accepted with complete conviction the text which declares that "righteousness exalteth a nation." And he was completely unaffected by the sophistries, and by arguments which it would be shallow to call merely sophistries, by which other political leaders to his left and right exalted *raison d'État* or *raison de classe* above justice.

Jaurès was converted to Socialism not by any dry economic analysis of the inevitable contradictions of capitalist economy, but "by the Republic." That is to say, the establishment of political Republicanism in France, the erection into a national creed of "liberty, equality, fraternity," made the turning of these principles into a programme just and necessary, necessary because just. Jaurès was occasionally an effective exponent of the view that the inevitable trends of modern economic life would squeeze out certain obsolete forms of distribution and production. He did not, like his Radical allies, allow his sympathy with the small man to make him the political saviour of the small shopkeeper. He was not prepared to bid the sun stand still to save the *petits bourgeois* at the cost of the total progress of French economy. On the other hand, it could be argued that he was more tender of the rights of the small peasant proprietors, less ready to see that any rationalizing of French economic life would mean the lessening of the weight of the politically privileged small farmer, than he would have been had he

D

been either a Northerner or the representative of a Northern constituency. For the most promising and technically up-to-date part of the French agricultural system was just the high capitalist farming of the North. In other ways too, the fact that Jaurès was so typical a Méridional limited his economic vision.

But if Jaurès in his political life kept on insisting that man, even the working man, does not live by bread alone, it was not merely because social problems seemed less complex, less tied up with revolutionary technological changes in the Midi than they did in the more rigid, greyer, less ebullient North. Jaurès was consistent; he was a professional philosopher, a professional idealist philosopher; the tradition of the rights of man, of the freedom of conscience, of the rule of law was as living to him as was the Nonconformist-Radical tradition to so many founders of the Labour Party.

It was this absence of any dogmatic approach to politics, except the moral approach, that accounted for Jaurès's prestige. His disinterestedness was no greater, in the vulgar sense, than that of some of his colleagues. Jules Guesde made more sacrifices than Jaurès to the cause of the workers. But with Jaurès the virtue seemed to be a natural aspect of a rich, happy, generous temper, not the fruit of a sour, political puritanism. When Jaurès as a politician was forced to compromise with the Mammon of unrighteousness, to associate with Combes and Caillaux in some of the least worthy of their activities, Frenchmen—above all, old associates of Jaurès like those of the League of the Rights of Man as well as mystics of genius like Péguy—felt a special distress. That it was not for a handful of silver or for a ribbon to stick in his coat made no difference. The example of the contagion of the world's slow stain was all the more painful.

Yet the rank and file of the Socialists, of the workers, like the most critical of his colleagues of the Chamber like Maurice Barrès, felt that in Jaurès the stain was superficial; the heart and the head were sound because never separated. The last years of Jaurès's life were shadowed by the threat of war. He was a ruthless critic of the policy of his own Government and gave a hand to critics by a generous blindness to the realities of Imperial German policy. For him the Second International was the last, best hope on earth. His murder saved him from a bitter disillusionment. But it also prevented him from rendering his country and the world his greatest services. How much Vichy has gained by the disappearance from the French scene of the great men whose mere names would have been a challenge to its defeatism! Foch and Clemenceau would have been very old indeed had they lived to 1940. But Jaurès was born three years after Pétain. Had he lived, the treason of the Déats, Doriots and the rest would have been far harder to present as a "realist" acceptance of the needs of the situation, as the way to "real" Socialism. Because Jaurès had never separated Socialism from democracy, from the Rights of Man, these sophistries would have had no effect. The thirty years in which he might have been alive were changed for the worse by his murder:

"Untimelier death than his was never any."

XII
MAURICE BARRÈS:
THE PROGRESS OF A NATIONALIST

WHEN the young and still obscure representative of a little literary clique in Provence began to write in *La Cocarde*, then edited by the white hope of French literature, few people can have foreseen the reversal of roles which was to follow. In 1894, Barrès was truly the *princeps juventutis* for French literary aspirants. Maurras was unknown and there was nothing to suggest that he would ever quit the obscurity of a contributor to the *Gazette de France* or a member of the *école romane*, that he would ever be anything more than one of the leading intellectuals of Nîmes or Arles. Nevertheless, ten years later, Barrès had become, or seemed to have become, a man of letters and nothing else. He had been a deputy; he had played an important role in the Boulanger crisis; he played a still more important role in the Dreyfus case; he was to be the ally and successor of Déroulède; he was to be a member for Paris in the Chamber. But, in 1904, his function as a director of conscience was over; he was still a great writer; he was no longer a master. He had lost two types of disciple and he had not found any new ones. That he should have lost the respectful admiration of the young men of letters of the Left was inevitable. It was a necessary result of the great schism of the Dreyfus case. Léon Blum has told us of his profound disillusionment when he found out that his literary idol was resolved, in spite of all the evidence, to remain on the side of the barricade which he had chosen in advance; and Jules Renard has told us with what readiness the bright young men of the *Revue Blanche* took up the idea that Barrès had deceived them in more ways than one, that he was not only an enemy of justice and truth, but that his literary gifts had been exaggerated. Because Barrès had not been shaken by the revelation of Henry's infamy, the prestige of the *Jardin de Bérénice* and of *Les Déracinés* was bogus. Such an intrusion of politics into literary criticism is not surprising, above all in France; Barrès himself an ardent politician, and a political novelist as well, had no reason to complain. He did not complain.

But the desertion of his disciples of the Right was more surprising and more serious. Barrès neither did nor wanted to draw to him the clever young men of the "internationalist" *lycées* of Paris. But he did want to win over the young men who had the same background as himself, the young men whose problems he thought he had at least stated and, to some degree, solved. Yet he lost hold of them. He remained a great ornament of the nationalist cause. In the political field, his name was associated with that of Maurras by Bainville and other representatives of the school, but it was as an ornament and not as a leader. His troops had gone over to Maurras and, far from thinking themselves unfaithful to their old leader, gave increasingly obvious signs of impatience because he did not follow them.

Barrès saw that there was some justice in the decision made by the young men. Boulangism had been a movement, not a doctrine, and the lack of a doctrine which would compensate for the personal weaknesses of the General had some part in the failure of the movement. During the Dreyfus crisis, the amorphous organizations of nationalism, the *Ligue de la Patrie française* led by Jules Lemaître as well as the older *Ligue des Patriotes* of Déroulède, had made their doctrinal weaknesses very obvious. In *L'Appel au Soldat*, Barrès remarked on this weakness and sighed after an organized system of teaching that would save the French nationalist forces from another débâcle. The teacher came; he was followed by the disciples, but not by Barrès. And, as the sequel was to prove, Barrès was right, right as much by instinct as by thought. No disaster of Boulangism or the *Ligue de la Patrie française* was comparable in its disastrous results with the results of the realist policy of the *Action française*. When Barrès wrote *Au Service de l'Allemagne*, he could not foresee what meaning that title held *in potentia*! He could not foresee a time when the *Action Française* would not have a word to say on the abandonment of Strasbourg and Metz, and when disciples of Maurras (though not Maurras himself) would look with complacency on a French Legion in German uniforms taking the oath of loyalty to the Führer of Germany, a bastard version of the foreign corps of the ancien régime, like the Royal Allemand or the Regiment of Deux-Ponts.

What was it that saved Barrès from the rigours of a system that ended in such ignominy? It was not that he was exempt from some of the great intellectual weaknesses of the school. One of the two most important historical events in the history of Lorraine in his time was the discovery of the Gilchrist–Thomas process, which, by making it possible to remove the phosphorus from the Lorraine iron ore, transformed the poor rural province of Barrès's childhood into one of the great pieces of economic booty of the modern world. Barrès ignored this development, just as Maurras and his school have continued to ignore the whole problem of the influence of the technical revolution on the position of France in the world. In the same way, although Barrès had a knowledge of the frontier provinces between France and Germany to which Maurras has never attained and understood their state of mind better than Bainville, he never attached the importance it deserved to the work of modern history in these regions, to the effects of industrialization, of Prussian administration, of German nationalism, and modern socialism. He laid himself open to the criticism of Albert Thibaudet in *Les Princes Lorrains*. He not only thought it possible to make of the Rhineland a new Switzerland, but to make of it a Switzerland in which no memory of William Tell would trouble the dreams of the former subjects of the Reich. His solution for the question of the Rhineland, set out in the *Grands Problèmes du Rhin*, his "Let us go back to the First Empire," to the Confederation of the Rhine, is naïve enough. But it is no more naïve than the Maurrasian solution; and in any case, to return to the time when Jean Bon Saint-André and Lezay-Marnésia won the respect and devotion of his German subjects for the Emperor, is to go less far back and to rely on historical parallels which have more life in them, than this dream of a perpetual Diet of Ratisbon, managed by an eternal series of Father Josephs! No, it was not because he was less of a realist than Maurras or had less of that "tact des choses possibles" that Cavour thought the greatest quality in a statesman, that Barrès let his disciples slip away from him.

The opposite was the case; it was because his realism was superior to that of Maurras, because his activities, as a deputy, as a party chief, as a novelist who was not merely the pet of a small literary and political circle, had involved him too deeply in the life really lived by men, for him to believe, with all the willingness in the world, in the possibility of remaking France on a plan that presupposed that 1793 had not happened or had had only transitory results. The Revolution *had* happened; not only the royal reform of the old order which failed to come off in 1789, but the Revolution which had sent his grandfather all over Europe with the *Grande Armée*, which had brought the Bourbons back in the "baggage carts of the foreigners," and, with them, the courtiers, the Polignacs, the Blacas, the men of whom, even more than of their masters, it was true to say that they had learned nothing and forgotten nothing. Varennes, Valmy, could a Lorrainer forget all that or accept a version of French history which saw in them only negligible and corrigible aberrations?

The division between Barrès and Maurras was not merely due to the natural inability of a Lorrainer to share the emotions of a "Blanc du Midi." There was a more personal cause. Barrès, as a young man and as a Boulangist, had been much taken with the idea of solving the French problem by concentrating all power in one man. The author of *L'Appel au Soldat* was very much attracted by this remedy for the political "mal du siècle." But Barrès not merely was free from the dynastic sentimentality of Maurras, but had his own dynastic loyalty, loyalty if not to a family, at least to a name. He was a Bonapartist, forced by the course of history to find substitutes for his devotion.

When the Boulangist adventure had finally collapsed, when the politicians of the Republic had managed to survive the Panama scandals, Barrès continued to express his naïve enthusiasm in a dithyrambic evocation of Napoleon. Under the title *Napoléon professeur d'énergie* he expressed his Bonapartism with a warmth and a kind of crudity, rare enough in his writings:

"Je suis sûr que nous manquons d'énergie, de volonté, d'enthousiasme, et puis aussi d'une qualité moindre, de la flamme romanesque. Le vrai traitement, la réelle psychothérapie ne serait point de conduire nos enfants dans les maisons d'idiots et de leur dire: 'sois semblable à eux pour être heureux.' Mais racontons-leur la vie de Bonaparte. Même, n'ayez point de scrupule de leur dire: petit enfant, si tu le peux, sois semblable à celui-ci. Pour ma part, je considère que tout individu qui n'est point malade d'admiration, d'enthousiasme sans issue à la lecture du *Mémorial de Sainte-Hélène*, doit être jeté dehors à coups de pied. . . . Ah! s'il est quelqu'un de qui ces noms: Bonaparte! Napoléon! l'Empereur! M. de Buonaparte! ne fasse battre le cœur, je ne suis pas de sa race, il m'est plus étranger qu'un nègre ou qu'un sous-préfet. Quant à moi, j'entends bien en mourir que de mon cœur pour avoir trop aimé l'homme de Brumaire, et, avec lui, six ou cinq héros, des hommes qui surent marcher sur les flots et n'y furent pas engloutis, parce qu'ils avaient confiance en eux-mêmes. . . ."[1]

The choice of Brumaire as the Napoleonic achievement which touched Barrès the most is significant. His nostalgic recollection of men who, unlike Boulanger and his team, "surent marcher sur les flots," recalls to us the fact that Barrès had taken part in a Brumaire that failed, that he had been the companion of incompetent conspirators. But there was more than that in the Bonapartism of Barrès. He was not only the grandson of an officer of the *Grande Armée*, with the tradition of the "épopée" in his blood. He was a French bourgeois of the eastern marches who had only given up his old faith because its uselessness, its sterility were obvious.[2]

There is no reason to believe that the Bonapartism of Barrès was less genuine than the royalism of Maurras, but, unlike Maurras, Barrès knew too well that the French people had deserted the House of Bonaparte almost as completely as they had the royal house. And he had too much wisdom, too much human sympathy, not to notice that it was impossible to build a system of political architecture on a tradition that was not generally accepted; without the people, no political renaissance was possible. The *élite* could show the way, could inspire, could attract individuals, but if the people did not make an "image d'Epinal" of the doctrine, the reconstruction of France would remain purely formal, it would lack life, sap. So you must win over the soldier, for the military hierarchy kept its hold on the people's imagination. If Boulanger was a "music-hall Bonaparte," so much the better for Boulanger. Wasn't Béranger, from the political point of view, a more important poet than Baudelaire and Paulus than Verlaine? Barrès would have agreed with the wise Scot who thought it more important to make a country's ballads than its laws. Or to put it better, he would have thought that a nation whose laws and songs were flagrantly opposed,

[1] *Le Journal*, 14th April, 1893. Cited by Victor Giraud in: *Les Maîtres de l'heure, Maurice Barrès*, p. 62.
[2] An intimate friend of Barrès told me that he did not hide his former Bonapartist views from his friends, but that he thought that the death of the Prince Imperial condemned the Bonapartist party to being a mere historical relic.

was far from the strength that comes from union. As long as only a handful of Frenchmen knew the refrain of "Vive Henri IV," as long as only a tiny minority rejoiced in the thought of M. de Charette shooting the Republican partridges, it was meaningless to talk of the French monarchical tradition: traditions are not the business of intellectuals, but of the mass of the people; for it is the man in the street who puts flesh and blood on the skeleton built up by the ingenious political system of the theorist.

Barrès was incapable of that unworthy affectation of certainty with which Maurras, for a whole generation, has written and talked as if the King were on the point of making his entry into Paris any day now. His Lorraine was more a Platonic pattern laid up in heaven, than a given political and geographical unit. But if some of Barrès's faults as a theorist came from his genius as a writer, he had too much of the novelist's vision, too much of the spirit of the observer of men and of man to allow his tendency to be doctrinaire to destroy his power of seeing, in his enemies, men who were formidable and even admirable. So, when he described those Radicals involved in Panama whom, officially, he had to detest and despise, he could not deny to himself their virtue (in the Latin sense of the word). In an article on Clemenceau written in 1896, this sense of artistic justice does not desert him.

"C'est un homme. Considérons avec plaisir cette physionomie indomptable, son teint jaune et les plans violemment accusés de cette figure si vivante ou éclate le besoin de vous expliquer à vous-même ce que vous alliez lui expliquer."[1] The enemies of Barrès are not simple traitors or cowards, or fools or rascals, inexplicably succeeding, despite all their contemptible character, in destroying the army of the virtuous and enlightened defenders of tradition, always on the right road, but never victorious. The men who had beaten Boulanger and saved the Republic were *men*, formidable by their courage, their ability, their ill-directed faith.

Of course that is not all they were; the author of *Leurs Figures* was as little prepared as Dr. Johnson to let his political enemies have the best of it. But he was too much of an artist to set up mere targets to shoot at. So as a myth-maker he could not hope to rival the author of the new political demonology, Drumont, or later

---

[1] *Figaro*, 20th May, 1896, not reprinted. The quotation is from Giraud, op. cit., p. 65.

D*

compete with Maurras and Daudet, without mentioning Béraud and the other *sbirri* of the French political police of the Duce.

His "Lorraine," in spite of its resemblance to a Sorelian "myth," was a myth both more human and more full of meaning than the mutilated "France" of the Maurrasian school. The very limits of his understanding of the province on whose temporal realities he built his spiritual construction, had less deplorable consequences, simply because Lorraine was thought of as a part of something much greater. It was not a universe, a complete habitation for the human spirit, as the "France" of Maurras claimed to be. This healthy limitation Barrès owed partly to his ancestral connection with Auvergne, partly to his adoptive connection with Provence. Pascal and Mirabeau, with whom he had created such strong links, prevented him from identifying the primordial virtues of Lorraine with the possibilities of human or even of French nature. His ancestry and his way of life brought home to him—both in his heart and in his brain—the possible varieties of French experience, the possibilities of unity in diversity. This made him a poor heresy hunter. A heretic could even, like the hero of *La Colline inspirée*, be a valuable variety of the human spirit. He did not like heresy for heresy's sake, but he felt—as befitted the author of *Sous l'oeil des Barbares*—a permanent distrust for orthodoxy; he had none of the passion for definitions to be imposed by the secular and religious arm which was professed by his old disciples, now won over to Maurrasian rigidity.

Of course, the deliberate provincialism of Barrès has rightly laid him open to serious critical charges, at any rate from men who had put themselves above mere nationalism. There is some justice in the reproach addressed to Barrès by a man who, having passed through the school of Maurras, declared that it was Barrès who "par un jeu dangereux, en a donné le modèle dans le régionalisme lorrain, élevé pour des raisons qui ne sont pas que de prestige, au rang de province du goût et de l'intelligence, et par le mot funeste de *déracinés*, inventé pour flétrir le caractère universel de la pensée."[1]

Would Barrès have denied all justice to this criticism? It is improbable. We have too much evidence of the irritation with which he received the tiresome worship of simple young men who took too literally his preaching of provincialism. It was one thing to

[1] Louis Dimier, *Histoire et causes de notre Décadence*, pp. 190–1.

fear the tearing-up of one's roots in the ancestral soil; it was something else to oppose "Lorraine" to "France." Nancy was obviously
a healthier object of the ambition of most Lorrainers than Paris;
but all the same Nancy was not Paris; Lorraine, no matter how
valuable, how essential she was to the life of her sons, did not
replace France. There is, in reality, far more of the spirit of the
"petit clan" in Maurras, a far more marked tendency to identify
the principles of the "félibrige" with the totality of French culture,
than there is in Barrès, the preacher of particularism. Barrès
preached, without practising it, a doctrine that would have justified
cutting off of one culture from another and the erection of new
barriers inside nations. But he would not have exploited Mistral
to a grotesque degree as Maurras did and does. The very sullenness
of the *Voyage de Sparte* is less a sign of an attack on classical values
than a protest against the view that all that is valuable comes from
the words and deeds of the ancient world. A northerner, a man of
the frontier, Barrès knew that there are forms of art, cultural
achievements, that the ancient world and, for that matter, the
modern mediterranean world knew nothing of. If simple young
men misunderstood him, that was their fault, not his. For Barrès
didn't want to train up disciples, to found a school, to see his *obiter
dicta* turned into commandments by his faithful followers. For an
artist, this was a more healthy attitude than that of an inveterate
doctrinaire, but that attitude certainly lessened Barrès's influence
over zealots, who wanted a simple, dogmatic and unvarying
answer to all questions. Barrès doubted if such a catechism of
answers could exist and he did nothing to create it. If some of his
writings and his activities show him, at certain moments, implying
that such a catechism existed or revealing regret that he could not
write it, his increase in self-knowledge and in knowledge of the
world cured him of this obsession. For, in this very different from
his rival, Barrès made progress. The world was less simple, less
malleable than it had seemed at first. Such an attitude is a mark of
the artist, but it is a weakness for a political leader who thereby
becomes incapable of providing "principles" sufficiently rigid and
easily digestible, which will spare those who accept them the
trouble of thinking and criticizing.

   The fundamental realism of Barrès appears in the way he accepted
the facts of the Revolution. He regarded them as a "good thing";

his views on the Revolution were closely linked with his views on Lorraine. Without the Revolution, Lorraine would have been not his "little country" but his "great country," his fatherland. But the equation, Lorraine–France, is an isolated theme. Even if Barrès had not been a frontiersman, if instead of being half Auvergnat he had been all Auvergnat, his central position would have been the same. The Revolution had *happened*. Any political theory based on an evasion of this fact was destined to sterility. On this point, he agreed with Napoleon.

"Je ne dis pas que ce qui s'est passé en France est juste, je dis que c'est un jubilé qu'on appelle une révolution. L'ordre social a été remanié, le roi a été guillotiné qui était le sommet de la législation. Si veut le roi, si veut la loi; c'est un ancien axiome en France. Tout a été bouleversé. . . . Vous ne pouvez revenir sur ce qui s'est fait."[1]

The distance in time between the Lorrainers, finally united to France by the Revolution and the epoch of King Stanislas, was no longer than that separating Barrès's generation from the murderous mutilation of 1871. How could you ask of a Lorrainer a spontaneous adhesion to the House of France in which that province had seen for centuries a determined enemy and, for a single generation, a rigorous master? That instinctive respect for the Bourbons which his friends felt or professed to feel, it was neither in the power nor in the will of Barrès to feel. He refused to submit to it and he had doubts, too, of the value of an emotion so intellectual as the rationalized monarchism of the converts to the doctrine. For Maurras and Daudet it was a different matter; they were "Blancs du Midi," descendants of men who had rejoiced at the news of Waterloo. If it was absolutely necessary for Barrès to have feelings of this kind, there were the descendants of the ancient dukes of Lorraine still reigning at Vienna! But all this was a proper theme for a novel, not for a serious political campaign. "Vous ne pouvez revenir sur ce qui s'est fait." This maxim of the Emperor was a constant guarantee against succumbing to the Maurrasian arguments. France was what the Revolution, the Empire, had made her; she was also what the Church and the Monarchy had made her. But a nationalist theory that assumed that her formation had stopped with her last king was an archaeological theory. It was a

[1] Adrien Dansette, *Napoléon Vues politiques*, p. 23.

way of despairing of France far more fundamentally than did all the pessimists and *dilettanti*. It was a decision to await the resurrection of the dead and not the improvement of the living.

While Barrès was still alive, his firm refusal to join the orthodox Maurrasian church was annoying and gave colour to the view of him as an amateur politician rather than a conscientious actor on the political stage, or even a serious critic and observer. But the posthumous publication of his *Cahiers* has shown how unjust was this reproach, how Barrès improved his political education and with what application he sought instruction from his own life and his own career. For Barrès, as man and as writer, there was a great deal to learn, to learn from Pascal, from the experience of life, from his experience as a father, even from his experience as a deputy. For the main source of knowledge for Barrès, as a politician, writer and political thinker, was that body so despised by his natural allies, the Chamber. The Chamber forced him to face, every day, the fact that France had gone through the Revolution, the fact that a theory of France had to explain the Chamber, not merely explain it away. It was not a mere piece of mechanism, a simple trick invented by the "four confederated nations" to cause the ruin of France. It had its Jews, its Protestants, its *métèques* and its freemasons. And the Barrès of *Leurs Figures* and of the *Scènes et doctrines du nationalisme* was always ready to hit them in the solar plexus with all his energy and courage when he got the chance. But he was too keen an observer not to see how French the Chamber was, whether it was for good or ill.

Above all, there was Jaurès. A political system which did not find a place for Jaurès, as a type, as a representative figure, typifying millions of Frenchmen, with powers far above the average, but characteristic all the same, such a system would have been so incomplete as to be worthless. It was not enough to treat Jaurès as a simple pathological symptom, as a growth to be cut out. He could be no more suppressed in this way than he could be discredited, deprived of his power over the mind of Frenchmen by shabby slanders about his appetite or his imaginary château. What was his secret, what forces in French life and traditions did he represent? He was the enemy of much that Barrès stood for; his uncritical internationalism was dangerous; he had been the ally of enemies of the army and the dignity of the nation like General

André. Nevertheless, there he was, and while he examines Jaurès, we can see Barrès enlarging his conception of his country, becoming ready to accept Jaurès, of course not uncritically, but nevertheless accepting him as the spokesman of a group of French ideas and attitudes which could not be excluded from any nationalist doctrine which professed to be complete. As in the case of the Revolution, it was too late in the day merely to regret the fact that Jaurès was there; he had to be used, corrected, instead of being excluded from French life by denying his right to exist.

So we see Barrès in the *Cahiers* weighing the case of Jaurès and the case of Maurras, seeing in each of them a typical specimen of the great French tradition, regarding the two southerners with some of the ironical wonder of a man of the north, but refusing to mutilate his view of France by refusing, to either of them, the attention and weight which was his due. And this dialogue between Barrès and Maurras, between Barrès and Jaurès, is only the most striking example of that process of self-criticism, of reconstruction of doctrine that make the *Cahiers* such fascinating and instructive reading.

Reading the *Cahiers* of Barrès, one sees a man looking for his road, who seeks, in perplexity, an explanation of himself, of his time, of his country. The member for Paris neither wrote nor talked in the manner that the self-analyst of the *Cahiers* used to write. He was a party man. But, alone with himself, he was something more and better than a party man. Like Pascal, he reacted against the casuistry of the *Action française*. He was not the kind of man to let himself be induced to deny his sentiments. And he knew (as a good Pascalian) the importance of sentiment.

It was very natural that the *Action française* should wish to win over Barrès to a complete acceptance of its doctrine. Although Barrès was no longer the idol of the literary youth, he was still the great literary figure of the Right. For he awakened an interest and he exercised an influence over the feelings of the young intellectuals that neither Bourget or Maurras could equal. Barrès had admitted the necessity of a doctrine; he had seen Maurras manage to create one and one whose power he did not deny, any more than he condemned its success, its critical success at any rate. Nevertheless, he resisted all attempts to get him to join the new orthodox political church. He was shocked by the "compel them to come in" attitude of the leaders of the school and surprised by the blindness of a school which boasted of being realist, but which was incapable of recognizing a reality as obvious as the psychological consequences of the divorce that had come about between the French people and its great dynasty. This separation was a fact which the apparent *dilettante* saw and felt, while it was denied by men who called themselves positivists, who set themselves up as professors of political science and not as practitioners of political aesthetics.

It was not for nothing that Barrès was a disciple of Taine, among his other masters. No more than Taine had done, did Barrès always rigorously follow out, in practice, all his own doctrines of intellectual discipline. But he had learned from Taine that respect for the facts which is the beginning of intellectual virtue; now this separation of France from the House of France was a most evident fact.[1]

The disciples of a great man are often more revealing than they intend to be; they play the role of Balaam's ass, who was, after all, a very intelligent animal. So in a study of Barrès which had the honour of a preface by M. Maurras, an important truth on Barrès—and Maurras—is expressed, perhaps unintentionally. The Barrèsian condemnation of a certain type of doctrinaire affects much more than the school criticized; it is an attitude of the mind, rather than a defined doctrine, that is in question. "Nous l'entendons condamner en peu de mots la froideur des Lassalle et des Karl Marx, théoriciens précis, mais glacés, qui ont éliminé 'toute notion de pitié, de justice, d'enthousiasme.' Quoiqu'il reconnaisse dans ces élements 'de vraies parcelles de l'humanité,' il tient ces doctrines comme erronées, parce qu'incomplètes: 'Des demi-bienfaiteurs sont aisément des malfaiteurs.'"[2]

"Half-benefactors are easily malefactors." If Maurras has ever remembered this verdict, when he looks at those disciples whom Bernanos has so well called the "petits mufles réalistes," he may have murmured *de me fabula narratur*. But the founders of schools of political orthodoxy don't permit themselves this kind of self-criticism.

[1] M. Petitbon remarks (*Taine, Renan, Barrès, Etude d'Influence*, p. 90) that it is the solid Roemerspacher, respectful of the facts, who had refused to follow Sturel in his Boulangist adventure, who stays, rooted in Lorraine, and in France, and "c'est à ce vrai disciple de M. Taine qu'échoit—recompense symbolique—la douce Mme de Nelles, la petite Lorraine que Sturel n'a pas su garder."

[2] A. Blanc-Péridier, *La Route ascendante de Maurice Barrès.*

Another disciple of Maurras, who has yet found it possible to carry on the "defence of the West" in the mutilated and gagged France of Vichy, has very clearly defined the dilemma of young Frenchmen of nationalist origins and opinions. On one side, there was the sensitive, intuitive, emotional doctrine of Barrès, or rather, for the word doctrine isn't apt here, the emotional attitude of Barrès in face of the problem of faith and life. As an inspirer of French sentiment, as a professor competent to teach his students how to cut themselves free of the facile materialism or the facile cynicism of some of the official teachers of French youth, Barrès was without a peer. No crude belief in progress, no self-styled wise acceptance of baseness in public affairs could easily get possession of a disciple of the training given by Barrès, a training of the emotions rather than of the mind. But was this training enough? Not for the system-makers; not for Massis.

Massis sets out, fairly enough, the case for Barrès. "Cette recherche de l'idéal, cette revindication du spirituel, voilà la part qu'il s'était reservée. 'Chacun a son rôle notait-il alors.' 'A Maurras la forme didacticque de la leçon, les conseils à autrui, des polémiques, du système. Qu'on me permette ce que je me surprends à faire sans en avoir le projet: la méditation!'" But this "meditation" which Barrès practised had, as he knew very well, the power to give young men a sense of direction, the power to excite them to live, by communicating to them a kind of spiritual awakening of which his art had the secret.

In this field, where he felt himself to be a master, Barrès felt some disturbance at the possible results of Maurras's influence. It was not that he distrusted his clear intelligence, but he feared that Maurras's influence would incline the young men towards a kind of fanatical exclusiveness, by forcing them to submit to a training which, he believed, left too many things outside its system. And his objection which Barrès would perhaps have hesitated to formulate in the case of general ideas, he did not hesitate to express under cover of discussing art and literature. "Vous les faites trop nier par vos disciples, ces romantiques," he wrote to Maurras in 1912. "Vous, vous les connaissez, et je ne suis pas inquiet que nous autres, vous, moi et les gens de notre âge les meconnaissions réellement. Mais vous formez de durs petits ésprits qui mépriseront trop profondément les Gautier, les Baudelaire."

These "durs petits ésprits" were going to despise, in life and in French tradition, in experience and in human values, things more important than Gautier or even than Baudelaire! Barrès's instinct did not betray him when he judged the dogmatic disciples of Maurras who had a systematic answer to every question, but whose positivism had, as little as his own agnosticism, an answer to the fundamental problems of life. And they did not notice that the life of a man or a nation had to be very mutilated to make so many positive assertions possible, assertions which reduced the scope of human life to the preoccupations of the citizen of a modern state! Men do not live by politics alone, and if they believe that they can, their very political life will itself dry up.

The revelation in the *Cahiers* of the tolerance of Barrès for what was for so many political thinkers the intolerable, has left the critics of the Maurras school in an awkward position. For they have not dared to deny one of the glories of the nationalist school; they have not been able to deny, either, in face of the evidence, the power of the *Cahiers*. It is odd to see Robert Brasillach trying to evade the consequences of that human tolerance of Barrès. "Rien de plus curieux, par exemple, dans ses derniers cahiers, que les notes politiques. Il cherchait une musique, fût-elle grossière, même au Palais Bourbon; il se laissait amuser et retenir par la seule chose sincère qu'il reconnait à Jaurès, son 'animalité' (et le page est magnifique). Bien avant que le fameux 'violoncelle' de Briand fut devenu un dogme d'état, Barrès discernait chez 'ce dur jeune homme' chez cet arriviste qu'il meprisait, une part de faiblesse, d'émotion devant le succès, qui s'exprimait par une 'poésie de qualité assez basse, mais pourtant assez réelle.' "[1]

In this petty explanation of the interest which Barrès took in men and which was an inherent part of his formation, one can see all the sterility of the criticism dried up in the herbarium of Maurras, and deformed by the spirit of system; as for the consequences of the desiccation, the rest of the career of M. Brasillach shows us clearly enough what they were.

It was the strength of Barrès in his last period as preacher and practitioner of the nationalist doctrine to have perceived that France, with her people, her history, her problems, was one and indivisible. It had not always been like this. But, by 1914, Barrès

[1] Robert Brasillach, *Portraits*, p. 57.

had made great progress. He had arrived at a position not quite above but, in a sense, on both sides of the battle. France was not an ideal construction to be modelled according to plans that were purely aesthetic or doctrinaire: it was a seamless garment which you could not tear without dangerously threatening its French character. French history neither began nor ended in 1789; the most distant like the most recent past had made France, assailed at the moment by an enemy not merely foreign, but barbarous. This enemy wished to ravage the spirit as well as the soil of France. And during the great crisis of 1914, at the turning-point of the Marne, Barrès despaired neither of France nor of her cause, and he found the words in which to sum up her long history as the guardian of her own civilization and of all the western inheritance.

"Vous souriez, vous dites qu'au départ des Allemands il y a d'autre raisons plus positives, plus tangibles. Je le crois avec vous. Avec vous je les entrevois. Mais avant de les dénombrer je salue cette puissance mystique d'un peuple sûr de sa durée, et qui a vu Attila reculer devant Sainte Geneviève, les envahisseurs devant Sainte Jeanne d'Arc, le duc de Brunswick devant la sainte Liberté."[1]

"Before Saint Liberty. . . ." Can we doubt what would be his attitude to-day, when the destiny of France is more than ever bound up with that of freedom? And when the masters with whom he had shared the empire over so great a part of French thought have come to the point, after having despaired of liberty, of despairing of France? As Barrès noted a few days later, it was not for nothing that Péguy had plunged into Michelet's *History of the Revolution*, and rising from it had gone on and upwards to the mystery of Jeanne d'Arc. The time for dialectic was over; the time for decision had come. And no matter what were the faults of taste and judgment that Barrès showed during those great and terrible years, he proved at the same time that "l'union sacrée" had for him a more profound meaning than a mere political truce, than a simple agreement to put off quarrels till the end of the war. It was a union in a whole—past, present, future—bitter and glorious, an inheritance that must be accepted in its entirety. Some days later, Barrès told his readers the story of the composer Albéric Magnard, son of Francis Magnard of the *Figaro*. Magnard had fired on two uhlans who tried to break into his house; he was seized and shot.

[1] 8th September, 1914, *L'Union Sacrée*, p. 151.

"Lui, le fils du grand sceptique, Francis Magnard, lui, l'enfant du *Figaro*, il a resolu de donner sa vie plutôt que d'accepter ce qui ne doit pas être." In 1940, it was the son of his great friend "Gyp," the surgeon Thierry de Martel, who killed himself on the day the Germans entered Paris, as a protest against the acceptance of "ce qui ne doit pas être." Can we doubt that Barrès would be with those who refuse to accept the intolerable? In spite of his faults of taste, in spite of a type of patriotic rhetoric that rings a little theatrically to-day, in spite of his errors of judgment, his premature optimism, Barrès shows in his "chroniques de guerre" that sense of the unity of France and of Frenchmen which raises an occasionally bitter polemic above mere bitterness. It is a tragic thing that "l'ennemi ait su se faire servir par les hommes mêmes chargés de le dépister et qu'il ait trouvé dans les organismes institués pour le combattre des complaisances."[1]

But how much more tragic Barrès would have thought it that leaders, masters who had set up as guardians of the integrity of the soil and the life of France, should have become the allies, the approving and silent witnesses of a work of treason towards France far more dangerous than anything planned by the defeatists of 1917! Barrès thought, in 1917, that it was easy to discover who were the enemies and the friends of Germany. He did not live to the end, made dark by despair, by hate, by party spirit, by the naïve calculations of self-interest. Had he lived to this day, can we believe that he, any more than Clemenceau, would have despaired, that he would, any more than Péguy, have tolerated the petty prudence of those realists who had found his teaching too sentimental, his doctrine too vague, his faith in the totality of France too tolerant?

[1] *En regardant au fond des crevasses* (1917), p. 5.

XIII
CHARLES MAURRAS:
THE POLITICS OF HATE
(1944)

On 11th July, 1888, a young Provençal literary aspirant was admitted as a member of the Société des Félibres of Paris. And to those defenders of the culture of the *langue d'oc* Charles Maurras gave a definition of his and their task: "Voste Félibrige es lou mantenamen de l'amour dóu pais," or to give his own translation, "le Félibrige consiste à maintenir l'amour du pays."

Nearly sixty years later, Maurras has been condemned in a French court at Lyons for treason, on a charge that might, in fact, be summed up in "the maintenance of hatred of Frenchmen for Frenchmen," ending in the final doctrinaire infamy of denouncing men who were fighting to free France, to the agents of the invader. It would be absurd to credit Maurras, great as his influence has been, with being the inventor and propagator of that hatred of Frenchmen for Frenchmen that Bodley noted a generation ago; *homo homini lupus* was not invented to cover the case of Maurras; but no book of his was given a more revealing title than *Quand les Français ne s'aimaient pas*. It was no fault of Maurras if they, for a brief moment, forgot their secular feuds. For the impression made by a study of the long life of this master of polemics is that of a drying-up of what little love there was in Maurras's view of the world and the final growth, to a malignant perfection, of a politics of hate.

At the very beginning of the Maurras problem lies the apparent mystery of his attitude to the national religion. Maurras tried to claim for himself the title of "Catholic," but he was too honest—and too proud of his own ideas—to hide for a moment that he had "not the honour to be a believer." He was a sceptic who saw in Catholicism the national religious tradition of the French people; he was the intellectual captain of a party that numbered tens of thousands of believers among its zealots. He professed, in public, respect for the traditions of his own and all truly French families; traditions which, if they had no other merit, marked him off from the inferior breeds who were ruining France, the "four confederate nations," the Protestants, the Jews, the Masons, the Métèques. They were "anti-France"; "France" meant a respect, formal or doctrinal, for the church of France. This was the position of a good many Frenchmen like Fustel de Coulanges, as a formal Protestantism was the counterpart in the case of Taine and others. But there was, in the case of Maurras, a further difficulty. Whatever formal respect he might impose on himself, he was not a mere unbeliever; he was a hater of Christianity and of all the specifically Christian elements in Catholicism. Mr. Wallace Fowlie has asserted (*à propos* of Baudelaire) that "once a Christian, it is impossible to dispossess oneself of the spirit of Christianity. The sacraments leave an indelible mark." If so, Maurras, who was at least baptized, confirmed and made his first communion, is an exception to the rule. For there is nothing in his attitude that recalls that other strange fruit of Catholic education, Joyce. There is no *odi et amo*. There is only hate. Mr. Santayana has recently told us that "Catholicism is the most human of religions, if taken humanly; it is paganism spiritually transformed and made metaphysical." For Mr. Santayana, the Catholicism of a reasonable man is a superior form of paganism; for Maurras it is an inferior form of paganism, tainted with Judaic infection, with the seeds of humanitarianism, with romanticism. It is as hard to imagine Maurras calling, like Mr. Santayana's free-thinking father, for "La Unción y la gallina," as Mr. Eliot found it to imagine that American semi-Maurrasian, Irving Babbitt, calling for that equivalent of Socrates' cock for Aesculapius. In each case pride was too strong.

From the moment that Maurras became an important influence in the French Church round 1900, the dilemma was pressed on him, and on his clerical and lay followers, by hostile Catholics and ironical neutrals. He had, unfortunately for his partisans, given hostages to the enemy; in his collection of "contes philosophiques," *Le Chemin de Paradis*, and in the essays later grouped under the title *Anthinéa*, Maurras made some concessions (with what bitterness we may guess). In a new edition of the tales, he claimed that his ideas were sufficiently "paienne et chrétienne pour mériter le beau titre de catholique qui appartient à la réligion dans laquelle nous sommes nés. Il n'est pas impossible que j'aie heurté, chemin faisant, quelque texte brut de la Bible, mais je sais à peine lesquels. D'intelligentes destinées ont fait que les peuples policés du sud de l'Europe n'ont fait guère connu ces turbulentes écritures orientales qu'extraites, composées, expliquées par l'Eglise dans le merveille du Missel et de tout le Bréviare." Those who have read the book will know how adequate a defence is this sufficiently disdainful explanation. Nor is there much evidence that either the Missal or the Breviary played much part in Maurras's literary or political equipment, except for one item which he detested and which, by itself, must have seemed to him to justify the hatred he bore the inexpugnable Christian elements in the Catholic tradition. There was always the memory of the revolutionary canticle, with its prophecy of the Jacobins, and the modern world, to excite his horror; *deposuit potentes de sede et exaltavit humiles.*

But it was not merely the Bible or the *Magnificat* that the political commander of so many of the faithful hated. In one of the Athens museums he had seen, in 1896, a statue which, as the catalogue noted, "nous rapelle l'image de Jésus-Christ." And Maurras declared his emotion with a passion worthy of Julian. "Je sentis pourtant le besoin de courir au grand air pour dissiper le trouble où me jetait ce brusque retour du nouveau monde et du Nazaréen par qui tout l'ancien monde s'écroula. . . . Je me couchai au sol et regardai, sans dire ni penser rien, la nuit qui approchait; *il me semblait qu'ainsi sous la croix de ce dieu souffrant, était arrivée la nuit sur l'âge moderne.*" It would be difficult to be more precise, to reveal a basic hatred more candidly. And, again, the apology to his allies was made from the heights. A note in a new edition of *Anthinéa* marked the suppressed passage: "Il m'a paru satisfaisant pour la pensée d'un certain nombre d'amis catholiques vivants ou morts et pour mon temoignage de profonde reconnaissance de sacrifier ce chapitre en mémoire de la grande âme du Pape Pie X." He had reason to be grateful to the dead Pope who had saved his works from the *Index* to which vigilant theologians had condemned them. But even suppressed, the words remained—strange testimony to the power of a man for whom the greatest Jesuit theologian of modern times was to risk the good name of the Society and to lose his seat in the Sacred College. Cardinal Billot was only the most eminent of the numerous French Catholics and Nationalists who made Maurras the keeper of their political consciences. And even those who had taken comfort in the suppression might have noted that in the luxurious edition of the *Voyage d'Athènes* of 1939, the suppression was maintained, but there was now no mention of the Pope. Who knows? It was perhaps only a matter of respect for the great company to which Charles Maurras, now able to write on his title page "de l'Académie française," owed some concessions.

The great feud with the Vatican that led to the condemnation of the *Action française* revived, on a lesser scale, the old scandals of the bull *Unigenitus*, giving comfort to the profane who found it hard to decide what side to take, that of Pius XI, who condemned what Pius X had protected, or that of the political heresiarch on whose side the anti-clericalism of the Left found it hard not to cheer. But when peace was made again (a half-Cannosa for Maurras who had, it is believed, been overborne by the fighting zeal of the officially Catholic Léon Daudet when the decision to defy Rome was taken) one old enemy remained unreconciled, unforgiven. Of all Maurras's polemical works, perhaps the most formidable, the one that gives the highest impression of his powers, is the attack on the Catholic democrats. And from *La Révolution religieuse* through the attempt to pin the guilt of the murder of Jaurès on the *Sillon*, down to the denunciation to the Germans of Georges Bidault, now Foreign Minister of France, and, as editor of *L'Aube*, an heir of Marc Sangnier, the hatred of the Athens museum has found ever deeper and baser expression.

How was it that such a man could, in fact, have become the political spokesman of the right wing of French Catholicism, the idol of the *bien pensants*? He was united to them by something as humanly important as ideological consistency, common enemies. It was with a certain historical justice that, at his trial, Maurras cried that this was revenge on him for his role in the Dreyfus case. As François Mauriac has recently pointed out, it is difficult in this new iron age to understand the emotions which convulsed France in the crisis whose formal cause was the question of the guilt or innocence of a not very interesting or attractive Jewish, bourgeois officer. Maurras has always insisted that Dreyfus was guilty but that it didn't matter anyway. The real question was this: should the safety and unity of France and her army be imperilled for the life or liberty even of a more attractive victim than Dreyfus? It was all very well to assert the maxim *fiat justitia ruat coelum*, but, remember, "there have been States without justice but no justice without the State." The sky might fall, would fall, and then would justice have much chance?

It would be very uncandid not to admit that Maurras was far more of a prophet, understood the spirit of the coming age far better than did Jaurès, Romain Rolland, or Anatole France. The proof is all around us to-day; possibly only in the remote and comparatively untouched United States can we find, in the schism among the American intellectuals over the guilt or innocence of Trotsky, a faint parallel to the great French debate. It was this intellectual boldness that gave Maurras his position. He defended Henry and the methods of Henry as later intellectuals defended Yagoda and the methods of Yagoda, as others preferred to ignore the murder of Matteotti or the probable identity of the patrons of the assassins of King Alexander or of the Roselli brothers. Many of the older Conservative leaders in France were intimidated by human respect; respect for the *Institut* or for their reputations in enlightened circles at home and abroad. Maurras was not; he had then a genuine and ferocious contempt for all the *notables*, royalist and republican. He despised them all as "les princes des Nuées." Round him, the young, angry militants of the ever-defeated army of the French Right rallied. He gave and wanted no quarter. And he found echoes in more circles than those of the declining royalists and depressed Catholics. It was not only young reactionary intellectuals who enjoyed the spectacle of "Criton," killing the flatulent and easily winded apologists for the *république des camarades* in the *Action Française*. That weekly and then daily "hour of truth" gave the *aficionados* of controversy a real delight. It seemed, on the eve of 1914, that the young men of the great schools of Paris were choosing between Maurras and Marx; it was a dilemma that Socialists like Marcel Sembat delighted to force on their less rigorous colleagues of the Left. By the time of the first war, Maurras was secure in a position held by no one since Joseph de Maistre, as the great "master of the counter-revolution." It was a great career for the minor Provençal poet and *littérateur*.

Whether Maurras would in any event have remained a mere man of letters may be doubted. His literary talents were formidable rather than attractive and he suffered from the narrowness of his education and tastes. Indeed, the reader is sometimes as astonished at his narrowness as was Doctor Watson at the limitations of Holmes's knowledge. Like Holmes, Maurras occasionally quotes Goethe and he professed to know English. Dante is given a formally central position as one of the glories of the Latin tongues; Mistral is, of course, preached and praised by the *félibre*. But basically, Maurras's literary culture is that of the old-fashioned French clerical *collège*, the French classics, Latin and rather more Greek than the average *fort en thème* of the old type usually had at his command. The culture produced by this education had curiously narrow limits. It was not only that Maurras has none of the cosmopolitan culture that was at the command of such close associates as Léon Daudet, Jacques Bainville and Louis Dimier. Although his own style was often most effective when it was freest from the traditional atticism of French rhetorical teaching, his admiration of Anatole France for having "defended the French tongue" was genuine enough to survive all political feuds. His deafness would have saved him from the cult of Wagner and of German music in general if his political principles had not done so, but his taste in the visual arts seems to have been limited to an admiration for the traditional perfections of Athens. He despised both Mycenaean and archaic art; the work of Humfry Payne would not in the least have diminished his anger at the English for removing the Elgin Marbles to London and, stranger still, he seems to have thought that the artists of Chartres and of the other glories of medieval France would have been indisputably better, not merely different, if they could have gone to school to Phidias.

There has surrounded Maurras a good deal of the servile admiration given by a self-conscious minority to its leader and chief public asset. So there has been more formal praise devoted to his poetry than, one suspects, there has been real devotion to it.   He was a member of the *école romane*, whose name may stir faint memories in readers of the defence of his own *poétique*, recently published by M. Louis Aragon. But whatever may be the long-term place of *Les Yeux d'Elsa*, *La Musique Intérieure* may well be a mere entry in a bibliography. Much the same may be said of the novel,

Les Amants de Venise. But this has another interest as a fictional presentation of the literary and social criticism of *Romantisme et révolution*, and *Barbarie et poésie*. That hatred and contempt for the private and public confusion bred by "romanticism," in letters and in love, must be considered central to the Maurrasian doctrine of life. And, with this in mind, we should remember that a close associate has testified to the scandal caused by the brutality of Maurras's private conversation on sexual matters, by his view of women. It was no mere matter of *gauloiserie* or *grivoiserie*, not the mere pornography of Daudet's *L'Entremetteuse*, but a savage and dogmatic return to a Greek view of women that a Greek would have found absurdly pedantic and systematic, but not novel. Maurras was worlds apart from the humane, easy-going Provence of Alphonse Daudet, or even of the lyrical landscape of Mistral. He had very little use for "dance and provençal song and sunburnt mirth." He was more a countryman of Cézanne than of less austere artists.

He was, nevertheless, by far more than literary affectation, a man of the South. He has always denied being a "Blanc du Midi," a man whose royalism was a mere family conditioned-reflex. But though his family did, for a misguided generation, rally to the Second Empire, he was indelibly marked with the spirit of the feuds of the South. He has told the world more than once of his pride that his native "Republic of Martigues" held out for the Catholic League against the "army of the Protestant King" (Henri IV) in which Malherbe served. He has told us, too, of the bitter winds from the Cevennes that strike the undefended town; winds from the country of the Camisards; and not far away is the country of the Albigeois and still not far away, in space or time, the memories of red terror and white terror, of Representatives on mission and of the murder of Marshal Brune. The Provence and Languedoc of Maurras is a hard, vindictive country. He has always refused to see in the Emperor anything but a disaster for France or in his claim to be French more than the most extravagant impudence of the greatest of *métèques*. And nothing less in the true spirit of the Maurrasian Midi can be imagined than the young Bonaparte's successful appeal to the Marseillais on the evening of the 10th of August to save a wounded Swiss Guard. Maurras was on the Swiss Guard's side, but he might have despised the republican soldier for his preposterous mercy.

The war of 1914 greatly increased his prestige. He had predicted it; he had indulged in no dreams of amity with Germany or universal disarmament and peace. There was truth in his affirmation (in the dedication of *L'Etang de Berre*) that "avec vous si mon corps avait valu mon âme, contre le barbare germain je me serais armé et battu pour le sol et l'intelligence de la patrie." As the war lasted, the influence of Maurras grew. It is true, as Louis Dimier has pointed out, that there was something ludicrous in the injured innocence with which Maurras denied plotting against the régime. If it was bringing France to ruin, why wasn't he? But the *Action Française* played a really important part in preparing the way for the dictatorship of Clemenceau, and that unrepentant Jacobin, with his own tenacious power of hatred as well as his origins in the Vendée, was not an intolerably strange bedfellow. He was certainly less strange than Chautemps and Peyrouton and Laval, necessarily tolerated by the defender of Pétain while Clemenceau's right arm, Georges Mandel, was in prison before being murdered by the French agents of the invader.

Against Versailles, Maurras launched a campaign that might attract more sympathy now than it did then. *Le Mauvais Traité* is not Maurras's best book by a long way, but what he said was not mere bile or folly. But it revealed, as all his writings revealed, what was his most serious intellectual as apart from moral defect, his ignorance of the real forces of the modern world. Even for a French intellectual his economics were remarkably naïve. He never seems to have noticed that the relative decline of France in the nineteenth century was at least as much due to geology as to stupid politics. The balance of power went with coal. Inside France, the balance of power, even on the Right, began to move against Maurras. As the most formidable of the many Maurrasian disciples who have later denied him has pointed out, the French people found their victory denuded of moral meaning, largely through the influence of the "positivist" politics of Maurras. And if Bernanos moved away in one direction, less creditable disciples moved away in another. Taittinger and Bucard and Doriot had by 1939 taken away much of the most noisy, combative support from Maurras. The militant "camelots du roi," one of the undoubted ancestors of the *squadristi*, of the S.A. and of various militant Communist organizations, were socially too exclusive, too *muscadin*, to compete with their children. Then the royalist doctrine was a handicap. Few people really believed in a restoration. Maurras had asked "is the *coup de force* possible?" All Europe was full of the answer "yes," but there were no General Monks, only more or less plausible imitations of Bonaparte. Inevitably the triumph of Fascism was an irresistible temptation to Maurras to begin to make those compromises that led him to treason. He was too intelligent to hide from himself that Italian Fascism was Bonapartist in spirit, far from the Capetian caution of the "forty kings who made France." But Mussolini was an enemy of the principles of '89, of parliament, of the freemasons, then of the Jews. He was also an enemy of France. Maurras tried to evade this aspect of the Duce's policy by claiming that he was no more Gallophobe than Crispi or Nitti, and that, in any case, he was an enemy of the decadent republican France, not of real "Latin France." This was the kind of defence Maurras had attacked when French republicans used it against French clericals. That the devotion of republicans to France was conditional on its being *their* France was treason. But Maurras was well on the way to the "France mais" of Arthur Ranc before the birth of the Third Reich complicated his already difficult position.

On the one hand, there was the renascent danger of German barbarism; on the other, the enemies of the new Chancellor were Jews, intellectuals, liberals, the four confederate nations. Maurras tried to escape by distinguishing between Fascism and Nazism. Part of the uncontrollable rage he felt at the alienation of the Duce by the Abyssinian crisis arose not merely from his contempt for "ideals," especially "Anglo-Saxon" ideals, but from the acuteness of his personal stresses. It was difficult to separate the Duce from the Führer if he refused to be separated. The murderous attack on Léon Blum, for which Maurras was sent to prison as instigator, was proof of crisis. The Spanish War was another testing time. That he should have been against the Spanish Republic was consistent enough; the follies of Spanish republicanism had been an old story with him since the restoration of 1873 had been held up as an example to the French. But an authoritarian Spain, armed by two hostile Powers on the flank of France, was that an unmixed good? And Maurras had not only to risk treason to the interests of France, he had to commit treason to the traditions of the *Félibrige*, to rejoice in the most brutal of Castilian triumphs over that glorious province of the *langue d'oc*, Catalonia.

The war, but only for a short time, enabled him to make a new patriotic virginity for himself. But with French defeat and the triumph of Vichy, he finally succumbed. He had always hated England next only to Germany; Protestant, liberal, triumphant England, paymaster and controller of all French internal seditions from La Rochelle to the *front populaire*. He could no longer speak his hatred of Germany, so England and its new instrument, "Gaullism," were attacked with all his vehemence and power. For a short time, Vichy seemed to be under Maurrasian direction, and the political preacher to have, at last, found an arm. But Vichy was a German creation; the Marshal had to take back Laval; the few feeble efforts at a national and traditional reconstruction were abandoned. Yet Maurras continued to give to Pétain a devotion and obedience he had never given to any of the Pretenders or Popes to whom he had paid formal service. His passion was now monarchical in the strictest sense of the term. Government by one man, even a senile and heirless man, was better than the "headless state" as he called the restored republic when on his trial. The spirit of the Catholic League revived in him and he gave to Pétain the same fanatical support that the Catholic demagogues of Paris had given to the senile Cardinal de Bourbon, "Charles X." De Gaulle was for Maurras what Henri IV had been for his spiritual and fleshly ancestors.

It was a tragic end for the prophet of "integral nationalism." Of course he was supported by illusions as well as by pride and hate. He was attracted by the merely literary dream of the "Latin bloc." He had, in 1922, quoted Mistral on the divided Latin race:

> "Si tu n'étais pas divisée
> Qui pourrait te faire la loi?

Oui, toutes nos faiblesses resultent de nos divisions, la verité a été vue du poète sacré." He was back in the dream land of his youth when he and the historical charlatan, Frédéric Amouretti, had dreamed dreams less preposterous than the madman's illusion of making of Pétain's France, Franco's Spain, Mussolini's Italy a counterpoise to the Third Reich or the British Empire and the United States. No "prince des Nuées" had ever preached a policy so straight from cloud-cuckoo-land as that. His venomous zeal was unflagging; he was still financially incorrupt and personally fearless.

He did not even take the easy way out when Victor Emmanuel, for once, justified some of the monarchist doctrine by getting rid of the Duce. He now refused to see who it was, in fact, he served. His official French nationalism was like those inverted and diabolic symbols that are, it is said, to be found in some Provençal churches. By the time liberation came, there was no turning back.

As far as Maurras was affected by a poet, he was affected by Dante and the Greeks. And he would have been at home among the bitter exiles of the Black Guelf party or in the Corcyra of Thucydides or the Athens of the Thirty Tyrants. Like a passionate Greek, he had finally sacrificed all to be the unregarded counsellor of the tyrant of his city. But unlike Dante, he had no notion of the role of Beatrice, his journey ended long before the *Purgatory*, much less the *Paradiso* where is to be experienced "l'amor che move il sole e l'altre stelle." Maurras, in prison, may think of his lost province, of the golden urbanity of Nîmes, of the majesty of the Pont du Gard. But his real home is not with the Roman ruins or Greek foundations of Provence and Languedoc, but in the ruined castle of Les Baux, in the fantastic valley where, so some have thought, Dante found the landscape of the *Inferno* in whose deeper circles he has thrust, with admiration but no dubiety, the great sinners who fell by pride. Even at this moment, of all the men whom the French nation has rightly tried and condemned, Maurras is put in a different class from the Suarez and Bérauds, Lavals and Doriots. It is only a few weeks since a resistance leader, in private, expressed his understanding of the power of the unshaken old man. And in refusing to appeal, to retract, to repent for a moment the odious role he had adopted for himself, Maurras has a sufficiently dignified and illustrious exemplar. As long as he lives we may be sure that his pride and confidence in his doctrine will sustain him:

> " . . . What though the field be lost?
> All is not lost—the unconquerable will,
> And study of revenge, immortal hate,
> And courage never to submit or yield."

XIV

BAZAINE[1]

(1943)

THE rank of Marshal of France is, or until very recent times was, the most famous military title in the world. It had around it the aura of great victories and most honourable defeats. Turenne and Villars, Saxe and Rochambeau, and then the constellation of the "épopée," the names mingled with the titles, the Duke of Elchingen and Prince of the Moskowa less glorious than Michel Ney at the Beresina or before the firing-party, the Duke of Rivoli and Prince of Essling less well remembered than the Masséna who had to surrender Genoa and who nearly won at Fuentes d'Onoro. But there are other marshals with more ambiguous fame. There were the old frivolous court marshals like Soubise and that Richelieu who captured Port Mahon and invented mayonnaise. And there are the marshals whose fame is clouded with the fumes of politics. There is Marmont, whose reputation, despite Sainte-Beuve's able *plaidoyer*, has not been freed from the imputation of treason in 1814. There is Bazaine, sentenced to death by a French court-martial and the victim of one of the most famous rebukes in modern French history —and administered by a Prince of the Blood. And to-day there is Pétain, surviving his fame and his honour till, at this moment, he recalls no one more than that shadowy Cardinal de Bourbon whom the dying League called King of France when Henri IV was still conquering his kingdom from the Catholic New Order of the Habsburgs.

Taken together, the lives of Bazaine and Pétain cover French history from the end of the First Empire to the end of the Third Republic, and Mr. Guedalla might have been content to write some elegant variations on the theme of the lamentable mutations of human and of national fortunes. But he has done much better. He has written a pioneer book. For this is the first adequate case for Bazaine. For obvious reasons French historians have fought shy

[1] Philip Guedalla, *The Two Marshals: Bazaine, Pétain.* (Hodder and Stoughton.)

of the subject, although the more objective among them have dismissed or discounted the more extravagant charges brought against him in the agony of humiliation that followed the *année terrible*.

Mr. Guedalla brings to his subject not merely an old interest in and knowledge of the Second Empire and the art of arms, but a special knowledge of the Spanish world and the Spain of the First Carlist War, and the Mexico of the abortive empire; indeed, the Oran and Tlemçen of the French *reconquista* are more relevant to our understanding of Bazaine than is the Crimea or Italy. No one has done more or as much to make intelligible to us the background and temperament of this taciturn, secretive, indomitably brave soldier of fortune. Had Bazaine died or been killed in Mexico his reputation would have been dim but untarnished. There might have been gossip about his matrimonial affairs, about his role in the turbid politics of Algeria or Mexico, but he would have ranked as one of the most capable products of the school of Marshal Bugeaud. But Metz put an end to a career of reasonable good fortune.

The disaster of 1870 was so complete, so shattering to the professional prestige of a class still living parasitically on the memories of the First Empire, that a search for a scapegoat was inevitable. For that role Bazaine was cast by his own past, by his origins as a promoted ranker, by his reputation as a political general, by the fact that, at the turning-point of the campaign of 1870, he was Commander-in-Chief. Even if the leaders of the French army had wanted to do him justice, it would have been difficult to do so. The day when a defeated army could put all the responsibility on the civilians, on the state of public opinion, on the politicians, on anybody but the *grands chefs*, had not yet come. Such a miracle of impudence as the Riom trial was beyond the imagination and the resources of the rulers of France in 1873. Bazaine was charged with various crimes. One was his conduct of the campaign in the open field, the choice he made of being shut up in Metz rather than make a desperate retreat westwards to Champagne or the walls of Paris. The defeats suffered around Metz were also imputed to him, to his wrong view of his duties as Commander-in-Chief, to a more sinister and premature despair. Against some of these charges Mr. Guedalla makes a good defence. But if Bazaine was neither the complete traitor nor the complete fool of the legend, he was, none the less, a disastrously incompetent general.

It is the contention, or at least the insinuation (for Mr. Guedalla dislikes the historical frontal assault), of this part of the narrative that Bazaine was made a scapegoat by the better-born, better-educated French generals for all the disasters of the campaign of August 1870. True, Bazaine has been blamed for not acting like a Commander-in-Chief before he was one. When he did become Commander-in-Chief the campaign was more than half lost. The disaster of Wörth and MacMahon's loss of Alsace had raised the odds even more overwhelmingly against the French. The hesitations of the last days of July and the first days of August had dissipated whatever chances there had been of a disorganization of the German plan of campaign by a sudden invasion of the Palatinate. Only a general of great energy, resolution and flexibility of mind could have hoped to redress the balance. Bazaine was not such a general, and Mr. Guedalla does not pretend that he was. But he defends him successfully against the charge of *deliberate* neglect of the occasional and so fleeting chances of success that were given to the French. He does not, indeed, make the nature of those chances evident to the reader who comes to the story of this campaign with no previous knowledge. That reader might be pardoned if he made a picture to himself of an almost infallible German general staff commanding an almost impeccable army. Whatever may have been thought by the credulous at the time, the campaign of August did not go according to any plan. Meckel was nearer the truth than Moltke.

It is with this in mind, that Mr. Guedalla's defence of Bazaine should be weighed. Unaccustomed to handling big formations, to the elaboration of staff work that such formations demand, Bazaine neglected his chief of staff, Jarras, and one consequence was the fatal congestion of the roads along which the retreating army moved. Perhaps Jarras would have done no better had he been given the normal authority of a chief of staff, but it is hard to absolve Bazaine from the responsibility for the logistics of the critical days before the decisive and fatal battles. Mr. Guedalla makes it easy to understand why the Commander-in-Chief, with his background, thought it his business to rally single battalions or direct the fire of individual

E

batteries, to fight his way out of a cavalry mêlée, to rely on the ocular demonstration of the fact that the Marshal accepted the old view of the duty of a commander, "payer de sa personne." But despite Napoleon at Lodi or at Montereau, that is not the main duty of a commander-in-chief. Napoleon (to whose practice Mr. Guedalla makes appeal) could afford the luxury of an immense knowledge of detail combined with a lucid and all-embracing view of the whole battle and the whole campaign. He could rebuke and undo the blunders of Ney on the eve of Elchingen, but he did not think it his duty to imitate Ney, to see in a command of minor tactics and in the exhibition of superhuman courage, the whole duty of a general. Sir Archibald Wavell, indeed, has suggested that the Emperor neglected minor tactics too much, and readers of such collections as Foucart on the campaign of Jena or Alombert and Colin on the campaign of Ulm will find it difficult to see much real resemblance between the methods of the Emperor and of Bazaine.

Sometimes Mr. Guedalla's zeal for the defence leads him to surprising historical allusions. There is a good deal to be said for, or at least about, Bazaine's preference for the strategical defensive. (The defensive battles he fought were often marked by local and ineffective tactical offensive movements, badly co-ordinated, ineffective, almost purposeless.) But the case for Bazaine is not strengthened by a remark like this: "All Lee's brilliance in attack had failed to win the Civil War for the Confederacy." Would it not have been juster to Lee (and to the Northern and Southern armies) to have written "Lee's brilliance in defence nearly won the war for the South"? Would it not have been juster to have contrasted Lee or Johnston with thrusters like Hood, or McClellan with Burnside—all to the advantage of the preachers and practitioners of the defensive? Of course that would not have closed the argument. For the critics of Bazaine (and Lee) might reply that more energy and less tact in dealing with Canrobert (or Longstreet) would have made the offensive pay; that the inferior side, if it cannot create impregnable lines that cannot be turned, loses, sooner or later, its key position, Saint-Privat, or Petersburg, as it was, a few years later, to lose Plevna, where the Bazaine policy was to be carried out with far more resolution and far more skill than Bazaine demonstrated—and yet Osman Ghazi had to surrender like his drabber exemplar. The Turkish Remingtons worked more wonders than the chassepots at Mentana or at Metz, but a superior army can avoid the traps laid for it by the inferior, if the inferior army perpetually waits for the spider to enter the traps set by the fly.

It is difficult to read accounts of these operations round Metz, with the blunders of Steinmetz more than offset by the blunders of Bazaine (or Canrobert), without reflecting that the only soldier present on these battlefields who had adequate experience of war in the age of railways, telegraphs, massed rifle fire and elaborate trench systems, wore neither a German nor a French uniform. For the reparable blunders of the Germans, the irreparable blunders of the French took place under the critical eye of a soldier who, five years before, had ceased to command a body of cavalry far better designed for real war than the German troopers who fell at Mars-la-Tour or the French who fell at Reichshoffen. Philip Sheridan, already, at forty, a veteran of a more modern and greater war than any known to Moltke or Bazaine, had seen the temporary demoralization of the Prussians under the murderous French rifle fire with the phlegm natural to the commander who had rallied his own shattered Army of the Shenandoah after Cedar Creek. He had, at Five Forks and Sailor's Creek, blocked the retreat of a greater general and a more famous army than Bazaine and the army of the Rhine. He had himself stormed Missionary Ridge with an élan far beyond the laborious Prussian assailants of Saint-Privat. Sheridan only saw the war from the German side, but had he been with Bazaine he might have written off the Marshal as, at best, a gallant divisional or corps commander like Burnside. No strategical ideas and poor tactical practice—this was not war as it was known to the Armies of the Potomac and of Northern Virginia. And had Moltke's army commanders been faced, not with Napoleon but with Lee, the dreams of the exploitation of the defensive that drifted through Bazaine's mind might have been more than dreams.

But the real case against Bazaine is not that he was an incompetent or unlucky general, but that he despaired too easily and too completely, once the professional armies were defeated. This charge necessarily involves an element of speculation. We cannot know what would have happened had Metz held out a few days longer when Gambetta's improvised Army of the Loire was marching on

Fontainebleau. We cannot know for certain how much the morale of the army in Metz was affected by its commander's pessimism and possibly excessive sense of discipline. But the case against Bazaine, that he underestimated the possibilities of improvised resistance, that he was too preoccupied with law and order, is a case that should have been discussed and, if it is possible, refuted here. But Mr. Guedalla again dislikes the straightforward approach; anything so bald as a political or military balance sheet is repugnant to him, so we are left to speculate upon the implication of the comparative figures of the garrisons which surrendered at Metz and Paris, the comparative wisdom of Gambetta and Thiers. Bazaine at Rezonville is not a mystery, Bazaine in Metz still remains to be explained against the lurid landscape of the autumn of 1870. But as an historical revision of a conviction too easily won, the life of Bazaine is a brilliant success. At the least, Mr. Guedalla has "broken" the verdict of the court-martial and ordered a new trial.

The section of Mr. Guedalla's book devoted to Pétain is of much less importance and interest. Out of three hundred and fifty pages only a hundred are given to the second marshal, and he is a lay figure, discussed along with the follies of MacMahon, the brief glory of Boulanger, all the serio-comedy of the pre-1914 republic in which the serious Pétain dutifully appears from time to time as a *figurant*. Only in his account of Pétain's role in the last war does Mr. Guedalla show the qualities of judgment and justice that mark his account of Bazaine. Pétain on the road to Vichy is a subject more interesting, more difficult, than Bazaine on the road to Metz, but we are too near the subject, too deeply involved to be good jurymen, even if the prosecution had adequate materials for the case. Mr. Guedalla shows his quality more by what he refuses to say than by what he says. He is too acute to waste time building hypothetical schemes of treason on glosses on the text of Anatole de Monzie. Pétain is dismissed with an apt quotation from the Duke of Wellington, but Pétainism remains for future explanation, for future defence, but hardly for future forgiveness. For even if we and Europe forgive, France will not.

XV

"IL Y AVAIT LA FRANCE"
(5th July, 1940)

THE character of the French Government is now beginning to appear. Under the cover of two great military reputations the forces of class and personal selfishness, the forces of those who long ago despaired of France, of those who thought no cause worth fighting for, of those who fear the revolutionary consequences of a continuation of the war, playing on the temporary despair of the average Frenchman so deceived, so betrayed, by his political and military leaders, have decided to try the daring and despicable experiment of saving all but honour. The chances of even temporary success depend on the self-restraint and tact of Herr Hitler, on the degree to which he can postpone the most humiliating demands of the enemy whom the French hate more than they hate the Germans and despise more than, for the moment, they despise themselves—the Italians.

But there are no chances of permanent success. The Pétain Government may talk of moral regeneration, it may criticize, with justice, the weakness, the folly, the sloth of the old political parties, the enervation of the national morale, the mediocrity of the ideals preached by most French parties and leaders since 1918. But, as General de Gaulle has pointed out, the Marshal has his share in the military slackness of these years and the direct responsibility for the moral surrender of military honour falls on the soldiers. It may be true that Marshal Pétain has dreams of restoring order, of using his military authority to tighten the slack fibre of French life, but not only is he too old, he now lacks the moral authority. Always pessimistic, he is not the man to succeed in a task that would require the energy and courage of a young and not discredited man. Nor can General Weygand replace him. The High Command of the French army has not and certainly does not deserve the prestige that would make a "national regeneration" possible.

Still less can it come from the politicians. The role of M. Pierre

Laval is proof enough of that. M. Laval, it is true, is consistent. He was against war in 1914, in 1935, in 1939, in 1940. But his motives are not likely to be thought edifying when his accumulation of a great fortune in a few years in the service of the State is remembered. Moral regeneration from such a source is open to suspicion. M. Laval's career, its worldly wisdom, its practical sagacity, make him an instrument, an intelligent instrument, of German or Italian policy, but France is not bemused enough to be taken in, to see in the *Gauleiter* anything more than that.

The Pétain Government will try to turn French anger and French shame against us. It will, at first, have some success. But its success is bound to be limited. Even if all France, or the majority of Frenchmen, had no higher ideals than those of M. Laval or M. Déat (it is unfair to lump the two together, but for the moment they are allies or accomplices), the necessities of the war, if we hold out, will force the Germans to strip France of that wealth, that internal security, that rest, that its present governors have foolishly thought to buy at such a price. The vision that may haunt some French minds of France as a willing partner in a Fascist Europe is baseless. Fascism needs some spiritual food, it needs the psychological support of patriotism. What can the Pétain Government do to supply that need? Against it speaks the most varied patriotic tradition in Europe: Joan of Arc and Richelieu, Danton and Gambetta, Foch and Clemenceau. Even the Bourbon Restoration of 1814 and 1815 had more to offer French sentiment than that. Louis XVIII bore only the shadow of the great name, but there had been the great name.

The new Government can only appeal, and could only appeal even if its political members were more personally reputable than they are, to a mean and timid selfishness, always present, indeed, in France, but always vanquished by the national spirit. And what that mean and timid spirit will save from the wreck depends on Herr Hitler and Signor Mussolini, neither of them magnanimous, neither of them quite a free agent. Herr Hitler may very possibly turn from the mere property-owners' syndicate represented by M. Laval to such able Fascist demagogues as M. Doriot. But as our resistance continues, the action of the Pétain Government will be seen for what it is, the resignation of old-fashioned professional soldiers to the fortune of war, combined with the false sagacity of the political agents of all those sections of French opinion (on the Left and on the Right) which despaired of their country the moment that continued faith seemed likely to be costly.

These men, these sections of all classes in France, can build nothing; their authority will more and more depend on direct German and Italian support. They will make their excuses; Marshal Pétain has dreams, so it is said, of "restoring order," of undoing the evil things done in the last twenty years. Such dreams haunted the mind of another and less distinguished Marshal. Bazaine, besieged in Metz, thought more of restoring order than of aiding the amateur armies that Gambetta was creating out of nothing. When he was court-martialled he defended his inaction on the ground that there was no legitimate authority in France to which he owed obedience. The President of the Court was a Prince of the Blood, and it was to the Duc d'Aumale that it fell to give the answer to Marshal Bazaine and, in anticipation, to that other Marshal who has accepted for France a position of ignominy she has not known since the Treaty of Troyes. "*Monsieur le maréchal, il y avait la France.*" There *is* France; it is to that eternal France which we should appeal, to military honour as well as to the powerful rational case against this fantastic trust in Hitler and Mussolini. To that France through all adversity, and till the day of her resurrection, our friendship will perpetually be extended.

XVI
DE GAULLE
(1st February, 1943)

THE movement associated with the name of General Charles de
Gaulle began as a radio appeal. In the last desperate week of French
organized resistance, when the new Pétain government was preparing to surrender, General de Gaulle, speaking from London,
where he had gone on an official mission, attacked the policy of
surrender because it was a policy of despair. His argument was
simple, only in the most fundamental sense political. The war was
not over and was not lost. And the policy which was soon so
appropriately associated with the name of Vichy was based on two
propositions: that the war was over bar a little unimportant English
shouting, and that it was lost. Nothing remained to do but to make
the best and quickest peace possible—no matter how harsh the
German terms, they were better than a continuation of a futile
massacre in France, than the pointless extension of the war to the
Empire, especially to North Africa, the only part of the Empire
which has really close ties with the metropolis.

At the moment that de Gaulle spoke, all that could be done was
to deny these assertions. Somebody had to do it and there was no
one else available. All attempts to renew the war in Morocco, or
Algiers, all attempts to find a spokesman for France failed. There
was only de Gaulle. And he had two claims to speak. He, more than
any other French professional soldier, had been free from the
Maginot-line complex and the Maginot-line mentality. He had, too,
been one of the few French generals who had added to their
reputation in the brief campaign of 1940. But, it must be admitted,
few in France knew this about him; not many knew anything about
him, even his name. He was a rising soldier, an interesting man,
known outside professional military circles as the military brains-
trust of Paul Reynaud, and that was all.[1]

[1] If I may be permitted a personal note; I was first conscious of de Gaulle's
name when he entered the Reynaud administration as a junior minister. Yet, when
clearing out books I had accumulated for a book on modern France, I found that
I had owned, read and annotated *La France et son armée*. I had quite forgotten
the author's name—and even the fact that this book was dedicated to Pétain.

To expect miracles from a practically unknown soldier appealing against the professional opinion of Pétain and Weygand to a nation overwhelmed by unprecedented and unexpected disasters was a folly—if it was committed. But I am not at all sure that it was committed. What was expected (wrongly as it turned out) was a violent political and military reaction against the policy announced by Pétain in his disastrous broadcast. No "honourable peace between soldiers" was possible. Resistance was possible and it was hoped that this truth would be appreciated by "les grands chefs." They, as is their wont, did nothing, said nothing, accepted the fact of military defeat as final. Putting one's trust in senior officers is a perennial civilian illusion. That trust was put, in vain, in June 1940.

It is not necessarily to the discredit of the senior officer that he despairs rather easily. For one thing, if he despairs he can always claim to be right; for if he despairs he loses the battle. Then, as a professional, he sees the weight of forces on each side; he can compute in military arithmetic better than civilians can—and as long as that is the only computation that counts, he is right. So Ludendorff was the first German to despair in 1918, Pétain the first Frenchman in 1940 (though in the Marshal's case despair was as much a personal habit of mind as a professional attitude; he despaired on the eve of victory in 1918 as he did on the eve of defeat in 1940).[1] There was nothing surprising in the refusal of the senior generals in Syria or Morocco to follow a lead given by a junior general who, in addition to committing the crime of speaking before he was asked, had been reasonably pessimistic in March 1940, when the Maginot illusions were all the rage, and so was inoculated against the despair that overcame men who had put their faith in an irrelevant system of war. To be told what to do by a junior was bad enough; to be told what to do by a junior who had been right was even worse.

Whatever the reasons, with one or two exceptions, no French higher officer in a position of independent command resisted the policy of surrender. The exceptions are worth noting. For one of them, General Catroux, was free from the criticisms brought against de Gaulle. He was not a junior "two star" general, but a "five

[1] The soldier is not always wrong in refusing to follow civilian heroic—and foolish—policies. The classic case of Lee v. Jefferson Davis is admirably put by Charles Francis Adams II in *Lee at Appomattox*. We can hardly doubt that Lee was right in 1865.

E*

star" general (a *général d'armée*, the rank just below marshal). And he was not a new-comer to statecraft, a mere under-secretary. He was the Governor-General of Indo-China, the richest French colony, the colony furthest from German power. Yet Catroux, one of the best known French generals, was not able to bring over his own colony or to shake the trust of the colonial officers and officials in the Marshal's policy. Legentilhomme, Governor of Jibuti, equally failed. And Jibuti remained loyal to Vichy, although following on the British victories of the winter of 1940–1, it was entirely surrounded by British territory, cut off from France and from all other French colonies and, one may assume, particularly animated by anti-Axis feelings, since Jibuti was the most obvious and certain Italian gain from an Axis victory. Not only was Jibuti held for Vichy for two and a half years (despite numerous desertions of individuals and small groups), but even after the invasion of North Africa and the *volte-face* of Darlan, it held out, and when it finally gave in, its officers and men rallied to de Gaulle, not to Darlan or Giraud. Once they took the decisive step, they took the rest. "Ce n'est que le premier pas qui coûte." And the first step of revolt against the Marshal was a revolutionary step that involved others.

This was probably not realized by anybody in the early days of the de Gaulle movement. Up to the catastrophe of Dakar (where, as in North Africa in November 1942, over-optimistic estimates had been made of the readiness of the local authorities to see reason) the calculation may have been that once it was obvious that England was not making peace, a sense of national honour and national interest would lead to a series of local rejections of the armistice, that the French Empire would re-enter the war which the event showed it need not have quitted.

The calculation did not fail entirely. Very important territories did join de Gaulle, territories important for their resources or for their strategic position or both. French Equatorial Africa (so important as an air route as well as for its economic resources) was won over by an able Negro governor, M. Felix Eboué, though some fighting was needed before it was made available to the anti-Axis war effort. The very rich and very important island of New Caledonia rallied to the cause locally represented by Australia, despite the temptation to follow the example of Admiral Decoux in Indo-China or Admiral Robert in the West Indies. In the first case, New Caledonia was saved from being another back-door to Japanese aggression; in the second, it was saved from being a Capua where officers and men like Candide can cultivate their gardens in an atmosphere of *dolce far niente* that recalls the pleasant isle of Aves more than a territory of a nation occupied, robbed, humiliated. The State Department may regret that it was not given a chance to make a deal that neutralized Libreville and New Caledonia, that took as many French assets out of the war as possible. But the Navy Department which, thanks to the de Gaulle movement, has these bases and, in addition, Tahiti and the Marquesas, probably thinks differently. Nevertheless, the policy of bringing all the French Empire (and the French fleet) back into the war by means of patriotic appeals, even brilliant patriotic appeals, failed. General de Gaulle is almost as much a radio wizard as the President of the United States, but there are many things that cannot be done by a radio talk. One of them, it proved, was to shake the authority of the government of Vichy, even in vast, remote islands like Madagascar, controlled by the British navy, immune to German threats and, as was believed before Pearl Harbour and Singapore, to Japanese threats.

The reasons for this failure deserve some examination. One is of temporary importance for the present and future policy of the United Nations. Because we talk of the British, French and Dutch Empires we confuse very different kinds of polities. The British and Dutch Empires, though in differing degrees, have independent and semi-autonomous governments and a tradition of independent action which is totally lacking in the French Empire. This is not necessarily a discredit to the French Empire. That as an imperial power they have got something is shown by the astonishing fact that, at the lowest and most disastrous point in French history, French authority has not been challenged from within by tens of millions of subject peoples. But this power of command is exercised by a small group of officials, themselves trained in absolute and blind obedience to the constituted authority, whatever it is.[1]

[1] A French naval officer, a friend of mine, who had his destroyer sunk under him at Dunkirk and who joined de Gaulle, leaving a wife and three children in Brest under R.A.F. bombs and German rule, asserted again and again at this time: "You are confusing the British Empire and the French Empire. These people will obey any orders that come from Paris or the successor of Paris." Another friend, a deputy who joined de Gaulle, told me of the sensation he caused when before the war he visited Dakar as a private individual, refused official hospitality or guidance and asserted truthfully and incredibly that he simply wanted to see what Dakar was like.

That so many men trained in this tradition rallied to de Gaulle is a ground of wonder, not that the whole Empire did not do what it had never done, resist the latest decision of the political authority in France. And even if the title of that political authority was doubtful, if it had come into existence through a military defeat and an illegal delegation of power, that was one of the ways by which legitimate governments had been established in France since 1789. The Government of National Defeat of 1940 came into existence more legally than the Government of National Defence in 1870. Both were provisional, both were irregular, but in France it is "only the temporary that lasts." But there is another aspect of the French Empire that is of greater and more permanent importance. The French colonial empire had its acute problems as all empires have and it had its acute political problems as all empires deserve to have. They were not less political for being disguised as economic. The French Empire, for reasons that on the whole are to the credit of France, had less mere political trouble than the British Empire had, but it had its basic troubles all the same. Was the Empire to be exploited by the methods and in the interests of high capitalism? It was an acute question in Indo-China (with the rubber companies); in tropical Africa (with the aftermath of the great concessions); in North Africa (with the question of land tenure, of the role of the landless Arab labourer). In North Africa (and in Indo-China) there was also a straight nationalist movement; a movement for independence in Indo-China, a movement for equality in North Africa. And all these questions were urgent; all could be settled one way or the other. The armistice gave a chance for settling them one way. For, naturally enough, French egalitarian principles were less active in the Empire than in France. Rigid democratic principles ruin empires. Moreover, the conservative elements in French society, more or less excluded from politics and not sure of their prospects in the internal administration, crowded into the colonies, both as officials and as settlers, that is, as planters. When the disaster came, the first reaction of many of these officials and settlers was to resist, and if the legal government had gone to North Africa, they would have obeyed and fought, but the Laval–Pétain palace revolution deprived them of the temptation to enter in the dangerous path of fighting a war of liberation from an imperial base, dangerous not as much for the mother country as for their ideas of the present and future of the imperial base.[1]

While the attempt to provoke or encourage a revolt in the Empire (by which the white officials and officers were meant) was failing, the de Gaulle movement acquired, not suddenly, not unexpectedly, but, in the time and circumstances, rather quickly, a function as a focus of resistance in France. The original thesis of the movement was that the Empire plus Britain would liberate France. But the logic of events was too much for the plan. The Empire did not move and Britain, from being only less unpopular than Germany (and not always or in all places even that), became not loved but respected with a new respect, admired with a new admiration. From being a handicap, the British affiliations of the de Gaulle movement became an asset. That the movement had to start from London was a handicap. But it reflected an unwelcome truth. Too seldom have we the place and the men and the situation all together. There was in the summer of 1940 only one place for a fighting movement preaching armed resistance to Hitler. It could not be located in Moscow. It could not be located in Washington. For Moscow was wrapped in a silence on the issues, the importance, the future of the war that the local Communist commentaries made even more baffling, and in Washington there was not only neutrality but a presidential election to allow for. It was impossible to run a movement insisting on the duty and profit of fighting Hitler from a country committed to all means of stopping Hitler—except fighting him. The gamut was run in Vichy from all aid to Britain short of renewing the war to all aid to Hitler short of entering the war

[1] I think that I have read every "inside" story on the fall of France, even the few written by Frenchmen. I am not convinced that there was, except in narrow circles, a premeditated treason or a spontaneous welcome for German victory. Had Vichy not had other supporters than the hacks of Brinon and Abetz, the pathological anti-Semites and Anglophobes, it would not have been so formidable. I take *The Chicago Tribune* more seriously than I take William Griffin of New York or even Father Coughlin. And I don't believe that Col. Robert R. McCormick doesn't want to win the war, or would not even welcome a brilliant American victory won under Mr. Roosevelt. So I don't believe in a fascist or cagoulard conspiracy turning over the Empire to Vichy. I do believe that there were—and are —elements in France and the Empire who argued that since there was defeat and disaster, what little good was possible ought to be extracted from them. It was not a case of "better Hitler than Blum," but "since we have to have Hitler, it would be a minor gain to smash any chance of a new *front populaire*." As far as France is concerned, this view is based on fairly wide knowledge. As far as North Africa is concerned, it is based on a three weeks' visit in 1939, a visit hardly long enough to justify even an English visitor in writing a book on the United States.

again on the other side. (There were great differences between the attitude of any important section of American opinion and either pole of Vichy opinion, but you cannot run revolutionary movements on shades of differences.)

When the de Gaulle movement started there was only one place it could start and that was London, because there was only one possible base for an organization that proposed to *fight* Hitler, not to vote against him, not to write manifestoes against him, but to fight him. If de Gaulle had been Colonel McCormick and had wanted to fight Hitler he would have needed to move his headquarters from Chicago, even if all his views on the English remained unchanged. Yet, having an English headquarters was a regrettable necessity. Relationships between allies are always difficult; the relationships between allies whose joint campaign has failed are even more difficult than ordinary inter-allied relationships; relationships between allies who then begin fighting each other (as the English and French did at Oran) are worst of all. The de Gaulle movement had to start from London and yet there was hardly a worse place to start from.

What saved the situation was the defeat of the German aerial invasion of Britain (which showed that a German victory was not inevitable) and the German raids on London, Coventry, etc., which showed that the British people were ready to stand the shock of German power, not merely to fight to the last Frenchman. The moral value of this fact in the winter when lots of Englishmen (and women and children) were being killed deliberately by the German air force and only a handful of Frenchmen (and women and children) accidentally by the R.A.F. was very great. The propaganda appeals from London had a weight that they otherwise could not have had. They may not have kept it, but they had it at the critical moment. And the moment was very critical. For it was the moment when the French people, the man in the street in the occupied zone, were beginning to realize that there was no easy way out of the war. On 25th June, 1940, Pétain had said on the air: "I hate the lies that have done you so much harm." By the end of the year in Paris and Rennes and Lille, the Pétain policy was simply a new lie (possibly innocent) which had done as much harm as any previous one. And men began to listen to the radio, "*Içi Londres*," and to identify resistance with the practically unknown general who, from the very beginning, had pointed out the inconvenient truth about the honourable peace between soldiers promised by Pétain.

But more than that had happened. The revolutionary character of the situation had become obvious. It was unfortunate but not fatal that the Communist line was still "a plague on both your houses," still a refusal to see any important difference between present German and potential British imperialism. For the French workers had a real revolutionary situation before them which no slogans could conceal. They had the mere *status quo* of 1939 minus political liberty, national dignity and material well-being which was all that Vichy had to offer—and they had resistance which was bound to be more than mere patriotic resentment. If the French government had gone into exile, if the classes in France which had made a profession of patriotism had lived up to their creed, patriotism might have been enough. (It has been enough, however the fact may distress liberals, in most European countries.) But in France there was a confusion that forced Frenchmen back to first principles. It forced and—right down to January 1943—continued to force Frenchmen of all classes, including men who held high office under Vichy and knew as much of its innermost secrets as if they had been Ernest Lindley or even George Sokolsky, to join de Gaulle openly or to work for him secretly. But above all, it forced the French workers and *petits bourgeois* back to their old principles and old passions. For the upper classes, in many individual cases in complete innocence and helplessness, were forced to become partners in German exploitation. I could name men of the highest character and competence who have been forced to collaborate in circumstances which do not allow me the right to judge them.

But the French people, humiliated, starved, butchered, will not forgive. There were many Tories of high character who had to go into exile in 1783, leaving their lands to Cabots and Lowells who were luckier, not better or braver. With the French Tories are mingled profiteers, mere grafters, mere success-worshippers, all marked as men who could get along with the Germans. It was a European statesman who knows Europe as well as most State Department officials, and America better than many, who said to me that the great division to-day in France was between those who could survive on the official rations and those who could eat well on the black market. And the second class consists of the rich and the friends of the Germans. From this point of view, the higher Vichy officials, even if they do not take advantage of their privileges, are privileged in the public eye. Without any planning, the de Gaulle movement became the chief, not the only but the chief, symbol of the underprivileged, the people of France, the people Admiral Leahy and Robert Murphy did not meet. It may not have deserved to be the chief symbol; it is not and never has been the only symbol. Its role was threatened when Hitler invaded Russia. With all European peoples (including the English) the Russian resistance has been the great, heroic theme of this war. But the effect in France was to help the resistance movement, that is, to help de Gaulle. The Germans aided by shooting people indiscriminately as Communists or de Gaullists. Often their victims were neither. But the identification stuck. The Russians were the people who knew the answers concealed from Gamelin, Weygand and Pétain. The de Gaullists were the people who had never spoken well of the Germans, unlike MM. Pétain, Darlan and Laval.

I repeat, the identification may have been unjust, but it was made; in France and all over Europe. It was made by Radio Paris, by Radio Vichy, by Radio Maroc. The main organizations of popular resistance in France faced this fact; willingly or unwillingly, I know not. But they made their terms with what was then called *La France Libre* and is now called *La France Combattante*, with the National Committee which sits in London. There was a corresponding evolution in London. Whether de Gaulle was originally a reactionary, again I cannot say. But the failure of the mere counter-pronunciamento forced the movement into really revolutionary channels. The docility of French soldiers and officials forced a reconsideration of the French social structure. The most unpopular class in France (as everywhere in Europe) was the conservative social class, "*les riches*," "*les gens bien*," whether they were bankers or soldiers. This class had, it appeared, no thought for the old unconditional patriotism when following out the old patriotic, no-surrender policy threatened its privileged position. Jacobinism, that is, revolutionary patriotism, was forced on the de Gaullist movement, especially after the beginning of the Russian war. (It is purely a guess on my part, but I am inclined to think that de Gaulle has been personally influenced by his admiration for the Red Army, so much more like the army of his dreams than the French army of 1940 which was created and commanded by the military chiefs that French society produced.) Internal resistance to the Germans, not diplomatic manœuvres or administrative evasions at Vichy or Wiesbaden, but the reaction of the French people in the occupied zone and even in the unoccupied zone, became identified with de Gaullism where it was not identified with Communism—and where the two were not confused in the minds of the Germans, of the men of Vichy and of the people of France. It is a thought that occasionally gives me some *Schadenfreude*, that it was the French higher bourgeoisie who failed in courage in 1940 who have made it certain that while the old order may be restored, with minor modifications, in some other countries, it cannot be restored in France. *Noblesse oblige*, as they said before 1789—and when it was discovered that the only obligations accepted by the nobility of France were privileges, the day of the Fourth of August was inevitable.

American policy, as far as it can be judged from the outside, is backing the old privileged orders in France against (among other forces) a movement that at any rate is not trying desperately to fight the tides. It is late in the French day to ignore all that has happened since William C. Bullitt left Paris. It is quite true that the State Department has sources of information that we private citizens, American or British, do not have. But the assumption or assertion that in all this question the State Department, and the State Department alone, has been cooking with gas, will provoke some ribald souls to a Bronx cheer and more refined persons like myself to polite doubt. I do not assert and do not believe that the French National Committee is representative of all that counts now or will count in the future in France. But it does represent some things that are important. It represents, first of all, the refusal to admit the thesis that France should or could make peace, even temporary peace, with Hitlerism. (That has involved strained silence, at best, in face of the massacres in Lidice, in Warsaw, in Nantes. What hands Pétain and Darlan and others have shaken in the last two years!) It represents the principle that a France which withdrew from the conflict, even to return when the tide appeared to be turning, was a France that could be politically but not spiritually restored. The tricolour has been flying in the fleets and armies opposed to Hitler since September 1939 to this day. That was the doing of the de Gaullist movement.

And, perhaps unwillingly, perhaps unconsciously, the movement has been forced to become political, to admit that this war is about other things than the territorial security of France and the Empire. It is not the only organized force that has claims on the future of a France freed from Hitlerism by the United Nations. It may not be the most important claimant. But it is among the runners in that race. The "good, the wise and the rich," to quote the old Federalist classification, are not. As the war has moved to its crisis, as the issues have been sharply drawn, I have been more and more impressed by a favourite text of mine from Burke. Burke was, as we all know, the apostle of the counter-revolution. Yet at the end of his life he felt the force of the movement of history. "If a great change is to be made in human affairs, the minds of men will be fitted to it; the general opinions and feelings will draw that way. Every fear, every hope will forward it."

Basically, it is because the French National Committee is not fighting against this great movement of history that it is important. Because its history has been chequered, its early hopes deceived, its character made for it by events, it has its present symbolic importance in France, in the other occupied countries and in England. It is not by its very nature condemned to futility, although of course it is not guaranteed even temporary victory or power in a liberated France. In this grey and grim world, it is something not to be predestined to defeat, as any policy based merely on the support, in France or the Empire, of the French higher officials, *les gens nantis* as Vandal called the political profiteers of the Directory, is certain to be. Of course, the profiteers of 1799 did turn the Revolution to their profit. But the Revolution had happened. Brumaire could not have been worked in 1793. And they had a chief with Arcola behind him and Austerlitz before him. He also had Waterloo before him. If the State Department has a Bonaparte up its sleeve, it should produce him. Even so, the distance between Austerlitz and Waterloo will be a lot shorter than ten years, if he or any other general or diplomat or even banker gets in the way of the great movement of the peoples of which the President of the United States has hitherto been so brilliant, so successful and so trusted a leader.

XVII
FRANCE: 1940[1]
(1940)

"C'est embêtant, dit Dieu, quand il n'y aura plus ces Français.
Il y a des choses que je fais, il n'y aura plus personne pour les
comprendre." Mr. Werth puts this saying of Charles Péguy on his
title page, and it gives something of the atmosphere of those
dreadful days when the best friends of France were distressed, not
merely by the military but by the apparent moral collapse of the
nation that has been central in European history for at least six
hundred years. Of the three records, the least valuable is M.
Maurois's. He has bravely reprinted some of the innocently
complacent stuff he wrote when all was quiet on the Western Front,
amiable evocations of Colonel Bramble, records of royal visits, of
officially conducted tours in England, of all that *bourrage de crâne*
of which he seems to have been a less critical victim than were
Messrs. Werth and Waterfield. It is very readable, but, except at
the end when the disaster had come, it is all too official, too
academic, too like a more elegant version of the official spokesman.

With Mr. Werth and Mr. Waterfield we are on a different level
—that of the first-class, critically minded reporter, resenting the
censorship that made him say only smooth things, but candidly
revealing how much even professional sceptics were taken in by the
smooth surface below which much was rotten and all was fragile.
Mr. Waterfield was with the Army while Mr. Werth was in Paris;
the first has given us a record of things seen, the other of things
heard. The one recounts the decline of the morale of the French
Army as month after month passed in increasingly determined
avoidance of action, the other the revival of the old political game
in all its rigour just as the blow fell—that blow which Mr. Werth so
well called "the invasion of the Martians."

[1] André Maurois, *The Battle of France*. Translated by F. R. Ludman. Draw-
ings by Edward Ardizzone. (John Lane.)
  Alexander Werth, *The Last Days of Paris*. (Hamish Hamilton.)
  Gordon Waterfield, *What Happened to France*. (John Murray.)

The Maginot complex, about which Mr. Waterfield writes with such just bitterness, was deplorable but natural in a country which had suffered so terrible an invasion—and so recently. So when it was discovered that the famous barrier was next to worthless, that another invasion, another bleeding of a highly anaemic people of what little young blood was left, was the price of fighting on to victory years ahead, the sword of France, unbroken under more formidable pressure twenty years ago, snapped. France was like the wounded English sailor Cardinal Newman tells of who, when he had submitted to have one leg cut off, was told he must lose the other. He said: "You should have told me that, gentlemen," and deliberately unscrewed the tourniquet and bled to death. Such, at first sight, is the lesson of these diaries. But it is not the real lesson, for it is made abundantly evident that, where a lead was given, where the *gradés*, civil or military, were up to the level of their responsibilities, Frenchmen and Frenchwomen were ready to fight upon their stumps as had been their wont.

Of the two diaries Mr. Waterfield's has the advantage of describing a little of the actual campaign, Mr. Werth's of conveying the increasing perplexity, fear, panic that came over Paris. Mr. Werth's diary has its main historical value in recorded conversations, sometimes attributed to eminent persons by name, such as MM. Comert and Laugier, sometimes to otherwise unknown figures like the permanently defeatist journalist "Percy," or "Marion" whose good temper seems to have been one of the few bright spots of the black days, or "Basil" who banged on the table while emphasizing the difference between moral and animal courage. They are all interesting as samples, but no doubt would be even more interesting if one knew them as Mr. Werth does. But the cumulative effect is attained, the end of the old order, of Camille Chautemps and Maurice Chevalier, of Georges Bonnet and Lucienne Boyer; all of whom may have a role to play in the future, but who cannot play the roles they filled in the *temps des cerises*—now gone for ever.

Mr. Werth and Mr. Waterfield, however, are not mere reporters. Each has his ideas of the causes of the débâcle, ideas rather too briefly and dogmatically stated, but ideas full of interest all the same—and not merely because they reveal the temper of the time. They differ a little in their interpretations; but both, escaping from France in the liner *Madura*, believed that the future of France as

well as of Britain was involved in the battle that now rages, the
battle to save ourselves and the future of European civilization. In
that battle France, though not Frenchmen, is at the moment a
non-combatant.

In the first weeks that followed the collapse of France there were
endless rumours of eminent Frenchmen escaping to England;
repeated expressions of surprise that X or Y had stayed behind.
Yet there could be nothing more natural than that Frenchmen
should stay on the soil of France, for French patriotism is rooted in
that soil to a degree unknown in any other great Western nation.
The French are Jews who have not quit Jerusalem and can have
only in one place their abiding city. Indeed, French Jews are very
French in this very point. Mr. Werth tells us how a distinguished
French scholar, despite the obvious signs of an anti-Semitic drive,
left the safety of the *Madura* (the ship that took the British refugees
away from Bordeaux). "A few hours before the ship sailed Julien
Cain, looking very agitated, asked me if he and his wife couldn't
get back to the shore. 'C'est un drame! ma femme ne veut pas
quitter la France; et moi—eh bien, moi non plus.'" And other
passengers behaved in the same way. "When it came to the point,
they decided, for better or for worse, to stay in their own country."
It is an old trait, natural in a country where *émigré* is a term of
abuse. It is, indeed, hard to think of a more un-French sentiment
than Rupert Brooke's belief that his body could turn a corner of a
foreign field into a part of England. The French have left their dead
in all corners of the globe, but with no notion that Wandewash or
Lang-Son or the Tell or Austerlitz or the Beresina or the Monon-
gahela are, thereby, made any less remote or barbarous. "It is a
long way to Carcassone" said the soldier dying on the retreat from
Moscow:

> Sternitur infelix alieno volnere, caelumque
> Aspicit, et dulcis moriens reminiscitur Argos.

And it is not only the soldier but the pioneering peasant who clings
with Wordsworthian fidelity to the kindred and hardly separable
points of heaven and home. The French in North America have
been the great adventurers, the great pioneers—and have combined
with their roving a fidelity (almost unknown in the English settlers)
to their original base. The valley of the St. Lawrence is to the

Canadien what the valleys of the Loire, the Indre, the Seine were to his ancestors, and the *voyageur* might make his own the lines of du Bellay:

> Heureux qui, comme Ulysse, a fait un beau voyage,
> Ou comme cestuy là qui conquit la toison.
> *Et puis est retourné, plein d'usage et raison,*
> *Vivre entre ses parents le reste de son age!*

After all, it is very much what Marshal Bugeaud, conqueror of Algeria and terror of the Moroccans, declared to be his aim in life. But for Bugeaud, the possibility of a peaceful old age in

> le clos de ma pauvre maison,
> Qui m'est une province, et beaucoup d'avantage

was bound up with the possibility of a free and great France. It is this double condition that the Pétain régime cannot meet—and their failure to meet it justifies the men round General de Gaulle. But we must never forget what a temptation assails a Frenchman when he has to choose between the concrete, tangible, so admirable, so beloved soil of France and the idea of France. He is no romantic Ulysses, *à la* Tennyson, wandering vaguely about the "untravelled world, whose margin fades for ever and for ever when I move," but a man who has been taught at school (if he needed to learn) that the very shape of his country was as admirable as a great line in Racine, as a drawing by Ingres, as a landscape by Cézanne or an early Corot —none of them vague things appealing to the undefined margins of the spirit, but as definite as a great *route nationale* or as the Puy de Dôme or the Montagne Sainte-Victoire.

It is surely this devotion to the actual soil of France which gave the Germans such a magnificent opportunity for blackmail. Mr. Werth rightly stresses the possibilities of "the fearful blackmail" which the Germans could have exercised "on the Government of North Africa and the soldiers and sailors there. Anything from the massacre of the two million war prisoners to the massacre of the entire French population." It was a Nazi asset that no story, however outrageous, beggared credulity; there was no reason to believe that, if it paid him, Hitler would stop at anything. But even if, stopping short of massacre of the French people, Hitler should threaten merely a savage reprisal on the soil of France, that evoked

dreadful memories of the last war. It was France whose towns had
been levelled to the ground, whose fields had been ploughed by
shells and deliberately devastated in the spring retreat of 1917, a
dreadful experience never forgotten by the French people, even if
it was only a debating point for smart Oxford undergraduates in
1940. Again, Virgil, celebrating the bare survival of Roman society,
hoping for national redemption from the follies so bitterly expiated,
illustrates the French mood. As a French scholar wrote when the
collapse was certain:

> Nec fuit indignum superis, bis sanguine nostro
> Emathiam et latos Haemi pinguescere campos
> . . . Satis iam pridem sanguine nostro
> Laomedonteae luimus periuria Troiae.

It is this revulsion from a second struggle that accounts for the
acceptance of defeat, and for that aspect of it to which Mr. Werth
and, still more, Mr. Waterfield devote attention, the refusal to
defend Paris. In one way Paris was too beautiful, too precious to be
defended. It was more than Warsaw was to Poland (there was
Cracow) or Madrid to Spain (there were so many rivals). Paris was
a cause (as Andrew Marvell said of the issues in the English Civil
War) too good to be fought for. Yet French pride, the old Parisian
pride, would have seen Paris in ruins rather than tamely surrendered.
What had changed? One thing was the disappearance not merely of
the hope of victory, but of the belief in victory—that is, the belief
that victory would have made much difference. After all, in 1914,
Paris and France had held out in the belief that victory would
repay the cost of attaining it, not merely the physical cost but the
spiritual cost. But what had victory brought? Disillusionment after
disillusionment. The soil of France, the face of France was barely
restored (it was only two years since the reconstruction of the
cathedral of Rheims was officially completed) and the spirit of
France was hardly restored at all.

Mr. Waterfield stresses the political timidity that prevented the
arming of the population of Paris to defend the city. No doubt
General Weygand and M. Baudoin feared the results of arming the
Paris worker. The workers of the Paris industrial region were, for
the most part, members of a party that, having advocated in words
and in deeds a foreign policy which would force France to measure

her forces with the Nazis, and probably with the Fascists, and having promised the aid of the innumerable legions of the Red Army, found all its basic hopes deceived. Although the Communist leaders had supported the entrance of France into a war whose occurrence they had not made less likely, within a week or so they recanted—under orders—and were all for peace with the accursed thing, for doing in 1939 what was done in 1940. That the majority of the Paris workers did not follow in the beginning their bemused or enslaved leaders is likely, but to ignore the deep injury to national unity and national confidence caused by the treason of Thorez and his brethren is to ignore one of the most important factors in the situation. The populace of Madrid did not consist, in large part, of people whose leaders were preaching a compromise with Franco, or whose effective chief was on ostentatiously good terms with Burgos. The most—it was skilfully argued—that the arming of Paris workers, belatedly converted from the belief in a mere Imperialist war, could have achieved was another Commune—and French Catholics could easily be terrorized by the vision of another Commune, another massacre of the hostages, with the Louvre going the way of the Tuileries. The servile admirers or hacks of Mussolini were not in a position to throw stones at *L'Humanité* and *Ce Soir*, but the average Frenchman was.

Further, the old suspicion of Paris had not been diminished by the role of the capital in recent years; or rather not the role of old Paris, but of the new industrial areas round it. To the provincial Frenchman it was intolerable to be given a lead by the rootless agglomerations of all nationalities which made up the population of Bobigny or Aubervilliers. Could even M. Laval have played his decisive role had he remained just another politician of the Paris suburbs instead of striking fresh roots in his native Auvergne?

That fear and illusion played a great part in the surrender is not doubtful. Fear of what a prolongation of the war might mean: it could hardly mean victory (here the old French neglect of sea power played a disastrous part); if it did mean victory, what then? As Mr. Werth points out, a war carried on from Africa would have meant a war primarily against Italy. And for many Frenchmen of the possessing classes Italy, or rather the Italian régime, had become dearer than France itself. Their treason was more odious than that of the Communists, whose love for a "strong, free, and happy

France" was too sudden to take in any but the most credulous of the class oddly known as the *intelligentsia*. It was on the native patriotism of the industrial workers, not on the Moscow veneer of Chauvinism, that the average Frenchman relied. But with the parties of the Right patriotism was quite enough, or should have been. For forty years the great and bitter doctrinaire of the Right had been preaching that patriotism was the beginning and end of political wisdom and duty. How much scorn had Maurras heaped on Left polemists who wished to weaken the wine of nationalism with the water of general doctrine. "La France, mais"—the "mais" of Arthur Ranc had been stressed and abused a hundred times. But as the hope of a Nationalist dictatorship in France faded, as competition on the Right became keener, infatuation with Italian Fascism became greater. There was a great deal to explain away in presenting Mussolini as a hero to the readers of the *Action Française*. It had been one of the great sins of Napoleon III (and of his uncle) that France had aided in the creation of two great and necessarily rival States on her frontiers. And Mussolini's Italy was obviously far more of a menace to the position of France than the Italy of Crispi, not to speak of the Italy of Giolitti, could ever be. Moreover, the Fascist régime was obviously much more like the Empire in France than like the traditional monarchy. Even the *Action Française* (whose courage in face of awkward facts had practically no limits) could hardly pretend that Mussolini was to Victor Emmanuel III what Richelieu was to Louis XIII.

Partly the infatuation was due to the literary bias which Maurras had inherited from the *école romane* and from the fantastic erudition of Frédéric Amouretti. The Latin race, the Latin nations were fictions whose comic side has been exposed by M. Louis Dimier, but which suited the Provençal vanity of Maurras and Daudet. And that they should think it possible for a combination of Italy and France to be more powerful to resist Germany than a combination of Britain and France, merely illustrates that anti-English bias, combined with a deep ignorance of the forces of the modern industrial world, which had always marked Maurras and his more credulous followers. And they were, after all, *Blancs du Midi*, heirs spiritual and fleshly of the mobs that had taken advantage of Waterloo to massacre their "Blue" enemies. To have fought on and defeated Italy would have been to aid the triumph of what they hated and the ruin of what they loved, if only as the enemy of what they hated. As for the Carbuccias and Bérauds and other adulators of the Duce whom Mr. Werth and Mr. Waterfield rightly pillory,

non ragionam di lor

as one of M. Maurras's literary heroes once said.

On the Right and on the Left there were doctrinaire, personal, financial affiliations with foreign Powers; brutal, "realist," cowardly in the case of the small but important group of Nazi partisans, venal, hysterical and illusion-ridden in the case of the partisans of the Duce, servile, credulous, fanatical in the case of the adherents of Stalin, who asked and got more implicit obedience from his devotees than Veuillot ever gave Pius IX. But all these elements, dangerous as they were, would have been as relatively impotent for mischief as were the Caillaux, Malvys, Lavals of 1914–18 had there been a central political authority to impose obedience and to produce a Clemenceau.

But what was fatal was that decline in the authority of the French State which, as M. Daniel Halévy has been preaching for ten years past, was the bad legacy of the early years of the Republic, the years when Gambetta was not allowed to do more than defeat Broglie. That atomization of State authority, described by all competent observers and praised by that typical Radical apologist for the easy way, Alain, had now to be paid for. The personnel of French politics was not wanting in men of ability, or even of character in the English sense of the term, but it was almost entirely wanting in men of intrinsic strength and weight. When one contemplates the men who, for twenty years past, have fought for what it became more and more absurd to call "power" in France, the bitter astonishment of Joubert comes to mind. "Combien d'épaules sans force ont demandé de lourds fardeaux!" And those politicians who had some strength of their own had none, or next to none, politically. How could a Reynaud or a Mandel compete with a Bonnet or a Daladier or a Malvy or a Marquet or a Laval, with their clans and their record of never letting their friends down? M. Bonnet, however, had not even this to recommend him. And so the Third Republic died because it did not breed Clemenceaus or even Poincarés any longer; it had feared great, dominant personalities, so it fell at the hands of a Laval; it had trembled at the shadow of a

ictorious general, and it was killed by the soldiers under whom
France had suffered her most ignominious defeat. It is too early yet
o draw up more than the most general balance sheet, but when the
ime comes to do more than that, these contemporary records will
e of great value, as they are at this moment of the greatest and
nost painful interest to those who, like all civilized men, have two
ountries, their own and France. But the France of all civilized
nen is not dead or even captive; she is where the spirit of France
s free, obeying the voices that bid her

> " . . . Sors de la poussière,
> Quitte les vêtements de ta captivité,
> Et reprends ta splendeur première."

XVIII
THE CASE OF DARLAN
(10th November, 1942)

OUT of Africa something new. The proverb has special appositeness this week, when to the welcome novelty of victory has been added the transformation scene that has made Admiral Darlan enemy of Britain, sponsor of collaboration, suddenly appear in the new role of defender of French Africa, enemy of the policy of Pétain of which he was so long the chief executant, and in the name of the Marshal, the agent of a policy that, if it succeeds, will ruin the whole edifice of Vichy. Or will it? That is the question; and, if for a moment the British public showed a human unwillingness to look the gift horse in the mouth, that moment seems to have passed. The news that MM. Flandin, Pucheu, Peyrouton and, possibly, other late leading lights in Vichy have had a sudden Damascus conversion has added to the bewilderment of the innocent spectator. All over the world can be heard the scuffling sounds as Vichy officials descend from the fence they had so long adorned, and, in the case of the more vehement friends of collaboration and enemies of Britain, the sound of ripping cloth as they leave behind them those parts of their garments too indelibly stamped with the swastika or the francisque.

In a time like this, the man in the street is right in refusing to judge the decisions made by his rulers. Only they have the means of assessing the price that has to be paid for such great military advantages as the easy occupation of North Africa. If accepting Darlan is the price, it will be paid, and it is reassuring, at a moment when reassurance is urgently needed, to learn from President Roosevelt that the arrangement is only temporary. But it is to the credit of the head as well as the heart of the man in the street that he recognizes that there is a heavy price to be paid for picking up some quick tricks. The men of Vichy are now imitating, rather late in the day, the French leaders who went to Morocco to rouse resistance there. They were thwarted by the fidelity to military

156

discipline of General Noguès. They are in French prisons; soon
they may be in German prisons. The prudent men of little faith
who made the armistice, who broke the obligations of the Alliance
with Britain, who trusted to the magnanimity of the Führer, are
now busy giving proofs of a conversion. But of a conversion to
what? Surely only to success?

It is, then, perhaps a pity that *The Times* has apparently found
it necessary to give General de Gaulle what our American friends
call the "brush-off." For he and General Catroux and General de
Larminat and General Koenig and General Legentilhomme paid
us the compliment of faith when the men of Vichy hastened to
make what terms they could before we, in our turn, surrendered to
Hitler. This may be forgotten in Printing House Square, but if so
it is the only place in London where it is forgotten—and nowhere
is it less likely to be forgotten than in Downing Street.

Trust in the courage and tenacity of the British people was the
great compliment paid to us by the Norwegians, by the Belgians,
by the Dutch, by the Free French and by the Greeks. It was a
compliment paid to us by the President of the United States, but
not, it is safe to say, by all or nearly all Americans. And it was
conspicuously not a compliment paid us by the men who took
over France at Bordeaux. Their judgment was bad then; if they
have learned better, well and good. But we need not and should not
welcome them as anything but sheep that were lost. We need not,
in most cases, doubt their good faith; but there is no reason to
forget that they had so little of plain faith in the future of their
own country and of ours in a crisis which tested and tried men's
souls. Indeed, we can go further than that. There were among the
Frenchmen who rallied to our apparently desperate cause in the
summer of 1940 men who had little more faith than Darlan. But
like the French officers before Waterloo, they advanced to the new
battle without fear and without hope. All was lost, they thought,
save honour. They were determined to save that, their own and
their country's. It will take a good deal to persuade me that a future
France, holding up her head among the nations, has more need of
the timid, the prudent, the despairing men of Vichy than it has of
the men who adopted for themselves and for their country, not the
imbecile craftiness of "*la France seule*" of Maurras, but "*honneur
et patrie.*"

It was left to these men, exiled, condemned to death, vilified b
Vichy and Berlin alike as paid agents of England (the Führer ha
just repeated the charge), to prevent the great political and mora
tragedy of the complete abdication of France before the odiou
Germanic incarnation of all that the best French tradition proteste
against. They were the true heirs of that great founder of Frencl
Algeria, the duc d'Aumale, who reminded another despairin
marshal, Bazaine, that "*il y avait la France.*" They were the heir
of MacMahon, another "*grand Africain*" who, from his priso
camp, behaved like General Giraud and rejoiced in every effort o
Gambetta to undo what the *grands chefs* had done. MacMaho
perhaps went too far when he refused to shake hands with Man
teuffel, the sympathetic and gentlemanly commander of the Arm
of Occupation. There was no precedent for Montoire in the caree
of that honest if not very intelligent soldier whose career is, in s
many other ways, so like Pétain's. Pétain was glad to shake the han
that Hitler deigned to give him; most, though not all, of his satellite
have been glad to carry out the most odious hints of their Germar
masters. Are we to forget all this and politely drop the men wh
saved the honour of France when it was besmirched by the Auver
gnat Laval? They made their choice; that of the old Régimen
d'Auvergne whose motto was "*Auvergne sans tâche.*"

These considerations are probably present in all our minds, anc
it may seem an impertinence to express doubts about our loyalt
to the men of 1940. But we are not alone in our French policy. W
have American associates who may be well disposed to take the lead
The State Department, so recently badly under fire, is now on to
of the world. Its French policy, it asserts, has been fully justified
That belief is open to serious question, but that is another story
What *is* relevant is the fact that, for good or indifferent reasons
the United States has been a moral supporter of the Pétain régime
from the time when Mr. Bullitt delivered the first effective apologi
for the policy of the men of Bordeaux, and M. Réne de Chambrun
with whatever prestige belongs to a descendant of Lafayette, begar
to sell his father-in-law, Laval, as a modern Washington-cum-
Cincinnatus. During the most critical period of the war the Unitec
States was neutral, and the majority of the American people was fo
"all aid short of war." Naturally, things look very different i
Dutchess County, New York or Illinois from what they do i

London or Paris or Rotterdam. But for that reason, the British Government has a means of understanding the psychological needs of fighting Europe that is not so easily attained by consulting the exiles in New York or Washington, some of whom found it convenient to pass through London in the summer of 1940. Too great jubilation at the success of the State Department's policy may have repercussions in Europe that are not as easily foreseen in Washington as here. If we welcome Darlan with too open arms, are we going to welcome repentant German military leaders, too? If we write off, as a matter for smart-alec jokes (as *Time* has just done), the fact that we and France declared war on Hitlerism, we may be abdicating a role of leadership in Europe in which no one can replace us. For Europe will notice (what we have been too kind or indifferent to notice) that the new Congress of the United States is fuller even than the last of men for whom this war began not a second sooner than the first Japanese bombs fell at Pearl Harbor. Such men are sound American patriots, but their past gives no great ground for expectation that they will see in an invitation to become good world patriots anything but another cunning English trick. That being so, we should be foolish to follow, without question, a European policy that ignores some psychological truths which no one here even begins to doubt.

It must have been an experience of a good many in childhood that one parable was difficult to reconcile with one's childish sense of justice. That the labourers in the vineyard should get the same reward whether they came to the task at the first or the eleventh hour seemed absurd. It may seem absurd still to the resisting peoples of Europe. But that is a point that we, who were among the early labourers ourselves, naturally feel more strongly about than we can expect the Americans to do. I hope that, if the question comes up, we tell them just the same.

XIX

FRANCE IN THE WORLD
(1943)

Translated from the French by NELL BURNETT

THE present state of Europe and the world is reminiscent of the famous banquet scene in *Macbeth*: France plays the part of Banquo's ghost. Upon the international scene a great absence is felt: that of a France, mistress of her own destiny, able to play her traditional role in Europe and in the world. The liberation of her Empire could in no way compensate for the enslavement of the mother country; no re-establishment of Europe is possible if it does not include the liberation and the re-establishment of France. But, fundamentally, this liberation and this re-establishment can only be achieved by France herself, by a French nation which refounds her institutions, regathers her strength, contributes directly to rebuilding the new Europe and the new world.

These are commonplaces upon which everyone is agreed. And yet, outside France there are few people who understand often enough or fully enough what the absence of France means, what is involved if France's return is to be as great an advantage to the common cause as we hope it may be. France will be physically liberated; officially she will recover her sovereignty; her rank as a great power will be recognized. But it is not impossible that her liberty, sovereignty and rank will be restored to her in a form which will make her re-establishment no more than a mockery, and France herself no more than *magni nominis umbra*.

What are the essentials if France is really to be capable of re-making her home and foreign policy? The time has come when that question should be asked, and it is fitting that it should be asked in *La France Libre*. For to-day the liberation of France is nearer than it was possible to hope in the dark days of the winter of 1940, when this review published its first number. Moreover, it is easier to-day to assess the true position of France; it is easier to gauge the gap left by her absence; its consequences are more apparent after three years of Vichyism.

The French problem comprises certain external and fundamental facts which must first of all be recalled, even if they appear to be commonplaces. It should never for a moment be forgotten that Vichyism has been a creation of the Germans, and even, to a certain extent, a successful creation. Of course, it was the French who decided to lay down their arms, throughout the homeland, and to ask for an armistice. But it was the Germans who determined the conditions of the armistice, who profited by them, who decided to limit their direct authority to a part of the territory, who (not content with tolerating it) gave their backing to the Vichy Government. It was the Germans who chose this policy in 1940, for reasons which, to them as Germans, seemed then to be good reasons. And even if they did not gain their main ends, they none the less profited in certain respects. They succeeded in creating great confusion, both inside and outside France; in spite of popular resistance (both within the homeland and without) a body which pretended to be the French State, a claim recognized by most foreign powers, seemed (from the mere fact of its existence, from its policy and from the arguments which it invoked to justify itself) to demonstrate to the world that France had finally abdicated. The Vichy régime was based upon the assertion that France could survive in so far as her culture was concerned, in so far as a society retaining its chances of happiness and even (to a certain degree) its dignity was concerned—but as a great nation, accepting the responsibilities, the duties and the dangers which comprise the life of a great nation, she had ceased to exist, had indeed ceased to exist well before 1940.

For, by libelling the governments of the Republic, by representing the defeat as the just penitence of a guilty nation, still more by proclaiming that France had sinned by presumption when she dared, in 1939, to assume her role of a great power, of a guardian of European liberty, by doing all these things, Vichy adopted a policy which could only be defended on the premise that France had ceased to be what she had been since the emergence of modern states. France was following in the course of Spain and Sweden, who have ceased to regret the splendour of the reigns of Charles V and of Gustavus Adolphus, and who recognize that the days of Philip II and Charles XII are over. It was better to cultivate one's garden and to allow the course of events to follow the channels traced by the masters of the Third Reich—so Vichy said.

F

That is a dangerous way of regarding the duties of France, her interests, her possibilities; and this way of looking at things is confirmed each time that France's *defeat* is spoken of as a *fall* or as a *collapse*—each time one yields to the temptation of postponing a study of the French problem until the day when France has been liberated—each time that the French problem is considered, even implicitly, as a simple problem of physical liberation comparable, for example, to that of Norway—in a word, each time that the problem raised by the fact that in 1939 France *declared* war is evaded. A France which collapsed, or a France which needed merely a material liberation, or which had not chosen to enter the war, would be just as deserving of sympathy, but would be far less worthy of interest. A fitting motto for such a France would be:

> "Men are we, and must grieve when even the shade
> Of that which once was great is passed away."

Peoples have short memories, especially in troubled times such as ours. The kaleidoscope of history changes so quickly that the man in the street can well be forgiven if he forgets certain truths which statesmen, for their part, would do well to remember. And one of these truths is that amongst the nations who are to-day lined up against the Axis, France is the only country, excepting Great Britain and the Dominions, to have entered the war voluntarily, of her own free will, and at the hour of her choosing, without waiting for a 22nd June or a 7th December.

It is not a question here of historic justice or of gratitude. It is a question of something of far more importance for the future of France and of Europe. For the result is that the misfortunes which have fallen upon France can be, and, in fact, are, represented as punishment for her sins, the outcome of her follies. And it is essential to take this view if one considers the opposite point of view as wrong or unimportant. There is no middle way: the declaration of war in 1939 can only be considered as a crime or a virtue; and if it was not pure folly, then it was pure wisdom. For France, and for her alone amongst the occupied nations, the war was not simply resistance to invasion, since, indeed, it was she who invaded Germany. It cannot be for her merely a question of expelling an invader who, it is possible to argue quite plausibly, would not have attacked her if she had remained passive.

It is not enough to reply that the decision of 1939 was natural, wise and inevitable, that Hitler had made his intentions so clear that only a government which was completely asleep, completely passive, completely incapable, could have refused to understand *Mein Kamf* and the lesson of Prague. But those critics who do not recognize France's merit in behaving in a way which was both courageous and wise (and wisdom in politics is a great virtue), are condemning, at the same time, certain great nations, and heads of State of world-wide reputation. They forget that Hitler's intentions *vis-à-vis* France were less clear, less publicly proclaimed, less completely in accordance with his political, economic and military needs than was his intention and his need to invade Russia and to crush the Soviet Union. Russia was a more dangerous power, Bolshevism was a political rival more to be feared than was Republican France. If the decision that France took in September 1939 was dictated to her by simple good sense, how can one describe the decision taken by the Russians in August 1939? And were they not asking for their rude awakening of 21st June, 1941?

If it was evident to the whole world that France was *forced* to fight Germany, how is it that it was not evident to the Americans that they were forced to fight the Japanese? And yet, despite the firmness of that country's rulers, a Congress which reflected American opinion faithfully enough refused to face up to this evident truth, and was still refusing when Japanese bombs came crashing down on Pearl Harbor. To consider France's declaration of war in 1939 as a fact without great importance, of no lasting interest, is to condemn Russia, the United States and most of the invaded countries, who, for their parts too, had refused to believe the evidence and had left it to chance to spare them the ordeals which obviously someone would have to undergo. Dare we say to the Dutch and to the Norwegians that the Swiss and the Swedes do not owe their good fortune simply to chance? Dare we ask tortured France to forget the choice she made, made with a troubled heart, with a fear which was not only justified, but not deep enough, a choice, in fact, that with the sole exception of the British Commonwealth, she alone made?

To ask her to forget it is to justify the Flandins and the Lavals, to justify not only their policy in 1939, but their present policy. For, if that decision was not one of supreme wisdom and almost unique, it was quite simply a stupid decision. Those advocates of prudence who contend that it was necessary to let the Nazi storm burst somewhere (and that it would certainly have burst in Russia) might, it is true, argue that the liberty, the dignity and, indeed, the very existence of France depended on the crushing of the Third Reich. But the weakened France of 1939 was no more capable of crushing the Third Reich than is the conquered and still weaker France of 1943. On the other hand, it was natural and even inevitable that Russia, the United States and Great Britain, all stronger than France, all further away from Germany, should have combined their efforts to break the Axis. A France which had remained neutral would perhaps to-day be in a position to contribute more to the Allied victory. What could Germany have done against Britain without the aerodromes which the Battle of France put at her disposal?

Of course Germany could have invaded France in any case, instead of turning immediately against Russia; but in that case France would have had a certain respite, Germany would have been clearly the aggressor, France would have avoided the cruel disillusion and humiliation of seeming to have undertaken a task well beyond her strength. Like Belgium or Holland, she would have been simply a victim and far more united than she is to-day. There never would have been a Vichy, for Vichy was not only the liquidation of a defeat, but also the disavowal of a policy that the outcome of events had condemned and upon which the country was deeply divided. That national unity which alone could have authorized the transfer of the powers of government to North Africa did not exist in June 1940. It did not exist because the Germans could say to the French what they could not say to the Belgians or to the Dutch: *Vous l'avez voulu.* Laval found himself in a far stronger, a far more defensible position than Quisling, because he could say that he, personally, had not wanted war. And Pétain could pose as a saviour and denounce "the lies which have lost France," because the whole policy which made of France the shield of Europe against the Third Reich had been one of those "lies." A France which had only been a victim would have found more pity abroad, more unity at home. How is it possible to refute this sophism without insisting upon the nature of the decision taken by France in 1939? And it is not possible to defend that

decision by producing arguments of prudence, by asserting that
victory was mathematically possible, and by urging that given the
military illusions harboured by the General Staff, the government
was right to take that decision. For such a defence takes no account
of two facts of cardinal importance, that France has reason to be
proud of her policy of 1939, and to expect some measure of
gratitude.

By refusing to play a purely passive role, and still more, a role
comparable to that of Italy (who waited for the moment when
victory appeared certain and cheap), France took a decision which,
for herself, is to-day and will be in the future of the utmost
importance. Thanks to that decision, which was to confirm the
resistance of the French people to collaboration and even to
attentisme, France remains a great nation, a great power. A policy
of neutrality or of *attentisme* would have meant a final abdication
on her part, and there could have been no going back. Because
Munich, and the mistakes and stupidities which preceded Munich,
would then have appeared as the natural stages in a progressive
decline, a progressive abdication, instead of being aberrations since
repented and expiated. To put things in their worst light, France
played the part of the Apostle Peter, whereas if she had remained
neutral in 1939, she would have played the part of Judas.

The consequences of such an abdication for France may be
judged by the case of Italy. Why is it that Italian patriotism, with
all its grandiloquence, has ever been fated to have its claims received
with irony, even by Italy's most complaisant allies? Why is it that
at the very time when services of all kinds were being bought from
her Italy has never been unreservedly recognized to possess a status
equal to her ambition? Why is it that the *volte-faces* in Italian policy,
worthy of the *condottieri* of the fifteenth century, have caused no
indignation, but have been received with resignation or amusement,
or with interested approval? It is most certainly because, despite
Carlo Alberto's programme, *Italia fara da se* has continued to be an
aspiration; at no time during the unification of Italy has it become
a reality. And a France who might have got out of her difficulties
by a simple *combinazione*—who, in 1939, or in 1940, or in 1943,
could have played the Italian role quite naturally—such a France
could not be really liberated.

Such a France would have found herself, when the war was

over, in the position of a new state which had to be created, and which would have had to have made herself accepted, to have sought for herself a modest place amongst the second-class powers. A Europe or a world in which France were to resign herself to such a role would no longer be either the Europe or the world which we have known; it would no longer be that modern society to which the motto *gesta Dei per Francos* applied, no doubt imperfectly, but better, none the less, than any other national motto. And we foreigners would do well to remember that what seems to us at times to be nothing but touchiness, nothing but egoism, nothing but national vanity or rancour, can be both all those things and at the same time something more, something greater: a means of claiming passionately and immoderately (if you will), and yet with justice, France's right not to be treated as a "fallen" nation, as a victim who must be helped, but rather as an eldest brother would be treated who had been dangerously wounded in a fight into which he had deliberately thrown himself, whilst his younger brothers, stronger and more prudent than he, had waited until the storm should have spent itself, hoping that they might themselves be spared through his action. This is the dignity which France won for herself in 1939 and 1940; and it is this dignity which she has not allowed the "realists" of Paris or of Vichy to rob from her. There may be certain mutual reproaches which Frenchmen and Englishmen can make but which they ought not to let any third party volunteer!

But the way in which France, in 1939 and since, has refused to abdicate has another aspect. A Europe in which France had given in without protest to the hegemony of the Third Reich, would no longer have been the Europe we know, the only Europe in which it would be possible for us to live decently. I have already said that; it is of enormous importance, but it is not the whole of it. France and England, in 1939, did not only declare war on a dangerous aggressor; they declared war on something which was unceasingly attacking their principles, their traditions, their ambitions. Far more fitting to this "something" than to the incompetent tyranny of the last Naples Bourbons, is Gladstone's phrase: "the negation of God erected into a system of government." The France of St. Louis, of Henry IV, of Pascal, of Montesquieu, of Voltaire, of Proudhon and of Tocqueville, it is that France whose spiritual glories were threatened by the Third Reich, and threatened with death. It was those great names, as much as it was those of Richelieu, of Louis XIV, of Thiers and of Clemenceau, which condemned the Third Reich and those who, in France, had made themselves its apologists. A France which was ready to look on whilst all Europe was absorbed by Hitler's Germany, which was resigned to becoming herself absorbed or assimilated, would have been a France that had abandoned the Cartesian Line, and had ceased to be the second home of every good European.

That is why France's declaration of war, then the resistance she maintained on all fronts (intellectual, moral, military), and that in spite of Vichy, outside Vichy as well as actually under the Vichy régime, have saved not only France, but also Europe and the world. And it is hardly necessary to insist upon the impoverishment which the triumph of German power and treachery would have meant for us. Through the breach left by the abdication of France would have surged the intellectual *Panzerdivisionen* of Germany. Neither we British, nor the Russians, nor the Americans, could have taken the place of the French genius.

One indication of the truth of this is to be found in the sucess of *La France Libre*, which has been a rallying point for all free minds exiled from the Continent. Another is the trouble which the Germans have taken to seduce the French *élites*, and the joy which the treachery of certain French "clercs" has caused them. If the allegiance of MM. Chardonne, de Montherlant and Company has so much rejoiced the heart of Dr. Goebbels, it is not only because they are talented writers, but also because they are *French* writers. If the conquest of even such mediocre publicists as MM. Luchaire and Suarez has given him such keen pleasure, it is because they are French. Even on an academician like Abel Bonnard, or a "Universitaire" like Bernard Faÿ, the quality of being French confers an added value. To betray the French Academy or the *Bibliothèque nationale* was to deliver a key position to the enemy, and not merely an outer bastion of the Republic of Letters. When after the war the time comes to rebuild the cultural and intellectual life of Europe, Great Britain and the United States, not to speak of Russia, will have a great part to play. But all three are, to some extent, foreign to Europe. The United States is so even more than is England; and then they are the chief English-speaking nations.

The German language, for a generation at least, has lost the freedom of the city. France, the French language, French culture, will constitute, at the very least, one of the corner-stones of the new edifice. For the greater well-being of Europe, French culture has been saved by the French people, and that in spite of the efforts, alas, of too many of those who were its official trustees. The marriage of the French people and of French poetry, of which Aragon's success is but one proof among many, the way in which the French have learned anew what it means and what it is worth to be French, their rediscovery of the reality of France: all of these things are undeniable gains; for no more than an oligarchy or an autocracy, can a culture which is purely aristocratic contribute to the reconstruction of a Europe in which the enslaved peoples have rediscovered themselves as nations, and have not yet ceased to be peoples. Unique amongst the great nations, France has suffered the same ordeals, been trained in the same hard school as the small nations; that is why she is especially well qualified to be placed at their head, at the side of the great nations who, more fortunate than she, have not known the full horrors of the defeat and occupation, have not been hardened by the need to fight simultaneously against treason at home, against the brutality of their enemies and the sometimes tactless kindness of their friends. It is important to recognize the fact that France has experienced the same fate, the same sufferings as Norway and Greece; that is why if there are certain services that France is incapable of rendering to Europe, there are others which she alone can render, and which are in danger of passing unnoticed by those practical minds against whose simple-minded hedonism the resistance of France and of Europe has been an unceasing and unreserved protest.

This is not to say that France, liberated France, will never cause her admirers either pain or perplexity. It is not true to say that France was defeated in 1940 because she was divided; but it is true that she was divided, and that those divisions have made her defeat both more bitter and more dangerous. She will have to pay for the years of the Vichy régime, and for the confusion, not moral but intellectual, which will be the aftermath of those years. Certain conceptions of life, indispensable to a stable civilization, have become discredited by the treachery of those who were their protagonists. Déat on the one hand, Maurras on the other, have rendered suspect certain truths which France will none the less need to remember. The common people have proved to be healthier and more stable than many of the so-called *élites*. She is, and has always been a country of *élites*; she could not become a united, docile and mediocre people. To say that we ought to be ready to applaud French dissensions would be to exaggerate; and yet we ought to be ready to tolerate those dissensions and, if possible, to understand them. What a shock it would be to us if suddenly we were confronted by a France which in politics, in science, and in the arts, no longer produced any refractory elements! We must be prepared to accept the France that will emerge, purified by her sufferings, but never reduced to drab good behaviour, to drab prudence, to the drab calculations of common sense. Such a tamed and sobered France would be a France in the image of Vichy, a France corresponding to the dreams and to the needs of Germany. Such a France would really have capitulated in 1940; such a France would not have declared war in 1939; such a France would be incapable of becoming the guide which Europe and the world needs. No people are better able to understand this than the English, who, in 1940, refused to admit that two and two made four, and to bow before the arguments which throughout the world—in New York and Moscow, just as much as in Vichy—were convincing and uncompromising to so many objective and timorous observers. An unreasonable pride, an unreasonable refusal to accept the verdict of arms, the inexorable march of history, "the wave of the future" (as Mrs. Lindbergh puts it), here are the signs by which one recognizes a great people. As the English did in 1940, so do the French to-day refuse to be reasonable and to resign themselves to a secondary role. This war will not have been the *finis Galliae*, and in this the world can only find cause for rejoicing. It is not going to be easy to understand each other; a great deal of patience will be needed; but the goal is worth the effort, more than worth it.

XX
THE CASE OF FRANCE
(1944)

I

THERE is an old Horatian maxim that advises against calling in a God to provide a solution unless the case is worth his trouble. There can be no doubt that the case of France calls for the most serious intervention of the best political thought at our command. The spectacle of the brain of our western culture put out of action by the most barbarous of invaders, the silence of Paris, the profanation of the whole soil of France, the absence from the stage of the world of a generally recognized French government, the ambiguity that overhangs the present and the future of the French nation, here is *nodus* enough. But faced with this unprecedented catastrophe, the solutions, the explanations have been far from worthy of so great and tragic a theme. The gutter, the brothel, the boudoir, the lobbies of Parliament, the directors' rooms of banks and trusts, the dark council chambers of ignoble conspirators, all have been called in to explain what is commonly called the "fall of France."

And the first thing to do is to protest both in the name of decency and in the name of good sense against the term "fall." Conquest, yes, defeat, yes, disaster, yes. But "fall" both flatters Anglo-Saxon moral complacency and conceals from its users and from their listeners the true character of the catastrophe, conceals from them the important political truth that victory and defeat are not issued like Sunday school prizes or demerits. It is a vulgar and immoral superstition to believe that the good always win or that the defeated were defeated because of some moral defect—a point less novel in Virginia than in old or New England. It is a special form of the worship of the Bitch-Goddess, Success, to condemn from a superior moral platform, men or nations that have not succeeded in winning her favours.

So by insisting on talking of the "defeat" of France, one does more than make a pedantic point of nomenclature; one brings to the foreground the primary problem, the problem of the *military* defeat of France, the *fons et origo* of so many ills subsequent both in time and in logical sequence. Here we come up against another intellectual sin, the congenital refusal of the Anglo-Saxon publicist to give due place to mere military considerations. It is hard for one brought up in that tradition to accept the fact that military defeat has, as a rule, military causes; that if the military accountancy shows a balance, other defects in the total social economy do not count; and that no other moral or intellectual merits offset military weakness when it comes to the last argument of kings and peoples. And the military reasons for the defeat and conquest of France are simple and indisputable, but they are not often enough borne in mind.

There is surely nothing at all surprising in the defeat of a people of forty millions by a people of eighty millions? True, British and Dutch and Belgian armies were involved on the French side, but so was the Italian army on the German side—at the last desperate crisis when, for all practical purposes, the French army alone was in the field. Sometimes a power much weaker in ordinary military resources makes up for that defect by other assets: better armament, better training, a more homogeneous society, a better morale. Even so (as the South discovered) a competently directed superior power can always win if its resources are used with reasonable intelligence and vigour. Grant defeated Lee, even if Hooker didn't!

But apart from the primary statistical inferiority, the more the French case is examined, the worse her position is seen to be. Not merely were there two German subjects for every French citizen; there were more than two German men of military age for every Frenchman of military age. In 1914, France had the oldest population in Europe; she lost more men out of a smaller pool than any of the other great powers; her bad demographic situation was at its worst in the years when her active army had to be recruited from the generation born in or just after the war of 1914–18—i.e. in 1938–40. The situation from the point of view of military morale was no better. For the French had suffered a more profound disillusionment than the Germans. The Germans had only had the shock of not winning a war they expected to win; the French had had the shock of winning a war they hoped to win—and then of having to fight a new war in worse conditions so soon after the last war that a large part of the army defeated in 1940 had known the agonies and glories of Verdun. If the veterans of the Army of the Potomac had had to undergo a new Cold Harbor or Fredericksburg in 1884—with Grant and Sherman very ready to tell them that it was no good—the Union might not have stood the strain.

II

Why, if these things were obvious, did the French go to war with British support and American approval? Because they were not obvious except to the few (among whom I hasten to say I was not included) who understood the profound revolution in the art of war caused by motorization, the tank, the new force of air-power. It was an accident that the military technique of 1914 favoured the defence and consequently the powers that needed time to mobilize their resources, the more pacific, the democratic powers. In this sense, the magazine rifle, the machine-gun, the quick-firing field gun were democratic weapons. The tank and the 'plane were not, since they made quick and decisive victory possible, and so benefited those powers that could really in peace prepare for war, because for them peace and war were only different stages in the normal life of the state. The French had prepared for a war of 1918; so had the British and Americans as far as they prepared for anything. But even had the French General Staff understood the technical problem, had they adopted General de Gaulle's theories *en bloc*, French preparation would have been grossly inferior to German because the French nation and its rulers wanted peace, and only nations whose rulers want war can really prepare for it in modern times. No peace-wanting nation will stand, even in time of open danger, the kind of preparation called for. American economic mobilization before and after Pearl Harbor illustrates that point well enough. Danger of war is not, in a democracy, the same thing as war.

But there was an additional cause of French weakness which had no moral character and was, in the crisis of 1938–40, incurable. It was not merely a case of total mobilization of resources (impossible until war came) but of the inadequacy of those resources—and those resources were inferior to German resources in a proportion far more terrible than before. For modern war is a war of steel and machine tools, and France was an exporter of iron ore and an importer of machine tools. With all her resources mobilized, she was still a military push-over for the Third Reich. *In time*, she could count on the industrial resources of Britain and America— but Germany refused to give her time, and how much time was needed, the fifth year of the war shows beyond any doubt. How long would a fully-armed France have had to wait before British and American resources were available? Two years, three years? It was asking too much, far too much. The defeat of France was, given the nature of modern war, a certainty—a certainty concealed from us because we did not understand the nature of modern war. So we started looking for extraordinary explanations and began talking of the "fall of France."

Some of the criticisms of the French war plan would be justified if they came from rigorous and prescient military theorists. But coming from the run-of-the-mill exploiter of the military history of the last war, they are comic or impudent. The French General Staff of 1914 was bitterly criticized for not staying within its Vosges fortress belt; the General Staff of 1939–40 stayed in the Maginot Line; the generals of 1914 ignored the German threat through Belgium and did not extend their Left far enough; in 1940 they rushed into Belgium with their best troops and equipment and lost them in the Dunkirk campaign; Foch ignored the importance of material superiority and over-emphasized morale and the offensive spirit; Pétain knew better; in 1939–40 war was to be won on the cheap and the Pétain legend was ready for German use when it was proved that no war is won on the cheap. But what chance had any French Government or General Staff of arguing the question of the lessons of 1914–18 with novelists and publicists and military critics who thought wars could be won by luring the enemy into the offensive? And what would have been the Anglo-Saxon outcry against French militarism if France, in the interval between the two wars, had cultivated the military spirit and sacrificed all her resources to prolonging the Maginot Line to the sea? And what if the Germans in 1940, faced with a Maginot Line to the sea, had merely contented themselves with the conquest of Holland and Belgium, whose air-fields are quite adequate for the bombardment of London?

And let it not be said that these fairly banal reflections on the military causes of French defeat are superfluous. They are not, for the greatest barrier between the French people and their British and American allies is and will be the belief on one side that the French defeat was due to corruption, treason, bad civilian morale, to anything but its simple military causes, and, on the other, the belief that the British and American peoples (and their soldiers) forget that, so far, many more Frenchmen have been killed in this war fighting Germany than Englishmen or Americans have been killed, that no army, not even the Russian army, has in fact withstood, in the same dimensions of space and time, the prepared onslaught of the Wehrmacht. Russia could recover (among other reasons) because of her area and natural resources; Britain could survive (among other reasons) because she is an island. The other reasons are important, but the decisive reasons that gave them a chance to be important are geographical. If the Germans could have crossed the Channel, they would have found troops not merely armed only with obsolete weapons, but in many cases not armed at all. If the Russian army could have been pinned up against mountains and frontiers, say on a line from Smolensk to Kiev, there might have been for it and for the victorious Germans, that "battle without a morrow" which Hitler strove for in vain when his own resources were stretched and his enemy's made more available at the very gates of Moscow. The French could not retreat to Seville or stand siege in a fortress with a moat whose importance we realize now when we are planning to cross it in the opposite direction.

This, though the main story, is not the whole story. There were grave and not inevitable weaknesses in French equipment, strategy, and political morale. We can be quite sure that so ruthlessly self-critical a people as the French will examine the question of responsibilities with a rigour that may shock us. But it will be well for us to remember the basic fact that the first burden of resisting the Third Reich was imposed on Poland; the second on France; and both at a time when Britain had declared war but was not yet in a position to make it, and when the United States and Russia had not even declared war.

III

Nevertheless, the questions brought to the forefront by the French catastrophe are not merely military. Defeat was the occasion for the revelation of old strains and weaknesses; it entered into the composition of some problems; it was a catalyst for others. These problems face us now and face the French now, and they cannot and should not be ignored. First of all, 1940 revealed that political nature abhors a vacuum. In the catastrophe, there was no institution to which the French people could turn, in which they could put their trust. There was only a personal symbol of past glory and personal integrity, Pétain. The Third Republic had succeeded only too well in taking personality out of politics. The generation of Poincarés and Clemenceaus was dead. No civilian in a moment of greater disaster than 1870 even tried to play the role of Gambetta. That fell to a comparatively obscure soldier, de Gaulle. There is a lesson here; not a lesson that only soldiers can evoke national pride or give the emotional power needed at such moments, but that somebody must, some man or group of men, some sacred institution, not so drab a body or so ironically regarded an institution as the Parliament of the Third Republic. It is only true in a very limited sense that "ridicule is the test of truth," and what little truth there was in the maxim was excessively exploited in France. It was not a minor matter that honest men had to put up with the company of rogues, that the dignity of the incarnation of the sovereignty of the French people, the President of the Republic and the Parliament, was an idea so remote from reality as to be a joke without further elaboration. What France needed was not more of the wit of Georges de la Fouchardière, but the sense of the dignity of the *Senatus Populusque Romanus*. When that dull machine-politician, Chester Arthur, became President of the United States by the accident of the assassination of Garfield, his old pals were amused. But when one of them put his hand on Arthur's shoulder and addressed him as "Chet," the New York politician removed his hand and froze him with a glance. He was President of the United States with a new standard of dignity and duty. Here is a lesson; and if Frenchmen and French leaders in the next few years seem to insist too much on dignity, national and representative, on pride, on what may seem like mere *amour propre*, it should be remembered that they are repenting a national sin that seemed pretty venial in 1939 and was almost mortal in 1940.

But it was not only the dignity of the French nation that was compromised; it was its authority and power. From 1918 to 1939 there was a steady ebbing-away of the authority of the French state. It became harder and harder to get any policy adopted or carried out; the balance of power was only too perfect; all pressure groups cancelled each other out. And France was left to routine that produced results ranging from brilliant (in technical reconstruction) to abysmally bad (in foreign policy and in public finance). If Frenchmen, especially young Frenchmen, act the Jacobin, talk of a France *"pure et dure,"* remember that they have memories of a régime that even its friends hardly dared assert to be worthy of respect, even if it was worthy of love. The old reactionary parties in the first years of the Third Republic called it *"la gueuse,"* the "slut"; it was untrue then; it was not so untrue in the inter-war years. The young Frenchmen and the young Frenchwomen who have been resisting the Germans and their allies are now far more akin to the Republicans of the heroic period, before 1870, than to their immediate predecessors. They see the Republic returning:

> Pâle encore, et des plis de sa blanche tunique
> Cachant son front voilé.

What they see coming is an immaculate Republic, but a republic. For "the Republic" is an ideal that has new life in it since so many have died for it. Liberty once taken for granted and too often interpreted as a mere licence for a policy and a life of minimum effort, has been lost and is now being fought for. The old scorn of the reactionaries for the "mere" ideals of the Left, the contempt for the cloudy concepts of the republican tradition, the *nuées* of Charles Maurras, have no hold on the young now, who have seen men and women die for those ideals and have seen the hateful sterility of the Maurrasian doctrine and the open treason of many of its disciples. And on the other side, men have learned that words like "liberty" and "France" have meanings not exhausted and not easily replaceable by the latest slogans turned out by M. André Marty. In a more genuine sense than the Communists meant it, the French people want a France "forte, libre, et heureuse," and if they have to sacrifice any of these attributes, it will be the last—they have learned that without the first two, it is empty of meaning.

Our soldiers will soon be deeply involved in the affairs of a country that is suffering from the greatest ordeal in its history. It is suffering in pride, for the total impotence of France, metropolitan

France, is a complete novelty in history. It is suffering in a sense from the necessary reaction to that impotence. The Resistance movement, apart from its military importance, was a moral necessity for France. But a great underground conspiracy is an expensive remedy. The Ku Klux Klan may have been a necessity but its price was long paid by the South all the same. France in 1939 was a rich country in the old way slowly adjusting itself to the need of becoming a rich country in the new industrial way. She is now a poor country, stripped and weakened, with more need but less means of bringing about that economic transformation that is a condition of her free survival. Already a country too old in population, she is now a country in which the young and energetic have acquired ways of thinking and ways of acting that may cut them off from the middle-aged electoral majority. A country accustomed more than any other to unlimited free discussion, she has been gagged. A country accustomed to be a leader and liberator of others, she will owe her formal liberation mainly to Allies. Most of the problems of France can only be solved by Frenchmen; some can only be solved by Frenchmen in association with their continental neighbours; some are general to the whole free western world. But on the relations of France and the French people with Britain and America very much depends—for us as for them. And there is one absolute condition of that relationship being fruitful, that when we think or talk of the "fall of France" we should mean by it what we mean when we talk of a brother or a comrade who fell in a battle that he began and he alone could begin, a battle which we are now carrying on to a victory that is his as well as ours.

XXI
THE CASE FOR FRENCH
(1942)

In the September *Fortnightly* Professor Allison Peers, under the title "The Tyranny of French," attacked the quasi-monopoly which that language now has in our school system. He raised other questions too; he complained, with justice, of the inadequate provision for the teaching of modern languages in our universities and of the neglect of the scientific study of modern societies, a study naturally, though not inevitably, associated with linguistic studies.

The position of French in the English secondary system is due, first of all, to its replacing Greek and later, and not so completely, Latin in the standard curriculum. It has become the standard second language as Greek used to be. And its position is now endangered because of the very mixed reasons why a knowledge of French became, in the late seventeenth century, what a knowledge of Latin had long been, a mark of the educated man. Some of those reasons are now obsolete; some are not.

French, in the two centuries between the Peace of Ryswick, and the first Battle of Sedan, was the language of what was thought to be, and for long was in fact, the most powerful European state. More educated people, more people in the movement of the age, spoke French as a native language than spoke German or Russian, and many more spoke French than spoke English, Spanish or Italian. In French, the great conflicts of the flesh and the spirit were carried on. It was the second language of Frederick the Great, Catherine the Great, Gibbon, Grimm, Alfieri. It would be hard to name an eminent Englishman of the eighteenth century who could not read French, and some, like Charles James Fox, spoke it admirably. French was then a necessity. But it was also a luxury. Paris was the centre of more than intellectual fashions and this left its trace on the language of diplomacy, war, cookery and fashion as early Italian pre-eminence in music left its trace in the language of that art. We still write *hors d'œuvres* for the same kind of reason that we write *andante cantabile*.

The political, economic and numerical reasons for the pre-eminence of French are gone. France is a conquered country and may never be a great world power again; France is relatively a poor country; and French is spoken by far fewer people than speak any of the great European languages, except Italian. French may preserve and probably will preserve for a time, the kind of snob appeal that pleases head waiters and smart dressmakers, but the kind of French that astonishes the waiter or impresses the mannequin can be acquired in ten easy lessons. There is no reason for wasting school time on such frivolities. So far, the case against its old predominance can be considered made. But the real case for French remains and it is the same as the original case for Greek in the fifteenth century. French is a language whose acquisition immensely broadens the cultural outlook of the English boy and girl. Other languages could do this too, but not so well or so easily. And French is taught in schools mainly in order that our educated classes should learn to read one foreign language.

Professor Peers would contest this thesis for several weighty reasons, but he has also taken time to advance some reasons that are so frivolous that one is tempted, at first, to mutter a tag from one of his preferred romance languages and content oneself with a *non ragionam di lor*. There is, for instance, the strangely unworldly assertion that few "ever travelled in France *from choice* compared with those who went to Switzerland and Italy." Professor Peers conjures up a vision of a tourist industry in France dependent on "school-parties and penniless undergraduates," on whose meagre surplus the innkeepers of Juan les Pins and of Le Touquet eked out a narrow livelihood, while the rich, the cultured, the sophisticated, crowded Sienna and Lucerne. In fact, in the last twenty years the tourist attractions of France have been far more widely appreciated than ever before in history, and the Lido and Saint Mark's both fought vain battles against the equally potent but snob appeals of French plages and French Gothic and Romanesque cathedrals. As for Switzerland, who that could afford it ever visited that once fashionable country except belated Victorians, winter sports addicts, mountaineers, tuberculous patients or pilgrims to Geneva? And only the last class needed any linguistic equipment

and, in their case, the best equipment was French! Another argument tells against teaching modern languages at all. If with all the
prestige of French, with all the advantages of experienced teachers,
preponderance of university chairs and other academic advantages,
so bad a job is made of teaching French as Professor Peers asserts,
why should we expect better results from the teaching of languages
like Italian, Russian, Spanish, for whose study such inadequate
provision is now made? It may be that a speaking smattering of
German is more easily acquired than a speaking smattering of
French, but a competent reading knowledge of German is less easily
acquired. So unless we assume that the aim of linguistic teaching in
schools is a speaking knowledge of the language, we are back where
we were. Boys and girls will learn to speak a foreign tongue if they
are made to aim at that seriously. And it may be that more attention
should be paid to spoken French or spoken German, but that is
another story. Before we abandon French on these grounds, we
should have to have proof that by some miracle, the stout English
refusal to make a fool of oneself speaking a foreign tongue is going
to be changed into a German or Polish willingness to learn by speaking, merely by making the victim language Italian or Russian.

That the old predominance of French is gone and that it is no
longer a *lingua franca* must be admitted. But it has to a great and
probably increasing degree been replaced in that role by English
(or American), and a little attention to clear English enunciation,
some elementary grounding in phonetics, would be a better invest-
ment of the time of the mythical strayed reveller in Stockholm,
Shanghai or even Buenos Aires than any other European language
except that of the country concerned.

The argument with which Professor Peers concludes his article
is of a kind that it would be a meiosis to describe as "tactless." If it
was silly of the educationist of the last war to base the claims of
French on the great role of the French in the alliance against
Germany, it is surely rash of a champion of Italian, German and
Spanish to stress the fact that many Frenchmen in the summer of
1940 (like many Americans, Russians and others) thought that the
British chicken's neck was about to be wrung. For the Italian and
German Governments were the self-appointed wringers and the
Spanish Government a benevolent onlooker while the operation
was attempted. I do not forget that nations are not always fairly

represented by their governments, but Professor Peers seems to have done so. This acrid partisanship is his contribution to the debate, not mine, and if it has any value it pleads for Russian, Chinese, Modern Greek and, above all, English, the language of the chicken.

With another of Professor Peers's reforms I am in great sympathy. We do need, and need badly, more thorough, objective and understanding studies of contemporary societies and cultures. But, as Professor Peers would probably agree, it is not the job of modern language schools in the universities, *as their duties are at present interpreted*, to train such students or to promote such studies. Time spent on Marie de France or Walther von der Vogelweide is, of course, not time wasted from a general cultural point of view. But it is not an immediate help to the student of contemporary France or Germany. It is not, I think, accidental that the most profound French student of modern English society, Élie Halévy, was a philosopher by professional training. It is, at any rate, worth noting that although French is much less widely and thoroughly taught in American schools than in English schools, serious academic study of modern French history and political and economic organization is much further advanced in America than it is here. We should have more and better understanding of our neighbours if modern language schools made it one of their primary jobs to study the contemporary life of the culture which they are also studying from a linguistic and literary point of view. And if the production of such experts is a primary university job (as it is), the most important societies to study and languages to master are Russian and American. Spanish and Portuguese are runners-up, but at a great distance, and their importance is due to the existence of Latin America, not to the intrinsic importance of Spain or Portugal.

I shall try to give reasons, later on, why the quasi-monopoly of French is, in fact, a good thing in itself, but even were this not so, the fact that nearly all the "educated classes" in Britain have been taught the same foreign language (although some have been taught others as well) is a matter for rejoicing. It would be a matter for rejoicing even had the language been German or Italian. For such a monopoly has the happy result of giving our educated classes a *common* foreign culture or the minimum linguistic means of attaining it. Thus after reflection, I find that only one of my friends and acquaintances who can read any foreign tongue, cannot read French. Even were a knowledge of French less intrinsically rewarding, this unity in our educational system would be a good thing. It was a weakness of the French educational system that it did not, in fact, provide that common background so that *lycées* on the eastern side of the country studied German, *lycées* in the central part studied English, and on the south-east and south-west there was a tendency to study Italian or Spanish. The gains that come from a knowledge of the current discussions of problems in another tongue are greatly increased if the whole of the educated classes have a reading knowledge of the same foreign tongue, provided that language is rich enough in its current production to cover adequately most aspects of contemporary life. We have got this desirable unity; why should we throw it away, however much we may encourage the study of more than one foreign language?

For all that we can do for the schoolboy or schoolgirl is to give him one or more linguistic tools with whose aid he can enrich his own native culture. The study of language as such is to be commended. But that is an argument for a little instruction in the character of really different languages, like Chinese, Hebrew or Turkish, not for stress on more or less inflection, more or less elaborate systems of Aryan verbs. There will be, in every thousand schoolboys, a few natural linguists as there will be a few natural mathematicians. But the natural linguist like the natural mathematician will look after himself. The average boy will be content— and should be content—if he is taught to read one or more foreign languages well and so has been given access to a culture different from his own *and* intrinsically interesting and valuable. A reading knowledge of any of the great European tongues will serve this end, but not all serve it equally well and none serves it as well as French does. The most serious rival to French is, in fact, German. But German has never really caught on as more than a useful tool, because German literature is more voluminous than interesting. I base this view on the candid admissions of friends of mine whose German is excellent and who very seldom read any German except for immediately utilitarian purposes. The prestige of German literature is lower to-day (with no blame imputable to Hitler) than it was a century ago. Only Rilke has won the serious attention of our own critics and poets. In any case, Professor Peers's real case is not for more German, but for some Spanish and Italian in the schools.

Professor Peers asserts that "there are many who would not hesitate to place either Spanish or Italian literature above French." It would be more impressive to have the names of the many and to find among them scholars, poets, critics, who are neither Italians nor Spaniards nor teachers of those languages. For it is not the bias of the Board of Education that accounts for the demand for *translations* of French books and not translations of the French equivalents of Ibanez or Feuchtwanger, but a complete war-time edition of Proust. It was not the memory of what subjects they took for school certificate that caused so many readers of the *New Statesman* to badger Mr. Raymond Mortimer for a glimpse of the new poems of M. Louis Aragon or leads thousands to pay real money for *La France Libre* or a review like *Sur* to publish *Lettres Françaises* in Buenos Aires. It is genuine interest in French literature which is a tribute to the skill with which Professor Peers's villains, the teachers of French in our schools, have done their job. And it is an even greater tribute to the variety and attractiveness of French literature which has not, for three hundred years, known any of those long periods of occultation that mark the literary history of Spain, Italy and Germany. I cannot speak for Spain, but the translation-filled bookshops of Italy were not only a tribute to Italian broadmindedness but to the comparative meagreness of Italian literary output. And what is true of literature is still more true of knowledge. In what branch of learning is it more important or as important to know Spanish or Italian as it is to know French? Perhaps an economist would be better employed in learning Italian, but he would be still better employed in learning Swedish. And, as we do not know what a schoolboy is going to find professionally useful, we must choose his language for him on general cultural grounds. That is why we should choose French. It is a key to French literature, but it is also a key to French culture and a more complete key than most languages are to the cultures of the peoples who speak them.

In one sense, the culture of a nation or a society is all the manifestations of its power of expressing its personality or adapting its natural resources to its needs. But here culture is taken more narrowly, as covering the conscious arts; this culture is a key, often the only key, to the wider culture or civilization of which it is the artistic or intellectual expression. Inside a national culture of this narrower type, one art or skill may be predominant, either by influencing all the other arts or skills or simply by being the thing that the nation and its neighbours agree is done best or is best worth doing. And it is sometimes easy enough to determine what is the main contribution of a nation to the civilization of the world, or to determine that there is more than one such major contribution.

It is especially easy to do this in the case of France. France, like England and unlike Germany and Italy, is a country whose culture is predominantly literary. In the Middle Ages her greatest contribution to medieval culture was architecture; and it would be argued by some (but not by me) that her greatest nineteenth and twentieth century contribution has been painting. But like English, French culture is a literary culture. Italy is for most people more a home of the fine arts than of poets; Germany more the home of music and philosophy than of prose writers. But France is the country of many books. The approach to French civilization from the literary side is imposed by the literary character of the culture itself. And it comes easily to the English boy or girl, because his culture is predominantly literary too. Indeed, it is in a way more literary than is the French culture. For what English Victorian musicians or artists compare in interest or eminence (each in his own kind) with Debussy, Gounod or Bizet, with Delacroix, and Cézanne? Something is lost in studying French life purely from the literary side, more than is lost than in studying English life from that side, but far less than is lost in studying German culture and omitting Beethoven, Brahms, Wagner, Hegel, or in studying Leopardi, Carducci, D'Annunzio, Pirandello and neglecting Rossini, Verdi and Puccini.

A knowledge of French is not only a better instrument for the understanding of French culture than is a knowledge of German or Italian, but for an immediate political need of British society, it is as valuable as English (or American) and Russian. In the great debate which must follow the end of Hitlerism, much of the most valuable discussion will be carried on in French. This is not only because the French language is and has been for centuries a model language of discussion, nor because in most departments of life, except perhaps in pure economics, the richness of the content of

French discussion is worthy of the merits of the language. But in the reconstruction of Europe, the role of France as the greatest and most typical victim of Hitler will make French discussions and French solutions objects of passionate interest to the other victims. German, for obvious psychological reasons, will not be to the taste of the victims of Germany. And, more important, the German internal problem will absorb the energies of the German people. Their examination of conscience and, we must hope, repentance, will be of the greatest importance to Europe, but the German problem is a thing apart. Nor can we expect Europe to use Italian for its common tongue. Europe is, in fact, as likely to use English (in its American version) as any language. But even if this is so, there are enough experiences common to all the invaded countries and not shared by us or by the Americans, to make the Dutch or the Norwegians watch, with a sympathetic understanding, the French experiments. In the general and (apart from oral command of the language) efficient teaching of French in this country, we have an admirable common instrument of education, of great immediate political value and of permanent cultural value. To disrupt this existing, efficient and valuable educational system will be easy. But it will be much easier to lower the standard of French than to replace it by other modern languages, taught as well and, in themselves, as rewarding.

XXII

THE FRANCE WE NEED
(1943)

In the pattern of Europe that is being designed now, designed by events out of the complete control of any of the leaders of the embattled nations, the position that the movement of current history will assign to France is fundamental. For France must be a great force in the new Europe or be impotent. And a Europe in which France is not a great force is a very new Europe indeed; there will be a vacuum which political nature will insist on filling. How? That's anybody's guess.

What is less a matter of mere guesswork is the kind of France that alone can prevent the vacuum from being created, the kind of France that can alone justify the British Government in its policy of guaranteeing French independence and the territorial integrity of the French Empire. To make this guarantee a national policy for this country, a policy that will stand wear and tear, it must be part of a European policy which, in turn, means that France must have a European policy. And France can have only one European policy that has any chance of success. France must be again a leader and teacher of free Europe.

A natural if unfortunate insularity often hides this role of France from us. It was Matthew Arnold who reminded us that, wherever the French went, they carried with them the ideas of the Revolution; that more Bastilles than their own fell at the sound of their trumpets. France need not be a sectarian, dogmatic, intolerant crusader (as she was for very human and fairly forgivable reasons in 1793). But the France that Europe wants, and Europe needs, is a France that has not renounced 1793 or 1789, that is prouder of having destroyed the Bastille than of having built it. That is the France that won more love and trust from other peoples than any nation in modern history. It was that France whose overthrow was the great tragedy of 1940. It was the fall of "the Republic," not of the Third Republic, that was the political disaster of that year.

For what followed showed that France would be republican (in the most general and generous sense) or a mere satellite of the triumphant Fascist powers. The very title adopted by the Vichy régime was significant. French State! It was a title fit for a *société anonyme* suing in some international commercial court, good enough for the Banque de Paris et des Pays-Bas, but not for the claimant to the successions of the Kings of France and Navarre, the French Empire, the French Republic. It was not to learn lessons in docility, in subservience, in machiavellian power politics, in sacred selfishness, that Europe had gone to school to France. Germany and Italy were supplying all the demand for this instruction.

It was not a drill-sergeant's France that had turned the ideas of the young Heinrich Heine upside down as he saw the Emperor riding across the sacred princely grass in Düsseldorf, or that had taught him through the mouth of Sergent Le Grand, the refrain of "Ça ira." It was not a France where formal legal authority was all that mattered, which had won the admiration of Europe in the great People's War of 1870. And, as 1939 and 1940 had shown, it was not a France that was in doubt about its principles and some of whose rulers (on their own admission) saw in the war of 1939 a mere matter of policy, a mere choice of the better or worse course of prudential action, that could repeat the miracle of 1914.

In one of his torrential floods of rather excessive eloquence, Victor Hugo looked forward to the time when Paris would be, for a united and free Europe, a "volcano of light." That time will come, but only if we do not compromise light-heartedly, or in casual indifference to the great issues involved, the chance now open to France to take her due part in the saving and freeing of Europe, to take part both by her exertions and her example. Then, to amend Charles James Fox, we shall be able to welcome one of the greatest and one of the best events in the history of the world, the restoration to Europe of her chief teacher of the amenities of life—and of the dignity of man.

But it is not only amenities and dignity that France can teach in a way that no other country can. It is the organisation of the economic and political life of the continental nations on a pattern that will neither reduce them to docile beehives, nor leave them impotent victims of the beehive states. France must solve for herself

—and for her neighbours—the problem of liberty and power. For herself, because her chances of survival as an independent power depend on her own reorganization; for others, because French problems are far more like the problems of her smaller neighbours than ours are. France must save herself by her exertions, and her neighbours by her example.

We cannot. First of all, we have not been invaded, plundered, occupied, humiliated, driven to the edge of despair. We are not much more prepared than are the Americans to understand the kind of wounds that must be healed, the dangers of convalescence, the temptations to rush after quick, infallible—and fatal—remedies. We know a lot more about European problems than we did in 1939, but we still don't know enough. Secondly, we are a unique country, overwhelmingly industrial, an island, deeply embedded in Europe, but with stronger ties than any other European country with the other continents.

The countries whose reorganization is essential to the peaceful future of Europe are much more agricultural than we are, or are ever likely to be (Belgium is the only exception). And unless France solves her problems, they cannot solve theirs.

The reorganization of France raises far too many problems to be discussed and solved, even in an article in this journal. But there is one basic condition that may be neglected in a misguided and ill-timed fit of "realism." So much nonsense was said and written in the years before 1939 about principles and preferences in foreign policy—with no regard to the fact that a nation without adequate power cannot have a foreign policy at all—that we are in danger of falling into the opposite error of thinking that power alone counts. And so much naïve underestimation of the force of old-fashioned patriotism was fashionable that we are probably right in stressing that, without old-fashioned patriotism, nations die, that no substitute has been found for it.

Yet patriotism is not enough. For by concentrating our view of our duties and interests too narrowly on ourselves, it blinds us to the needs of the hour. Both France and Britain could have strangled Hitlerism in its cradle if they had wanted to. But exclusive national patriotism left them in the "let George do it" mood that gives Hitlers their chance.

So it will be again. Only a France that accepts her part of the total European responsibilities, that escapes from the Vichy folly of preaching "*la France seule*," can be a leader in a free and peaceful Europe. Only a France that goes back to her old tradition of being the teacher of Europe, the tradition of the Crusades as well as of the Revolution, can make or keep the Allies, can win the support that she needs—and we need. As far as we and the Americans encourage those forces in France that hate the tradition of French liberty, French humanity, French duty, we are preparing a material restoration of France that will last just as long as we put material force behind it. And we shall not do that for very long. But a France that is the corner-stone of the new free Western Europe, its heart as well as its head, that is an ally worth having.

Neither we nor any non-French power can decide whether such a France is to come to life or not. But we can very easily make its birth difficult and dangerous. If we do, we shall not have to live very long to live to repent it.

XXIII

NEWS OUT OF FRANCE[1]
(1944)

LONDON has an abudance of visual reminders that we live in an iron age; the devastation of the Temple and the streets crowded with the uniforms of exiled nations are two. But one place in London brings home to the passer-by the novelty, the intolerable novelty, of the situation of Europe, occupied, tormented, assailed by the brutality and the bribes of scientific barbarism, the empty continental side of Victoria Station from which we used to leave for Paris. Another is the rarity of French books and periodicals. Both mark an unprecedented silence imposed on what has been, since the twelfth century, the main smithy and market for European ideas. There were wars in the old days. At the very beginning of the intellectual primacy of Paris, an English student was awakened by the jingoistic and Anglophobe enthusiasm of two Parisian matrons celebrating the birth of that prince who was to be Philip Augustus, destined to conquer Normandy and win Bouvines. At all times, up to our own, there have been bickerings, intellectual as well as material. Victor Hugo and Tennyson both wrote foolish things; there were exchanges of abuse at lower levels too. But the commonwealth of letters and learning was not destroyed by force. Captain Cook and Faraday, Laplace and La Pérouse were admired and served in both countries. London housed Verlaine and Paris Wilde; 1940 made a breach in historical continuity unknown since

[1] *Fontaine.* Revue mensuelle de la poésie et des lettres françaises. No. 29. (Algiers: 43, rue Lys-du Pac. London: Care of *Horizon*.)

Lettres Françaises. Cahiers trimestriels de littérature française édités par les soins de la revue *Sur*. Buenos Aires.

French Public Opinion since the Armistice. By Georges Boris. Oxford University Press. London: Milford.

The Three Years of Fighting France. June 1940–June 1943. By Félix de Grand' combe. Wells Gardner, Darton and Co.

France. By Professor Jacques Métadier. Preface by Wickham Steed. Macdonald.

Three Years of Hell. By Harry J. Greenwall. W. H. Allen.

the days when St. Augustine was welcomed at the court of Canterbury by the daughter of the King of Paris.

But the ice age imposed by the German power has been brief; it is already receding. There is more news out of France, there is now, in Algiers, a new French capital. The mother country is still gagged, but some of her sons can speak for her. First of all and best of all, the poets. It was the arrival here of the text of *Le Crève-cœur*, landing among the lovers of letters with an impact like that of Rudolf Hess among the whole population, that awoke new hope for French cultural life, even under Vichy. And *Fontaine*, which made of poetry, good poetry, the most effective and subtle instrument of the recovery of French pride and French energy, has rightly pride of place here. It is not only because *Fontaine* was warned by the Vichy authorities that its dangerous tendencies were noticed, or because some of its chief collaborators have been leaders in intellectual resistance; it is not only because it has published poetry, like that of Aragon, which marked the reconciliation of the most sophisticated French culture with the simple patriotism of the French people; but it is because it has published good poetry, good criticism, good prose, because it has maintained and defended the French tongue in its darkest hour, that its place of honour is so high. And in nothing is its merit better shown than in the admirable severity with which a critic like M. Henri Hell judges the French collaborationist writers and the justice with which the real literary merits of a Montherlant or a Chardonne are admitted. Something of the same justice is to be seen in the admirable review *Lettres Françaises* published in Buenos Aires, when that capital was still hospitable to the true cultural tradition of Latin America —which is far more the tradition of Paris than the tradition of Madrid. With *La France Libre* in London, these three reviews have held the pass, sold or abandoned by some of the directors of the great Paris reviews.

The historical background to the catastrophe and the historical developments since have to be allowed for in any assessment of present French intellectual activity. So there is a welcome place for M. de Grand'combe's *Three Years of Fighting France*, a straightforward account of the Gaullist movement written by a Frenchman who knows England very well indeed and reminds us, if we need to be reminded, of the admirable generosity with which the news

of the armistice was received in England in 1940. It would be a pity
if less generosity, less wisdom were shown now when the liberation
of France is at hand and when our relations with her will call for
wisdom and forbearance—and even some lapses of memory. And
M. Boris, writing like M. de Grand'combe from a Gaullist point
of view but with great skill and adequate objectivity, reminds us of
something else that we must not forget. "The General's presence
in England, at a time when France had become a prison from which
no man bearing authority could emerge, will always be regarded,
come what may, as one of the happiest gifts of destiny."

The enslavement of France and the attempted enslavement of the
French mind since 1940 are an historical theme of the greatest
interest and importance. Any book that casts light on the social
history of that period, on the psychology of the French people, on
the spiritual history of their reaction to conquest and then to
betrayal by so much of their *élite*, is to be welcomed. Mr. Greenwall's book is no worse than most such books—which does not
mean that it is very good. Apart from his erratic spelling, the
summing-up of the recent history of France with which he ends is
inaccurate, complacent, and, if taken seriously, may offset the good
that other sections of the book might do.

For Mr. Greenwall's account of his life in France after the
armistice, his criticisms of the B.B.C. programmes for instance,
deserve attention. Even more interesting is his account of the
attitude of the numerous British subjects stranded in France and
of the prevalence among them not only of Pétainism, but of
Lavalism. It is also worth noting, as a novelty, that after the glowing blurb on the jacket, we now have the glowing blurb inserted
in the text. "We get the clearest picture ever penned of what
France was like on the inside looking out," so the reader is told on
page 119 by the publishers. That we could hardly get from a book
like Mr. Greenwall's, but we get a minor contribution to history all
the same.

The political discussion, for obvious reasons, is not yet conducted
at a level comparable with that so magnificently attained on the
cultural plane. For obvious reasons. French culture was not so
discredited as were French military and political institutions by
their collapse. The French people might naturally feel bitterness
against *les grands chefs* at the sight of a Marshal of France capitaliz-

ing defeat and even bitterly reproaching the French people (as
M. Boris reminds us) for refusing to join him in his disastrous and
increasingly odious speculation, "Frenchmen, it is from yourselves
that I want to save you." And Frenchmen, it may be suspected,
regard with a certain irony those politicians who can now find good
reasons for their abdication of 1940, for their role as the assenting
members of the only French Parliament that has peacefully abandoned its own functions, a degree of modesty and despair beyond
even such unimpressive bodies as the Five Hundred of 1799 or the
Corps législatif of 1870.

That the trend of French opinion is most decidedly to the Left is
confirmed by all competent observers; that it is in the widest sense
profoundly republican, democratic and politically idealistic is
indubitable. The influence of those disciples of Maurras whom
Bernanos called *les petits mufles réalistes* has been destroyed by their
treason, and the elegant political pessimism of Alain has few
attractions for the vigorous and undespairing young. But in the
absence of free discussion, free movement, in the inevitable dis-
tortion that necessarily accompanies any conspiratorial enterprise,
it is hard, indeed, to decide what France wants and needs—and
what she needs is and must be closely related to what she wants.
The living forces of future France are underground inside France,
and although relations between the underground and the outside
world are now far better and more constant than they were, they
are still communications from the catacombs to a free world for
which the French people have a most vivid nostalgia, a passionate
devotion, but whose necessary habits they may, to some degree,
have forgotten.

Political discussion outside France (and North Africa is outside
France whatever the legal status of Algeria may be) suffers from a
creditable sense of modesty in some cases, the modesty bred by
ignorance of what German occupation has meant for the body and
the soul; while, on the other hand, it also suffers from the survival
in some exiles of a conviction that nothing much has changed, that
controversies are where they were in 1939. After 1870 the younger
republicans got rather tired of the great exiles who never forgot what
they had said in 1848 or in 1851. They became known as the *trop
connus*. Possibly some distinguished exiles of this emigration may
incur the same epithet.

G

It is natural that this flavour should be more prevalent in French writing published in America than it is in French writing published in London. For London in the late autumn of 1940 when *La France Libre* was established; when men and women were rallying round General de Gaulle; when others were organizing the emotional resistance to German–Vichy lies that had been so great a force in France; London was then in the front line. Many of the men and women who then made London their base were not animated by any very lively faith in the power of Britain to resist successfully; they were convinced that, in this last desperate moment when the fate of freedom in Europe depended on less than a thousand pilots of the R.A.F., London was the place to be in. It was the new Verdun. No such flavour could be given to life in New York; the chief city of a country still neutral in form if not in spirit, a country in close official relations with Vichy, a country in which the Jacobin intolerance shown by the French in London might well have seemed out of place, almost excessive.

The basic French problems were not created by the war and defeat; they existed before 1939; they will exist after liberation. It is therefore essential that the British and American publics which have such an interest in the appearance of a France *forte, libre et heureuse*, should have these basic problems clearly set out *now*, that they should not be left under the impression that the French problem is merely one of "fascist betrayal" or even (though this is a less dangerous illusion) of German exploitation. To put these truths before the British public is presumably the aim of M. Métadier in his little volume *France*. Something of the generosity and generality of the French intellectual temper is conveyed. But M. Métadier is too uncritical an apologist. No fiction did more harm between the two wars than the survival of the English belief that the average Frenchman was a Chauvinist, dreaming of the Napoleonic "épopée," or the glories of Louis XIV or the Crusades. In no western country, happily, was there less Napoleon worship than in France. In no country was official education freer from Chauvinism (it could be argued, indeed, that a complacent in-difference to the realities of force in the world was the besetting intellectual sin of the *instituteur*, but that is a very different story). By stressing this truth and illustrating it from French text-books, M. Métadier performs a useful function, but he is not content with this. He discusses past wars (like the War of the Grand Alliance, which he calls the "War of Devolution") and shows that all or many were unpopular.

But that is not the point; the French State under Louis XIV was organized on such a basis that aggressive wars could be waged and were waged. It is important to notice that they were opposed and criticized by people like Saint-Simon and Fénelon; it is important to note that Louis XIV repented on his death-bed of his bellicosity. But it is dangerous to pretend that there was no bellicose flavour about the motto *nec pluribus impar*. It is dangerous because it is untrue, and it makes it harder to gain acceptance of a very important truth, that the France of the twentieth century was more thoroughly cured of the passion for glory of the old type than any other great nation. And one is entitled to suspect the historical judgment of a writer who thinks it odd and peculiarly French that, in the Middle Ages, Frenchmen wanted to be sure that they "had right on their side and this right was not weighed by a selfish or even national interest." It was far more important in the Middle Ages to have, or to pretend to have, general principles of right on your side than it is now. There was more meaning in *Gesta Dei per Francos* when it was first written than there has been ever since —though M. Métadier would be right if he insisted that this conception lived in French minds and policy for longer than it did elsewhere.

But it is in his treatment of political and economic questions that M. Métadier is most depressingly optimistic, and that the inferiority of his book to M. Maillaud's admirable work of the same title and scope is made most evident. France cannot become a great Power again, or play the role that it is necessary for our good and that of the world that she should play, unless there is a very profound alteration in her economic methods, her distribution of her resources, her system of public finance. To preach a return to the France of 1939 is to preach an abdication. To give aid and countenance to the dangerous superstition of the French intellectual that economics are a matter for literary manipulation is to preach a very dangerous kind of obscurantism—an obscurantism against which, from its foundation in London in 1940, *La France Libre* has brilliantly campaigned.

These discussions, these controversies, some admirably con-
G*

ducted, some less admirably, are signs of new life, of communication between Frenchmen outside metropolitan France and those who are still captive. It is a tragic but not desperate situation:

> Tous les Français ressemblent à Blondel,
> Quel que soit le nom dont nous l'appelions,
> La liberté comme un bruissement d'ailes
> Répond au chant de Richard Cœur-de-Lion.

XXIV
TRACTS FOR THE TIMES[1]
(1944)

THE metaphor of a tidal wave has been used often enough in the last few years to describe the state of Europe, and it suggests the problem that faces those who try to estimate how much of the old Europe survives beneath the waters, how much will be seen when the rapidly receding flood is sucked back into its original marshes, and what, if anything, has been gained by the catastrophe, what debris of old institutions have been swept away for good, and what seeds have been left in the mud. In the case of such a catastrophe there is a human temptation to expect that the destruction has been complete, that, in some fashion or other, a great material and moral disaster should bear fruit in proportion to its mere material size. And closely associated with this assumption that the moral and intellectual books will show the same gains and losses as the material books, is a resignation before the mere size of the problem, a resignation that may be pessimistic or optimistic, a pessimistic resignation to an unknown but fully determined future or an optimistic resignation before the laws of progress. "There must be a solution, but we don't know what it is": "There must be a solution, we know what it is; this is it."

It is against this attitude, in either of its forms, that the very remarkable polemic of M. Raymond Aron is directed. By an acute and remarkably objective analysis of the present situation and of its more recent origins, M. Aron hopes to dispel both the pessimistic and the optimistic illusions. The survival of civilization is not impossible; but it will not be brought about by the application of a few dramatic and dogmatic principles. We are not bound to pass into the hands of Mr. Burnham's managers, or of the officers of

[1] Raymond Aron, *L'Homme contre les tyrans*. (New York: Editions de la Maison Française.)

André Gros, *Les problèmes politiques de l'europe: réflexions sur la paix future*. (Hachette.)

P. S. Gerbrandy, *National and International Stability*. The Taylorian Lecture, 1944. (Oxford University Press. London: Milford.)

a totalitarian state socialism or of the agents of a new international of cartels. It is against a "sterilizing fatalism" that M. Aron fights. And so he is critical of all total solutions and of all total explanations. "En dissolvant ces nécessités massives nous parviendrons peut-être, non à substituer des prévisions globalement optimistes aux prévisions totalement pessimistes, mais *à marquer les points d'application de la volonté humaine.*"

The dissolution of Europe, its old nations and its common culture, into a new harmonized, integrated, economic, political and cultural unit need not happen if we do not want it to happen. It is not, in fact, likely to happen even if we do want it; there are too many living forces against such a solution. But what will happen will be better or worse, more or less hopeful, in so far as we understand what we are doing and what we have done, and in so far as we really *will* what we want. A Spanish statesman (naturally a pessimist by trade) once said that he did not know where Spain was going, but he knew she would not arrive. For M. Aron, Europe and the nations of Europe can arrive, but only if they know where they have been going so far—and that route map is not to be drawn up quickly in some well-intentioned slogan production office.

This work is full of matter, but the title of this "Literary Supplement" recalls us to order. For although M. Aron treats of economics and war, of sociology and law, a great part of his book deals with the role and the responsibilities of the intellectuals. In his title, M. Aron recalls that remarkable last book of Elie Halévy, *L'Ère des Tyrannies*, and in the creation of an age of tyrants the men of letters have a heavy responsibility. They, more than most, have exalted such non-moral systems of value as the nation and the class. For although M. Gros greatly exaggerates the degree to which morbid national feeling has been made to order by propagandists, the poets, historians, novelists and professors have much to answer for.

It is natural that M. Aron, a Frenchman specializing in German questions, should concentrate on German and French examples of this *trahison des clercs*. If there be any among us so foolish in 1944 as not to realize that the tone of a culture has profound importance for the life of the nation concerned—and of its neighbours—the section of this book called "guerre impériale" is what the Americans call "required reading." But of even greater interest is the discussion of the treason of so many French clerks, of the igno-

minious contrast between the resistance of the French people and
the acceptance of the German triumph of 1940 by so many of the
intellectual *élite*. This again is not a problem to be explained in a
few orthodox political formulas; it is too complicated for that. It
is not even to be explained in terms of personal feebleness of
character (though that counted for a lot). It raises more general
questions, and the analysis given here is most timely and, for
English readers, novel.

Central to M. Aron's theme and problem is the case of "Alain."
For Alain was both by formal and real profession a teacher—and
a teacher of politics. He was many other things as well, but the
basic doctrine was that of the famous "Eléments d'une doctrine
radicale." He was, as M. Aron insists, bold and original in his plea
for the politician, in his defence of politics. To defend a dim and
drab figure like Combes in the age of Lenin and Mussolini, that
was boldness. To be so critical of planning and great economic
agglomerations, that was boldness of a more startling kind. To
defend the standards of the provinces and of the less fashionable
part of the provinces was a kind of heroic gesture—in the beginning. It was no case of admitting, reluctantly, *à la* Renan, that M.
Homais was right. It was a matter of proclaiming, daily, that *of
course* M. Homais was right. And by dint of repeating this, year
in year out, Alain, like Maurras, acquired a vested position as a
political philosopher *en titre*. He, like Maurras, had a doctrine, a
doctrine that insisted on the pre-eminence—and sterility—of
political solutions.

A l'autre bout de la chaîne, Maurras parvenait, en quelques
dizaines d'années de prêches quotidiens, à convaincre une partie
de la bourgeoisie que de la restauration monarchique dépendaient
l'existence et la grandeur de la France et que, faute d'un roi, nul
espoir n'était permis d'un gouvernment raisonnable. Egalement
étranger à la situation de la France et de l'Europe, également
abstrait et théorique, Alain a convaincu une partie de l'opinion de
gauche que l'opposition morale du citoyen aux pouvoirs apportait
la meilleure garantie des libertés et de la paix.

What these two sophists had in common was pessimism. Maurras
advocated a solution that he made no serious attempt to put into
action and in which active belief was almost impossible. Alain did
not advocate any solution. He only provided elegant variations on

the theme of clearing your mind of cant about politics and patriotism. Alainism, Maurrasism were admirable doctrines for the
irresponsible young men who wanted to shine or score. They were
also, perhaps unconsciously, contributors to the deadly illusion
that any policy, any political philosophy was possible for France that
did not take daily vigilant account of the outside world. Maurras
sinned by looking at that world through the spectacles of his
increasingly outmoded Latin, Ultramontane, monarchical doctrine.
He lived far more in the clouds than did the enemies he was
denouncing as romantics.

Alain did not look outside at all. He was content to assume that
what was adequate for Rouen was adequate for the rest of the
world. While Maurras unconsciously revealed the grave limitations
of his knowledge of books and men, Alain rejoiced in his. And only
by reading the later aphoristic collections, things like the *Propos
d'Économique*, can the disastrous limitations of Alainism be appreciated. It was no great tribute to the clarity of the French mind
that the propaganda of the *front populaire* (a movement which, if it
meant anything, meant planning, authority, external and internal
vigilance, all animated by passionate faith) should have made of
Alain one of its symbolic figures, should have linked his name with
that of Langevin as one of the glories of the renovated republic.

For it must never be forgotten that Alain, this denigrator of
established authority, this preacher of systematic doubt, was an
official of one of the most important republican corporations, the
University. He was a paid philosopher, provided in his *lycée* at
Rouen and then in Paris with a succession of brilliant young men
to impress, to seduce, to sharpen his wits on and build his great
prestige on. For all his ostentatious scorn for the official hierarchies,
"Monsieur Alain" was a great figure in the Latin Quarter. Could
there be very much wrong with a political system that not merely
allowed the sons of small tradesmen to become ministers (and,
often, to be seduced in the process) but paid and honoured a
sophist for illustrating, in a few ingeniously varied forms, the thesis
of Doctor Johnson that "most schemes of political improvement
are very laughable things"? That the powers that be should do as
they were bound to do, and that people like Alain should be free to
say what they liked about them, this was, for some, the essence of
republicanism, a weak state subject to incessant criticism, one that

left the private citizen plenty of time to cultivate his garden. Alain had certainly taken to heart the advice of his eminent predecessor Burdeau. His pupils had little excuse for continuing

à rêver l'impracticable et à mépriser le practicable, à substituer la logique des idées à l'observation des faits, à faire reluire, aux yeux avides des foules, des visions de justice absolue, quand nous ne pourrons jamais réaliser qu'une justice boîteuse, limitée, imparfaite.

Some of them learned their lesson (M. Maurois was a disciple of the Rouen days). Some reacted violently, as Barrès had reacted against Burdeau, but around the man who had spent a life undermining respect there yet hung the aura of respect. That this way of life, this professional scepticism, this resignation to contemporary French limitations, was a luxury was hidden from Alain. And when the day of revelation came in 1940 it was too late. Langevin went to prison, and Alain entered that reconstructed *Nouvelle Revue Française* which was to be the Trojan horse by which Goebbels hoped to take the citadel of that French culture which German barbarism must slay—if it is to live unashamed.

The systematic scepticism and resignation that led Alain into resignation to Vichyism was, despite the prestige given to it by Alain's official reputation as a permanent *frondeur*, not the most dangerous source of seduction used by the Germans. Far more deadly was the impression made by the passionate faith of the Nazis. Some of the French men of letters were already half-Nazified long before 1940. In the case of Alphonse de Chateaubriant, a novel like *Monsieur de Lourdines* might seem a deliberate apologia for *Blut und Boden*, ordered as such by Herr Abetz, if one did not know it to have been written before 1914. An even more talented writer like Montherlant was prepared, by his temperament and his literary past, for an acceptance of the triumph of "virility" and "energy." Even Déat has a certain inner consistency. The failure of the Third Republic to provide a political authority adequate for the reconstruction of French economic life, aided, no doubt, by notorious non-intellectual causes, led Déat to his present desperate and despicable position. It was not want of ability or courage or energy that marked some of the most notorious collaborators. Indeed, all these qualities were present in some of their Nazi allies and paymasters. But in an age anxious for faith, in an age in which the Western peoples seem crippled by a crisis of faith that makes for extravagant external political credulity, it is well to be reminded by the event that faith, energy, courage are not enough. And if there is one text more than another that this problem recalls to mind it is: "If the light that is in thee be darkness, how great is the darkness."

This text might be but is not quoted by the Prime Minister of the Netherlands in his Taylorian lecture. It is a plea for faith, but not for a faith in faith. It is a plea, illustrated by great names (one of them a great German name), for an acceptance of moral standards in politics and for a rational scepticism directed against all systems that try to by-pass the necessity of moral standards in politics. The *ephori* to whom Althusius, like the other Calvinists of his time, wished to entrust a role recalling that given to themselves by the modern intellectuals, were saved from the worst temptations by their sense of responsibility before God for obedience to standards that they did not make or choose. The preachers of totalitarian solutions of any kind are reminded of the political realities that these solutions involve, of the risk of moral degradation that is inherent in Caesarism, whatever label it may wear to-day. Communities have a *ratio* that cannot be weakened without deadly peril to the citizens of that community—and its neighbours. We are our brother's keeper.

And it is a common and hopeful character of all three books that they do not accept, as the whole political duty of man, the picking of the presumed winner in the race and putting everything on the favourite. Favourites do not always win. The French collaborationists have found out that this realism does not pay in any form. We, the western victors, shall have comparable if not identical temptations; so these are very much tracts for the times.

XXV

TOCQUEVILLE[1]
(1945)

THERE are great books that wind into their subject like *The Republic*; there are others that strike their note at the very beginning, challenging the reader to follow out the implications of the theme. "Every state is a community of some kind, and every community is established with a view to some good"; "Je veux chercher si, dans l'ordre civil, il peut y avoir quelque règle d'administration légitime et sûre, en prenant les hommes tels qu'ils sont, et les lois telles qu'elles peuvent être"; "Nature (the Art whereby God hath made and governs the World) is by the *Art* of man, as in many other things, so in this also imitated, that it can make an Artificial Animal." It was a book adopting the second mode which appeared in Paris, in 1835, under the ambiguous and often really misleading title of *De la Démocratie en Amérique*. For the true theme of the new-born classic was not democracy as a system of government but the implications of equality. And so the theme is stated in the first lines of the introduction:

Parmi les objets nouveaux qui, pendant mon séjour aux Etats-Unis, ont attiré mon attention, aucun n'a plus vivement frappé mes regards que l'egalité des conditions. Je découvris sans peine l'influence prodigieuse qu'exerce ce premier fait sur la marche de la société; il donne à l'esprit public une certaine direction, un certain tour aux lois; aux gouvernants des maximes nouvelles, et des habitudes particulières aux gouvernés.

This was the true theme of the remarkable book that the young magistrate sent to study the American prison system, at his own expense, had produced. This was the theme that he continued to

---

[1] Alexis de Tocqueville, *Democracy in America*. The Henry Reeve text as revised by Francis Bowen, now further corrected and edited with introduction, editorial notes and bibliography by Phillips Bradley. Foreword by Harold J. Laski. In two volumes. (New York: A. Knopf.)
  Souvenirs d'Alexis de Tocqueville précédés d'une introduction de Luc Monnier. (Paris: Gallimard.)

ponder all the rest of his life, as a writer, as a deputy, for a short time as a minister. Tocqueville would have adopted as his own the counsel that Matthew Arnold insisted on repeating to his unattentive countrymen. But for Tocqueville, living in France, knowing America, it was not a matter of seeking equality. It was coming; it was there; its area of influence was ever spreading. The great moral and political problem of modern society was to adjust it to the inevitable growth of equality, without letting that equality serve to even out inequalities at a common and sordid level of greed. Accept equality and its consequences, ennoble equality; that was the counsel of the young Norman noble to the French bourgeoisie and notables, a counsel they refused to accept then, or since, with disastrous consequences to France.

Tocqueville was too much an aristocrat by blood, taste and education to welcome all the implications of equality. After all, he in his château of Tocqueville ("Tocqueville of that ilk" as they would say in Scotland), witness of the moral degradation of French political life that followed the destruction of the political power of the old aristocracy in the revolution of 1830, witness of the crudeness and banality of much of American life, was not confident that the rising tide of equality deserved nothing but welcome. But there was no promise in the role of Canute; no hope in such sand-barriers as had been erected by Louis-Philippe or Guizot against the encroaching sea; no security in the complacency, alternating with panic, of the bourgeoisie. "Historical continuity with the past is not a duty, it is only a necessity," said Justice Holmes. Acceptance of the Revolution, of its continuance, of its ineluctable consequences, above all, of the spirit of equality—that, too, was not a duty, it was a necessity, although the refusal to see the necessity was a wilful breach of the duty of the good citizen, above all of the good French citizen.

The dilemma of the conciliation of liberty and equality is no less urgent to-day than it was in 1835. Nor is it now easy, as it was then, for English readers and critics to dismiss as a mere French crotchet the preoccupation of Tocqueville with equality. Even England, where the religion of inequality had its most revered temple, has begun to succumb to the spirit of the age, the age which formally began in 1789, or in 1776, but in reality long before, when the feudal order was first sapped by kings, lawyers, merchants. Yet even to-day, even in France, the struggle is far from ended. And so there can be no question of the timeliness of this admirable new edition of the great book or of the propriety of the interest aroused by the publication, in Paris under the Germans, of the first complete text of those memoirs in which Tocqueville poured out for his own relief his bitter experience of the little wisdom and little nobility with which France had been governed. Now Paris is free and the revolution is again on the march. And it is fitting that, in America, Tocqueville should be again given his chance to teach. For near Tocqueville is the little town of Valognes, which Alexis de Tocqueville represented both in the rotten borough Chamber of Louis-Philippe and in the democratic Assembly of the Second Republic. And there, in the summer of 1944, a great army from the United States swept through the German lines and on, in a pursuit as magnificent as Murat's exploitation of Jena, freeing Normandy and France from the pollution of a rule based on inequality as a religion whose Moloch demanded sacrifices of all civic virtues as no order of government has done since Christendom was born. In a world that has seen the rise and fall of the Third Reich of the *Herrenvolk*, the lesson of the claims of equality as a political principle needs no very great excuse for being insisted on.

But it is equally idle to hide the fact that the compatibility of equality with freedom is not more certainly established now than it was when France turned from the tumult of 1848 to the acceptance of the (in the short run) efficient and prosperous tyranny of Napoleon III. Tocqueville had seen and insisted that the political conflict would merge in the economic. A year before the publication of the *Communist Manifesto*, he drafted a remarkable paper which his party colleagues in the Chamber of Deputies, very naturally, did not publish.

La Révolution française, qui a aboli tous les privilèges et détruit tous les droits exclusifs, en a partout laissé subsister un, celui de la propriété. Il ne faut pas que les propriétaires se fassent illusion sur la force de leur situation, ni qu'ils s'imaginent que le droit de propriété, est un rempart infranchissable parce que, nulle part, jusqu'à présent, il n'a été franchi.

In 1848 property was awakened from its confident security by the barricades of June, more effective alarm bells than the epigrams of Proudhon. Since then the possessing classes in France have shown many faults, but ignorant courage is not one of them.

For the selfish and ignoble politics of the age of Guizot and Thiers, Louis-Philippe and Louis-Napoléon, Tocqueville had nothing but condemnation, and we may be sure that he would have liked the "ordre moral" of the younger Broglie and the elder Caillaux, or of Pétain and Laval, just as little. He was too great a man to think that the creation of an *élite* such as that to which he belonged by blood and education, was worth paying for at the price of the misery and degradation of so many millions. He preferred the mediocrity of America to the ostentatious inequality of France. But he did not idealize the poor any more than he shut his eyes to the political death of his own order or the political incompetence and greed of the triumphant bourgeoisie. And we may be sure, in turn, that the decline in France—and not only in France—of the regard for liberty, for human freedom and dignity, would have made him as sombre to-day as he was in the last years of his life under the Second Empire. For Tocqueville was as much an ethical absolutist as Acton, as much an enemy of the mere *raison d'état* as his great-grandfather, Malesherbes. And he would not have been kept from seeing the reality of the murderous heresy by any of the modern disguises, even by the current fashionable one of calling a police state a democracy.

Apparently the brisk and, as the Americans say, brash young man who translated the first volumes of Tocqueville had not fully understood the importance of the book which was to make the name of Henry Reeve as well as of the author. Although English praise was lavish, it was not untendentious. The limitations of American society, the weaknesses of American government were stressed in many English reviews, and they led, as Professor Bradley suggests, to a curious if short-lived misapprehension in America. For American criticism was then "colonial" and touchy; it was immensely interested in what English writers had to say and ready to see in it yet more examples of what Lowell was to call "a certain condescension." So Tocqueville was, for a moment, on the strength of English excerpts, treated as another Mrs. Trollope, denigrating the country and the people he had visited. Of course, Tocqueville was critical; his view of the American press, for instance, did not

differ much from Martin Chuzzlewit's. But he preferred the world
of Jefferson Brick to the world of the far more sophisticated but, he
thought, far more harmful polemical journals of Paris. Tocqueville
was no sundial commentator, but he was a friendly and serious
commentator. He had taken pains to be accurate, he had taken
pains to be just and understanding, and this was soon seen and
appreciated. After America came France and within a few years
of its publication, *Democracy in America* was a classic. At least the
first part was; the second, which appeared in 1840, had not the
charm of novelty and was less an account of democracy in America
than the reflections of a political moralist on themes more or less
illustrated by America. Tocqueville was by literary taste and even
style, a kinsman of Montesquieu, and there was, in the second part,
something to justify the application of the famous gibe: Part Two
was "de l'esprit sur la démocratie" rather than a study of the working of democracy in America or anywhere else.

In other ways than this Tocqueville was half a man of the
eighteenth century. His descent from Malesherbes (which Professor Bradley neglects) not only gave him an hereditary vested
interest in the *Encyclopédie* which Malesherbes had saved from
suppression, but gave him a natural entrée into the minds and
methods of the nearest approach to Whigs ever produced by
France, i.e. the *noblesse de la robe*, of which his great-grandfather
was a greater moral, if not as great an intellectual ornament as
M. le président de Montesquieu. We know from Sainte-Beuve that
one of the very rare occasions on which Tocqueville showed passion
at a session of the *Académie française* was in a defence of Turgot.
But Tocqueville was only half a man of the *Encylopédie*. No more
than Joubert could he welcome the dominance of the Voltairian
spirit. He was *mi-croyant* at least. He saw in the force of
American religion one of the great safeguards of the republic. He
deplored the irreligion and frivolity of France. In his curious
correspondence with that prophet of inequality, Arthur de Gobineau, he argues against his contradictor the importance, the
novelty, the value of the Christian contribution to civilization and
is genuinely scandalized by Gobineau's penchant for Islam. But
he was highly critical, too, of the clericalism of his colleague
Falloux, as he was of the Gallicanism of Dufaure. He believed in
morality, in justice, in rationality, in moderation, in religion, in a

sense in Christianity and in the Church. All of these virtues and institutions were politically indispensable. They accounted for the success of republicanism in America, they accounted for many of the political and social merits of the English system, though that system was disfigured by the selfishness of the admirably skilled ruling class that had so fostered inequality to its own profit and the national loss.

It was the palpable purpose of Tocqueville to preach to his own countrymen, not to write a mere description of the American system of government as a going concern. This bias had serious effects on his methodology and there is justice in the criticism of Pierre Marcel. "Pour racheter l'insuffisance de ses documents, notre auteur profita de tous les prétextes qui lui permirent d'établir un parallèle avec la France et de tirer le plus grand nombre possible de leçons générales." But Tocqueville's methods, now made plain in that most learned and most acute study of Professor Pierson's, which does for him what *The Road to Xanadu* did for Coleridge, had other weaknesses. In *Tocqueville and Beaumont in America*, Professor Pierson has shown how much Tocqueville depended on a few informants and was sometimes led astray by mounting their hobby-horses too confidently. He thus overestimated the import- ance of the abolition of entail. So, too, he took over from Justice Story the most extravagant view of the range of the contract clause, the view that Story was soon vainly to press on his col- leagues in the Charles River Bridge case. Tocqueville's Federalist, or at any rate anti-Jacksonian entourage, led him to underestimate the importance of the presidency and led to his failure to see the practical and symbolical role of General Jackson. He seems, at best, to have thought of Jackson as he thought of Napoleon III. "Il s'y rencontre des moments où les plus mauvaises pièces sont celles qui réussissent le mieux." That there were two sides to the case of the Bank of the United States was not to be admitted.

In Part II the range of topics dealt with, from the role of the drama in a democracy to the place of women, gives Tocqueville a chance of saying things which, whether wise or foolish, are not to be dismissed by a confrontation with the laborious learning of modern jurists or historians. Even the now startling statement that "in America the independence of woman is irrecoverably lost in the bonds of matrimony" was not a fantastic paradox a century ago.

And though the famous prophecy about the revolutionary role of non-commissioned officers, like Rousseau's happy score about the approaching historical importance of Corsica, is a mere lucky shot, it has its interest in an age that has suffered so much from Gefreiter Hitler—for that rank is adequate for Tocqueville's thesis whatever military experts may think.

But it is not by defects or guesses that books live, and *Democracy in America* has lived by its moral dignity, its acuteness, its wisdom, its style. That style is not easy to render into English, and on this side of the Atlantic it will seem to many people that Henry Reeve did a better job than his pedantic corrector, Professor Bowen. But with great industry Professor Bradley has revised the reviser, especially pruning out the *faux amis* of which the self-confident Bowen was so revealingly fond. The result is easily the best edition of a great classic and an admirable tract for our times.

The Gallimard edition of the *Souvenirs*, apart from the interest that it gains from showing what could be published in a German-occupied Paris, has a more permanent value. For it restores the text that Tocqueville wrote for himself. He did not wish the recollections of his own political career to be published at all, and so he permitted himself a great deal of freedom in his character sketches of his colleagues and political friends and enemies. His nephew, the Comte de Tocqueville, was reluctant to show some of the leaders of the Right in so unfavourable a light and there were many and important excisions made, notably in the portrait of Louis-Philippe, so cruel, so convincing and so unpublishable when the old king's grandson, the Comte de Paris, had become, for all but a handful of fanatical "blancs d'Espagne," rightful King of France and chief of the party of order.

The Tocqueville of the *Souvenirs*, even of the expurgated version, was a more pessimistic, more disillusioned critic than the Tocqueville of the *Democracy in America*. All that he had feared from the moral mediocrity of the new ruling class had come to pass. Guizot and Louis-Philippe had ended as he had foreseen. But the hopes, the not very robust but sincere hopes that he had formed of the possible union of the best elements of the French people under the Republic, had been rapidly and bitterly deceived. A strong sense of duty, a noble ambition made him try to save what was to be saved from the wreck, to try to manipulate the vanity of Thiers, the private virtues or at least the private amiability of Louis-Napoléon, the possible return of good sense in the minds of the conservatives, of prudence and discipline in the ranks of the Left. Some solutions had been condemned out of hand by history; the attempted revival of the old régime under Charles X, the rule of the *gens nantis*, of a complacent and morally odious possessing class under Louis-Philippe. Tocqueville had no family and few personal reasons to admire the Revolution, but he accepted the fact that it had happened. He could have made his own the words of Napoleon I. "Je ne dis pas que ce qui s'est passé en France est juste, je dis que c'est un jubilé qu'on appelle une révolution. . . . Tout a été bouleversé. . . . Vous ne pouvez revenir sur ce qui est fait." Tocqueville put it with more eloquence (an eloquence which the translation renders well): "Those who hope to revive the monarchy of Henry IV or of Louis XIV appear to me to be afflicted with mental blindness: and when I consider the present condition of several European nations, a condition to which all the others tend, I am led to believe that they will soon be left with no other alternative than democratic liberty or the tyranny of the Caesars."

But Tocqueville sought liberty through democracy rather than the other way round. "The gradual growth of democratic manners and institutions should be regarded, not as the best, but as the only means of preserving freedom: and, without caring for the democratic form of government, it might be adopted as the most applicable and the fairest remedy for the present ills of society." "Manners" hardly gives the force of "mœurs," which modern American writers normally translate by the pedantic but exact invention of William Graham Sumner, "folkways." For Tocqueville was convinced that neither in geographical conditions nor in political institutions was the main secret of the success of free government in America. "Il faut recourir à quelque autre cause; et cette cause, où la découvrirai-je, sinon dans les mœurs?"

So he accepted the necessity of admitting, as soon as possible, the mass of the French people to political rights. Only by practice was freedom learned. But he had none of the naïve optimism of his colleague, Hippolyte Carnot, who, on the morning of the "Fête de la Concorde" of the 21st May, 1848, said, "avec cette niaiserie que les démocrates honnêtes ne manquent guère de mêler à leur vertu: 'Croyez-moi, mon cher collègue, il faut toujours se fier au peuple.'"

The worst days, the days of June, had not yet come, but 1848 was already educating Tocqueville, as it did that other Norman, the hero (and indeed, the author) of *L'Éducation Sentimentale*. For, as Tocqueville knew, most of the Representatives of the People had gone to this festival of "confusion fraternelle" armed.

The people could go wrong, wrong through ignorance, through foolish leaders like Ledru-Rollin, through the dominance in them, as in the bourgeoisie, of a mere "politique de ventre." Such an amoral attitude was more pardonable in a Paris worker than in a Louis-Philippe or a Thiers. But both sides in the imminent civil war were ready to sacrifice liberty to victory. It was Marrast who, by his example, taught again to Tocqueville the lesson he had never forgotten: "J'avais remarqué depuis longtemps que le seul moyen de mettre à l'unisson un conservateur et un radical, c'était d'attaquer non dans l'application mais dans le principe, le pouvoir du gouvernement central." Tocqueville feared more than what we should now call fascism; he hoped for more than a mere increase in material equality. He would have understood and shared the fear of a modern satirist, the fear of a world:

> Where men, like bees, must do as other bees;
> Where to be good is to be like the rest,
> But freaks and freemen are their country's pest:
> While he that's vicious in a way that's shown
> Serves more than he who's virtuous on his own.

There was no doubt something a little irritating, a little Aristides-like, in Tocqueville's attitude to his colleagues, to the various misleaders of all classes in French society. When the Duc d'Aumale got news of Tocqueville's death he wrote to Henry Reeve that "of all the men of mark in our deliberative assemblies, M. de Tocqueville was certainly the most stainless." The most brilliant of the sons of King Louis-Philippe cannot have been ignorant of Tocqueville's opinion of the political morals of the July monarchy and he can hardly have warmed to so severe a critic of his father's system. Nor can the various politicians with whom Tocqueville worked have enjoyed his contempt for their wisdom, or their character, or their knowledge, or all three. The "république des camarades" of the Third Republic existed long before the Third Republic—as it exists in all free governments. Tocqueville was a political rigorist, and politicians have always been, in practice, for the Jesuits against the Jansenists. His view of politics was too exclusively ethical and did not take sufficient account of the necessary and justifiable differences between public and private morals. It is not an attitude that is in any apparent danger of being overstressed to-day. And the main lesson of Tocqueville is not merely that equality is destined to come, or that it should be made compatible with liberty to which it is the only effective but not necessarily effective means, but that even liberty and equality are inadequate aims for a society which, if it forgets justice, forgets its greatest end.

XXVI
POWER
(1945)

In 1935 the *Normandie* crossed the Atlantic for the first time and on the return voyage one of the passengers was Comte Bertrand de Jouvenel. Another was Tom Pendergast, Boss of Kansas City (Missouri), and, on the advice of an American journalist, the young Frenchman, abandoning his store of books on American politics, set himself to study the phenomenon of the power politician in this (chemically) pure form. "I am told," said de Jouvenel, "that you are the ruler of Missouri, Mr. Pendergast. Can you tell me how it is that you do it?" In this long, acute, learned and, in general, objective treatise, M. de Jouvenel continues the investigation of which the interview on the *Normandie* was one of the early research projects. M. de Jouvenel in his essay does not recall this episode in the preparation of his book[1] (that piece of information we owe to Mr. Marquis Childs), but his time was well employed, for Tom Pendergast was a remarkable specimen of an important type not confined to American politics, the "unidea'd" politician, the pursuer of power for its sake or for its fruits. And as a lesson not to ignore the historical importance of such types, it was a decision of Pendergast that, a year before, had sent to the United States Senate Mr. Harry S. Truman, unconscious as both Senator and Boss must have been, that it was the road to the White House, in one of the decisive moments of American and world history.

In intention, and often in achievement, M. de Jouvenel is a naturalist. Even when he is a pathologist, he tries to attain and does sometimes attain the scientific passionate objectivity that can make "What a lovely tumour" a totally justifiable manner of expression. But in spite of the plan and in spite of the comparative success in the execution of the plan, it is easy to see that M. de Jouvenel is hostile to power or rather to the dressing-up of the crude, ineluctable facts of power in philosophical garments more or less

[1] *Du Pouvoir histoire naturelle de sa croissance*, par Bertrand de Jouvenel: Geneva: Les Editions du Cheval Ailé.

well-fitting, more or less attractive, but hiding in virtue of their fit and beauty, the crude, ugly facts of political life. The emperor *may* have clothes, but they are mere clothes, mere fig-leaves in the case of cruder doctrines, covering more or less successfully the fact that in its origin, and, in some cases, in all its span of life, political power represents the imposition of authority by force, represents the aggressive and egoistic elements in human nature, has no claim in its own right to more than the obedience bred of fear or resignation.

In his investigation of the genesis of power and of the child of power, the State, M. de Jouvenel goes far back into history, back to Rome, back to African tribes. But his interest is not primarily historical, his examples are, for the most part, modern. Indeed, one could go further; the theme of this book is power in general but the method of studying it is an analysis of the origins and growth of the power of the French State. It is in his analysis of the reasons that led to the creation of the absolute monarchy, the failure of alternative systems of power and the fruits of that success and failure, the Revolution and the Empire, that M. de Jouvenel displays most historical learning and, what is rarer, historical imagination. It is the case of France, the France of 1789, child of the France of Richelieu and Louis XIV, the France of 1945, child of the Revolution, but marked like the Revolution by remoter ancestors, that engages M. de Jouvenel's deepest interest and passions. And it is as a contribution to the problem of French reconstruction that *Du Pouvoir* is most valuable. But its value is great and not only for Frenchmen, since all that concerns France concerns western civilization and, in addition, in spite of many local variations, all western nations could and should say of much that is here described *de nobis fabula narratur*. It has been suggested that M. de Jouvenel from time to time writes as a pathologist rather than as a physiologist and that, even as a pathologist, he does not always achieve the objectivity of pure science. But if he succumbs at times to the temptation both to see in pathological terms and in terms of a rather censorious morality, he could plead that he is much provoked. For he has to face and to denounce the comforting sophistries with which, for many centuries, the truths of power have been concealed.

M. de Jouvenel is not an anarchist. He admits that much of

what we most treasure in our civilization, including the instruments of our resistance to mere power and our ability to resist its moral, if not its physical domination, we owe to the creation, by force, of the State. He would insist that the makers of the State had no such intention and an end-product must not be imputed to them for virtue by a complacent historiography. But for him, civilization seems to be bound up with power and there is no hankering after a past golden age, a lost Eden, an amiable and non-belligerent primitive society doomed to destruction by the users of bronze or iron. The State, founded exclusively on force in the beginning and with force deep in its foundations to-day, is with us for good. But to accept it, to assess its claims is one thing, to refuse to regard its real character, to find excuses for its waste, its crimes, its follies, this is political blindness and wilful blindness at that. What the Lisbon earthquake did, or should have done, for the optimists of the Leibnitzian school, the two world wars have done for M. de Jouvenel and should do for others.

The atomic bomb has come since to make the urgency of his message even more apparent and, presenting the rulers of the world with unprecedented powers of destruction, it may force us all to regard the Minotaur (as M. de Jouvenel calls it) in the face. The immensity and urgency of the problem may (it is hard to be hopeful) force thought on even the most complacent.

Outside the lands impregnated with Germanic traditions of authority and so fairly immune to the attractions of German system-builders, the Hegelian version of liberty, the Hegelian court costume that covers the naked forms of power, has little attraction. (Its more or less legitimate descendant, Marxism, has much, but that is another story.) So we do not get and do not need a refutation or an exposition of the ingenuities of political idealism; there is no need to repeat the argument of Hobhouse against Bosanquet, or to undertake to defend Hegel from the charge that he is responsible for his disciples and for providing the Prussian State with a convenient ideology.

It is in quarters much nearer home that M. de Jouvenel sees danger. Above all, in the illusion that democracy as such, the rule of "universal suffrage" as the French Radicals used to hypostatize the electorate, has any passion for liberty, any fear of the excesses of power. Because all voters have, or think they have, a share in power, because the political career open to talents stills the critical spirit and soothes the *amour-propre* of the ambitious, power in a democratic State grows easily—like a fungus or a cancer the libertarian is tempted to say. Can the sovereign people do wrong? It can, but it does not like to be told so. Can wrong be done to the sovereign people by its delegates, the effective manipulators of political power? Certainly, but the character of the wrong may not be noticed at all if its immediate effects are only felt by a minority. And if the effects on the majority are delayed, the chain of responsibility cannot be followed up by the simple voter. He is a Theseus with no thread of Ariadne to lead him through the labyrinth. In the old days the King had a right divine to govern wrong, but the people knew that it was he who governed or did not govern. "De par le roi" was a less mystifying formula than "République Française. Liberté, Égalité, Fraternité." The people might be reluctant to blame the King, anxious to find scapegoats for him in his ministers or mistresses, but the responsibility was not so easily evaded. Louis XIV, Louis XV, Louis XVI all knew different forms of it.

In the modern democratic state, above all in a headless parliamentary state like that of the Third Republic, responsibility was hard to fix or at least to fix *exclusively*. The Laval trial showed that. M. Pierre Cot might write of "Le procès de la République," but that was a metaphor.

C'est en vain que Proudhon a toute sa vie denoncé la diversion de la démocratie vers un simple compétition pour l'Imperium.

Cette compétition a donné ses fruits nécessaires: un Pouvoir à la fois étendu et faible.

Mais il n'est pas naturel au Pouvoir d'être faible. Il se trouve des circonstances qui font désirer au peuple lui-même de trouver à sa tête une volonté vigoureuse. Un homme, une équipe, peuvent alors, s'emparant du Pouvoir, employer ses leviers sans timidité.

Ils manifestent son accablante enormité. On croit qu'ils en sont les auteurs. Mais non! Seulement les usagers abusifs.

For the French problem (and it is not only the French problem) is the refusal of mankind to see the problem of power as a problem except when power is in the wrong hands, i.e. in the hands of others, of the other class, party, sect. And so we come easily to believe that unlimited and uncriticized power, in command of the unprecedentedly effective coercive machinery of the modern state, is no danger to human well-being and dignity if it is in the right hands, the rightness being proven by doctrinal or national or class tests. And in any society where there is no power independent of the current rulers of the state, human freedom, dignity and, since August 1945, mere human survival are goods whose security is lessened day by day.

Central to M. de Jouvenel's theme is the failure of the French *noblesse* to become or to remain an aristocracy and so an effective restraint on power. In their long war with the crown, the French nobles never developed the institutions or the *esprit de corps* that would have enabled them effectually to combat the King, his tireless lawyers and *commis*, the jealous and rising bourgeois, even the permanent resentment of the peasants. Each moment of weakness in the long history of the House of France was exploited but for individual ends, or even if they were class ends, the class was too limited, too ill-disciplined, too idle to rule. It may be, of course, that the alternative before France was not the creation of a ruling aristocracy allied to the bourgeoisie as in England, but the descent of France to the level of the Polish Republic, with the *noblesse* as a western *Szlachta*.

The failure was not so much the failure to come to terms, in time, with the King, but the failure to come to terms at all with the middle classes. There is a revealing passage in Sainte-Beuve where he discusses the possibility that Henri IV, had he lived, could have developed a fruitful partnership with the *noblesse*. His murder left only the absolutism of Richelieu as a solution. And Sainte-Beuve with all his interest in the old order and his pleasure in its aristocratic aspects had no doubt that it was well for him, the *roturier*, that the experiment was not tried, that the *noblesse* was put down, that the grand reign came and Versailles—and the Revolution.

M. de Jouvenel sees it very differently (after all he is not a *roturier*). In the destruction of the *noblesse*, he sees, rightly, a cause of that dislike of independent authorities which still marks the politics of the average Frenchman and its inevitable corollary, the reliance on the State to do all things, including the things which it is not the interest of the State, of any State, to do, the creation of independent sources of power. For him, the *fin des notables* began long before the nineteenth century, long before either Tocqueville or Daniel Halévy noted it. And the nobles were at least as much sinners as sinned against. For they showed themselves incapable (as even Saint-Simon had to admit) of ruling the State; they were only capable of living off it. So the Regent discovered in the brief period of aristocratic reaction that followed the death of Louis XIV. The King and the bourgeoisie could rule; the King and the *noblesse* could not. But the *noblesse* could and did prevent the King from ruling. All through the eighteenth century there was an increasing and, from one point of view, unnecessary alienation of the crown from its old ally, the bourgeoisie. The Great King's decision to create Versailles had much to answer for. There was now in a special sense a "court," cut off from France as the Louvre and Saint-Germain had not been. There were courtiers, good for little else except being killed in increasingly unsuccessful wars. Proust, in one of his most famous passages, describes the skill and grace with which the Duc de Guermantes helps on Marcel with his coat; it was the fruit of generations of court life. What Basin de Guermantes now did for the climbing bourgeois, he had been trained by heredity to do for the King. But the mere courtier, now without a court, was a long way from the Gilbert le Mauvais of the stained-glass window in the church of Combray. By 1789, the higher ranks of the French nobility recall the inbred nobles of the impotent Mikado's court, or, even more, the Manchu nobles and the eunuchs of the court of the last emperors of the Ch'ing dynasty. For the feudal nobility of Japan at least produced a collective Mirabeau to carry out the Meiji restoration; the court nobles of Versailles, greedy and inconsequent, were incapable of any collective action and, bred to isolation in Versailles, the House of France was now but the chief noble family submitting to the greed of its parasitic court.

In a sense, the *noblesse de l'epée* was almost innocent compared with the *noblesse de la robe*. For the court nobility was at least true to form; the intriguers of the *oeil-de-boeuf* were the spiritual as well as the fleshly heirs of the frivolous leaders of the Fronde. But for the great legal families, heirs of the jurists who had, in collaboration with the Capetian kings, made France, *their* alliance with the court nobility against the King was treason to their own traditions and *raison d'être*. The much abused Chancellor Maupeou was more truly in the tradition of the medieval *Parlement de Paris* than were his enemies. Because the *Parlements* sank into mere noble clubs, as blindly devoted to their selfish interests as the old court nobility in which they were now, by education, tastes, marriage, almost merged, they could not serve any useful purpose, could not be an effectual check on the excesses of royal authority. And, still more important, since in any case royal authority was every day growing weaker, they fatally discredited the idea of any check on the sovereign. The formal claims of Louis XV mattered little; the real heir of Louis XIV and of Richelieu, of Philippe le Bel and Louis XI was to be the "sovereign people." And that was a fiction covering the extension and strengthening of the authority of the State to an unprecedented degree. "The Revolution itself found formulas for the future enslavement of mankind," as Professor Butterfield has written, and the armies of the Republic and Empire taught them (with many better things) both to the peoples whom the Convention proposed to liberate and to the kings whom the Convention proposed to destroy.

Since then, all revolutions have made the same promises and given the same performance. So have the counter-revolutions. Who remembers, now, Lenin's insistence on the necessity of destroying the State or the almost Cobdenian flavour of much Fascist propaganda in the first years of the movement and of the régime? Power grows; its holders see to that, whether deliberately or unconsciously is not the main question. And although M. de Jouvenel does not quote, or, what is more surprising, misquote Acton, he too thinks that power tends to corrupt—and to corrupt the ruled as well as the rulers.

It corrupts the ruled by depriving them of the need and opportunity of responsibility. M. de Jouvenel is too wise to ignore the fact that, to apply in a different context the famous defence made by an English divine, economically helpless men are, as a rule, too poor to keep a political conscience. The craving for security is legitimate and, in any case, inevitable and almost universal. One of the justifications for inequality is that it diminishes in the privileged the pressure of insecurity. A head of a great and opulent family has less excuse than the poor man for justifying by his conduct the maxim that "le bon père de famille est capable de tout." But we should not blind ourselves to the fact that the price of security may be very high and, if we resolve to pay it, we should not abuse language by describing as a system of freedom, an organization of command in which the greatest of sins is dangerous thought.

It is not only the natural weakness of the ruled that tempts the rulers. Politics, ruling are a trade and a profession and like all other trades and professions have their share of "déformations professionelles." And the professional sin of the professional ruler is an excessive *esprit de corps* and an excessive and often dangerous neglect of the needs and feelings of that mass which the crude French word so well describes as "administrés." More politicians and bureaucrats than the liquidators of the kulaks have become drunk with success and there is an unconscious international of rulers, as there is a common understanding among the politicians of a country that often, if not always, cuts across all but the highest party barriers. Each country has its own type of Pendergast.

This political phenomenon, to whose description and explanation M. de Jouvenel devotes a rather Germanic solemnity, was admirably and succinctly described by his uncle in that brief masterpiece *La République des Camarades*.

Il y a moins de différence entre deux députés dont l'un est révolutionnaire et l'autre ne l'est pas, qu'entre deux révolutionnaires, dont l'un est député et l'autre ne l'est-pas.

A more rigid and more professional revolutionary organization, inside and outside the Chamber, has changed the scene, superficially. M. Duclos cannot publicly permit himself the professional solidarity that was possible to a parliamentary revolutionary in the remote age of 1914, but to be part of a governing machine is sobering, disillusioning and, paradoxically, also intoxicating and a source of self-deception. For the inner difficulties are revealed, the apparent irrelevance of items in a programme, articles in a creed are manifested, while the delights of power, prestige, the "inside view" may go to fairly strong heads and the pressure of driving ambition once relaxed by success, the passions and hopes of the rank and file may be easily and disastrously forgotten. Yet, and it is characteristic of M. de Jouvenel's fairness that he states the case, the ruler is not in modern times often a mere exploiter. He is usually affected by the terms, the flattering terms, in which his function is described and may and does try to live up to them, not always with good results it must be admitted. The ruler, even the tyrant, may, M. de Jouvenel suggests, be prepared to sacrifice his immediate and material interests to his passions and, still more noteworthy, to his principles. So Louis XIV committed the folly of the Revocation of the Edict of Nantes, so Hitler committed the folly of the Nuremberg Laws and of the persecution of the Jews. The cases have something in common, but less than is suggested here. Wise after the event, Massillon in his funeral oration on the great King might compliment him on the sacrifice he had made for religion, on his disregard of the counsels of those who foresaw the weakening of France and the strengthening of her neighbours by the Revocation. Perhaps the King did foresee this, more probably he accepted the ill results with the good; the economic and military losses endured by France were, he could deceive himself into thinking, more than offset by the religious gains of the conversion of so many thousands to the true faith, by the ending of the scandal of tolerated and even privileged heresy.

But it may be doubted whether the King at any moment before the event, really drew up a balance sheet of the kind suggested by Massillon. Long before the Revocation, the King had written for the eyes of the Dauphin:

Et quant à ce grand nombre de mes sujets de la réligion pretendue réformée, qui était un mal que j'avais toujours regardé et que je regarde encore avec beaucoup de douleur, je formai dès lors le plan de toute ma conduite envers eux, que je n'ai pas lieu de croire mauvaise, puisque Dieu a voulu qu'elle ait été suivie et le soit encore tous les jours d'un très grand nombre de conversions. Il me sembla, mon fils, que ceux qui voulaient employer des remèdes extrêmes et violents, ne connaissaient pas la nature de ce mal.

The deception of the King was one of the chief means of making a career in the administration adopted by intendants like Foucault in Languedoc and Béarn. That ingenious bureaucrat, so Sainte-Beuve tells us:

exposa à Louis XIV, dans une audience particulière et lui fùt agréer toute la partie ostensible et séduisante de son plan; il ne parla que de l'amour, de la vénération des Béarnais pour la mémoire de Henri IV, sentiments qui avaient passé à son petit-fils. De rigueurs, il n'en fut un moment question que pour en rejeter aussitôt l'idée.

We have good reason to doubt if it was necessary to deceive the Führer about the results of his Jewish policy. His passions, his zeal were less superficial than those of Louis XIV. He had probably very little hesitation at inflicting on Germany great losses in skill and devotion, as well as increasing the fears, resentments and resources of the nations he was determined to attack. If sincerity and freedom from the simplest forms of egoism are adequate moral equipment for the ruler, Louis XIV and Hitler had them. Had they been worse men, in the sense of being mere exploiters of power, they might have been more formidable. By leaving Hugue-nots and Jews alone they might have encouraged illusions and won admiration, even trust, among their neighbours. But the lesson is not that a tyrant will always give the show away, be a victim to his zeal, his folly, his hates. It is rather that a ruler may commit infamies with the general approval of his subjects (as Louis XIV certainly and Hitler in all probability had), once the principle of *raison d'état* is accepted and the healthy fear of unlimited authority has been conjured away by the successful encouragement of human credulity and passivity.

No one looking at the world we live in can doubt that the theme of this book is, or should be, on the agenda of every modern society. The technical developments that strengthen authority also make its extension necessary. It is mere cynical resignation in the manner of Alain to deny this. M. de Jouvenel is anything but resigned, though he neglects the pressure of modern economic and tech-nological necessities, or apparent necessities on the old political order, even in countries like England and Switzerland, which have escaped the worst effects of absolutist centralization. (M. de Jouvenel's optimism about the rights of the individual against the administration in England would startle Dr. C. K. Allen.)

As power has become more and more formidable, till it now threatens to involve in doubt the mere existence of the human race, the dangers of submission, under any guise, to a power not bound either by institutions or by the spirit of society to render any account of its intentions or performance, need hardly be stressed. Or one would say so, did not every day show that in the spirit of blind trust or mere resignation, more and more men and women ignore the dangers and accept the promises (so often betrayed) that this system, this party, this order of things will, at last, produce a system of rulers whom there will be no need to watch for our sakes and to criticize, even to rebuke and recall, for theirs.

These truths may seem to be not so much self-evident as platitudinous. But we must not neglect platitudes and we are neglecting this one. For all the movement of the age has been towards the uncritical exaltation of State power. Where to-day are the Pluralists, the Guild Socialists, the Anarchists? Reduced to tiny sects or transformed into uncritical acceptors of the saviour State. And nowhere is that transformation more marked than in M. de Jouvenel's France, the France of Proudhon and of Jaurès. But it is not only in France that the old wariness of the State, and the lesson of not putting unlimited trust in princes or parties, has been forgotten.

XXVII

FOR THE FOURTEENTH OF JULY, 1945

THERE are some events so heart-warming in themselves, that there is a real temptation to abandon oneself to a merely emotional enjoyment of them. And the good European would be very tough-minded, indeed, who was not touched by the fact that this year, 1945, will see the 14th of July celebrated in Paris, freely in a liberated city. How often since 1940 have those of us who have known Paris thought with bitterness of the pollution of its soil by the Germans, of the betrayal of its spirit by Vichy! For, under Vichy, memories were as dangerous as thoughts are in Japan, above all memories of those days when:

> "Death was on thy drums democracy
> And with one rush of slaves, the world was free."

In vain, Vichy tried to root out this nostalgia. In vain it cele-brated on the Plateau of Gergovia the triumph of Vercingetorix; the spirit of the great Gaul worked against Vichy, and the commune of which I have the honour to be a citizen will remember that General de Lattre de Tassigny lived there in the dark hours, not that a feeble imitation of the pagan rites of the Third Reich revealed the senile impotence of a sterile régime.

So when I saw, in Paris, last week, the stands being got ready for the great parade of the first free 14th since 1939, I was not censorious as were some strict moralists and economists. France, Paris, the world needed this celebration.

But there is another aspect of the celebration of the 14th on which we must lay stress. It is not a mere celebration of the liberation of the territory such as was held after 1870 and 1918. This July 14th could be, and should be, a celebration much more in the spirit of 1789 and 1790. For France has known and suffered in her inmost fibres in the past four years from a tyranny much more odious, inhuman, soul-destroying than any known in 1789. It is a matter of historical controversy how much the fall of the

Bastille in 1789 was a merely symbolic act. The prison was half or more than half empty; the great days of *lettres de cachet* were over. It was more a relic of the past than a present stronghold of tyranny that fell. But there can be no controversy over the power, the odiousness, the immediate and terrible importance of the fall of that vast Bastille which the Third Reich erected all over Europe. We may dispute whether the veteran prisoners of the Bastille were much better off liberated (I have no doubt they were, but it is arguable). There can be no controversy over the importance of liberating the captives of Buchenwald, Dachau, Ravensbrück, over the totally beneficent deliverance of these men and women from the prisons designed to dehumanize them, to illustrate the power of the Herrenvolk to take men and women (and an *élite* of men and women) and make of them sub-human creatures, mere prisoners, mere tools. In those Bastilles, death was a triumph for the prisoners, a defeat for the jailers. And yet the survival of men and women, as men and women, was the great triumph of the human spirit over its antithesis, the great heresy of National Socialism. In no place more fittingly than in Paris can that triumph be celebrated, in that city where one can meet and even learn to recognize men who, like Dante, have been through hell and by immense tenacity have earned the right to tell how they survived:

"e quindi uscimmo a riveder le stelle."

This *fête nationale* is one in which the whole world can join; it could be, and in its inmost spirit is, a canticle of liberation, a commemoration for the future remembrance of the people of France and the earth. And it would be appropriate to use in that celebration of the deliverance from a tyranny worse than Pharaoh's, as a proper counterpart to the anti-Semitic poison that the Third Reich has injected, the words whereby Moses bade his people remember this day, in which "ye came out from Egypt, out of the house of bondage."

In that celebration we should remember, too, the lesson of the four years of tyranny, the lesson of the power of the modern state, ruthless, scientific, devoid, in theory and practice, of any universal code of conduct, to debase men and women as well as elevate them in resisting it to heights of heroism that one could not have dared to hope for, before the ordeal. There *are*, we now know, men and women whom no tyranny can crush, though it can kill, but they are and must be a minority. It is too much to expect of the mass of mankind such heroic virtue, such continuous courage, such a power of enduring suffering not in ourselves only, but in others. And it was one of the most dreadful crimes of the Third Reich that, while it elevated some above all previous standards of heroism and constancy, it forced many more, by human but not ignominious weakness, to fall below their best standards, to suffer the pangs of conscience, to see themselves either forced to endure the interior conflict of self-approach or to take the other way out, to justify their weakness in a spirit of bravado, of cynicism that is no less harmful for being pardonable. In France and in all the occupied countries, there is a danger of a cleavage along these lines. The claims, expressed or not, of the heroes of the resistance can be a stimulus or a reproach. If they are a reproach, they may be a new source of division. The betrayal of France by so many of its self-styled *élite* is a crime, a great crime and one calling to heaven for vengeance. The odiousness of the spies and policemen who made themselves the agents of the Reich cannot be palliated. There will be no tears shed for Darnand's men as tears were, legitimately enough, shed for the Swiss Guards of 14th July, 1789 and 10th August, 1792. The need for a thorough *épuration* is clear; its speed is a national necessity. But no country can be governed (outside Plato's Republic) by a minority of saints and heroes. There are not enough to go round and, what is worse, in the exercise of power they often cease to be saints and, though less often, to be heroes.

So there is another aspect of the *fête nationale* on which it is wise to dwell. The first celebration of the fall of the Bastille, the *Fête des Fédérations* was an attempt, an unavailing attempt, to unite Frenchmen, to remake France in a spirit of tolerance, fraternity and love for a common country. By 1791, the 14th July was already a partisan occasion. And from that time on, French internal history has been, alas, a series of party triumphs, often stained with blood. The *grands jours de Paris* have been, and have had to be, triumphs or defeats in a perpetual civil war. It is possible that the conflict must go on; that the problem of giving to France political and social institutions in the spirit of the Revolution will not soon be solved. But it is worth dwelling, now, on the one great Paris "day" that was a totally national triumph, the liberation of 1944. It would be

to insult all sides in previous civil struggles, both sides of the
10th August, of Thermidor, Brumaire, 1830, 1848, even 1851 and
1871, to compare them with the handful of desperate traitors who,
in August of last year, prevented the liberation being totally a
French triumph over a totally foreign enemy. But the truth was
near enough the ideal. This was a triumph leaving no French
scars, in which all Frenchmen who had not totally divested themselves
of all right to the name, could rejoice and in which Frenchmen of
all parties, all classes, all traditions took part. Since 1789 such
united French triumphs have been external military victories,
gained by the French state and the French army. Here was a
triumph gained by the French people, in its most generous and
widest sense, and a triumph not only over a material but over an
ideal enemy—for the enemy defeated then, had his idea, infamous,
now vanquished but not dead, for evil has its own terrible power
of life.

This year, and in the future, July 14th can have new meanings or
renewals of the old meanings realized with a deeper passion.
Frenchmen and Frenchwomen have learned what it is that makes
liberty dear. They have learned what it is to be French in a France
totally subjected, corporally speaking, to the enemy of the French
body and the French mind. They have seen the most odious of
tyrannies at close hand. And faced with the terrible problems of
reconstruction, affected as they must be with the emotional damage
done by the occupation, tempted as they must be to brusque
solutions, to legitimate anger at the impunity of some base profiteers of the disaster, they will be subject to the temptation to fall
back, as did the Nazis, on force, on a party view of justice, on a
deliberate exclusion of a great section of the French community
from the national life. If that temptation is succumbed to, then
much of the heroism of the terrible years will have been, from the
national if not from the human point of view, in vain. Then we
shall see the terrible paradox that other countries may be able to
rejoice in and profit by that heroism more than France will be able
to do. But if that temptation is resisted and a new France is made
in the spirit of July 1790 and August 1944, then we and France can
celebrate every July 14th in the spirit in which Charles James Fox
received the news of the first. "How much the greatest event it is
that ever happened in the world and how much the best." And

that will be reward enough for those of us who through the dark years have like the exiled Jews—and at moments with not much more immediate faith—thought of this great festival and prayed "next year in Jerusalem."